KEATS

AS A READER OF
SHAKESPEARE

R. S. WHITE

KEATS
AS A READER OF
SHAKESPEARE

UNIVERSITY OF OKLAHOMA PRESS
NORMAN AND LONDON

Library of Congress Cataloging-in-Publication Data

White, R. S., 1948–
Keats as a reader of Shakespeare.

Bibliography: p.
1. Keats, John, 1795–1821—Knowledge—Literature.
2. Keats, John, 1795–1821—Sources.   3. Shakespeare,
William, 1564–1616—Influence—Keats.   4. Influence
(Literary, artistic, etc.)   I. Title.
PR4838.L5W45   1987)   821'.7   86–40532
ISBN 0–8061–2053–3

Contents

Preface

John Keats acknowledged Shakespeare not only as one of his greatest literary models but as his 'good genius' guiding him in his own poetic enterprise. This book is an empirical and critical study of the evidence concerning the nature of Keats's understanding and admiration of Shakespeare's dramatic texts. Primarily, the intention is to use Keats's statements in his letters, annotations and markings upon his own texts of Shakespeare, and his clear affinity with the critical principles of his contemporary William Hazlitt, to build up a detailed account of what Shakespeare meant to Keats as a creative reader who happened also to be a great poet in his own right. Although not intentionally a 'source study', the treatment raises many new suggestions about how Shakespeare influenced Keats's own poetry both in broad terms and in specific lines. It may ultimately be impossible to define the elusive 'Shakespearean' quality which critics have always detected in Keats's poetry, but at least it should be possible to be clearer about what Keats himself thought 'Shakespearean' poetry meant to him. I hope the study will be helpful to scholars of Keats (who are not always as intimately knowledgeable about Shakespeare's words as about Keats's), as well as, incidentally, providing lovers of Shakespeare with a unique kind of 'anthology' of phrases and passages which have been selected by the inimitable taste and judgment of a compatible and sensitive poet. The nature of this taste, fashioned and demonstrated in the act of reading, is the central subject of the book. In this sense I am aware of the larger questions of literary theory concerning the act of reading a text and the nature of literary influence which are raised by the subject as a whole. Although it is outside the scope of this book to tackle these questions directly, I hope the information provided and the presentation of the problems will provoke literary theorists into developing notions of the text as a body of potential meanings which are activated by individuals in the act of reading.

It has been necessary to address certain questions of methodology and I hope that a summary explanation of the approach adopted here will not be taken to imply that I cannot see the possibility of other modes of enquiry raised by the richness of the material. First there is the nature of the critical ethos in which Keats's thinking took place, a subject which must be dealt with without its being allowed to dominate discussion. Although Keats had no formal training in English criticism, he lived at a time of great changes in literary theory of which he was well aware. The proof of this lies in the undoubted, substantive similarity between some of his expressed ideas and those of Hazlitt, Keats's favourite critic. In this book the attitude is adopted that the public aesthetics and taste of Hazlitt provide some firm, analytical ground from which to build up a knowledge of the poet's assumptions. Keats was as much a child of his time as any other mortal, and his personal commitments were inextricably linked up with those of Hazlitt even though the personalities and modes of expression were as different as could be. It would be misleading to pretend that Keats existed in lofty isolation, communing directly with the dead dramatist in a perfect and 'universal' way. He had at least one mediator.

A more difficult problem surrounds the use of markings and marginalia on Keats's copies of Shakespeare. Sometimes he conveniently left us some general statement of interest in a letter which provides at least a starting-point when we look at the markings. However, it must frankly be admitted that certain questions about the markings cannot be answered. Usually the activity of marking cannot be dated. We cannot say what the precise intention was – whether to pick out passages for later attention or as an aid to memory, or whether they reflect the mood he happened to be in when he read the play. In the absence of definite evidence, the assumption adopted here (justified in the body of the text) is that it is still possible to say the markings are evidence of a selective attentiveness on the part of the reader which manifest his own taste in Shakespearean poetry, whatever that may mean in a particular context. This seems consistent with Keats's own attitudes. His theories of reading and writing outlined in Chapter 1 establish that the immediate 'intense' impression of a moment's concentrated reading is just as valuable as evidence of the imagination's predilections as the impression that survives through time. Keats's attitude towards Shakespeare changed from an idolatrous raptness in 1817 to the more wary distance held by the poet of 1819 who feared the inhibiting effect of 'influences', but this does not invalidate the earlier readings as important to his poetic memory throughout his writing career. To cut a long story short, I attempt to present the evidence of *what* Keats chose to notice, where possible to consider this in the context of his more discursive statements, and to use my own critical judgment as supporting evidence rather than as a primary perception. Sometimes it is possible or necessary to suggest *why* Keats marked something, but I try not to speculate unless it seems profitable to do so, and in a way which I hope will not prevent readers from thinking along other, equally persuasive lines. By and large, the significance of one marking will never be the same as that of another, and analysis must tactfully reflect this fact. Moreover, what is interesting to one reader will not be so to another and I have tried to present as much of the evidence as possible to stimulate other readings. Once again, if the Keatsian attitude is legitimate that a text is a potential which each reader will fulfil in a unique way, I hope my own text will be received in the same way.

In dealing with the influence of Shakespeare on Keats's own poetry, my main aim has been to define some general areas of contact – shared themes, ideas and kinds of language – in order to establish broad lines of approach rather than making the discovery of specific sources a priority. Inevitably, however, I have felt encouraged to make new suggestions of sources for particular lines in Keats which supplement those listed, for example, in the notes to Miriam Allott's *Keats: The Complete Poems* (London, 1970) and the pioneering work of C.L. Finney's unpublished Harvard PhD thesis, 'Shakespeare and Keats' (1922), much of which is absorbed into his *The Evolution of Keats's Poetry* (Cambridge, Mass., 1936). In making these suggestions I have tried to exercise due caution and have relentlessly excised many of my wilder hunches. All the time, however, the stress is upon general facets of poetic compatibility, since it would be quite wrong to give the impression that Keats's sources can be mechanically isolated. Even when there is an obvious echo, Keats can magically create something new, a process which I tentatively analyse at the end of Chapter III on 'Shakespeare's Hieroglyphics'.

In order to do justice to the detail of the wealth of material, I have imposed other limitations. Clearly, Keats read voraciously and widely, and, however tempting, it would have been an awesome task to accommodate assessments of the lines from his poetry and letters leading to Spenser, Milton, Wordsworth, Drayton, Beaumont and Fletcher, and a host of others. By and large I have also excluded detailed consideration of the non-dramatic works of Shakespeare, which is substantial enough as a topic to fuel another book, although not, I hope, so different as to deny the conclusions reached in the present enterprise. There is enough in the drama itself, as received by Keats, to keep us busy. There is a burning need for a complete study of Keats's influences, but in the present state of knowledge the attempt would be doomed to a certain superficiality.

All the problems gravitate around the special qualities of the two writers with whom we are dealing. Because Shakespeare is so diverse and wide-ranging in his field of reference, and because Keats is such a congenitally open-minded reader, capable of developing and even changing his thoughts, there is little that can be taken as fixed or solid except the very diversity of stimulus and response. One thing which I hope does not emerge is any great inconsistency, for even in complexity there can be substantial inter-relatedness. I take heart from Keats's own belief in identity expressed through fluctuating feelings and circumstances, in hoping that 'something of great constancy' emerges from the evidence.

R.S.WHITE

Acknowledgements

I have been helped by a large number of individuals and some institutions existing as collections of friendly people. I must thank Mrs Gee for facilitating my use of the resources of the Keats House at Hampstead, Rae Ann Nager at the Houghton Library in Harvard, the University of Newcastle Upon Tyne for giving me research funds to visit these libraries, and the Humanities Research Centre at the Australian National University for providing me with an idyllic six months of scholarly companionship in Canberra when I wrote the first and most voluminous of the many drafts of this book.

One whose assistance I cannot repay in person is the late Professor David Bonnell Green of Boston, whose PhD thesis was a transcription of Keats's markings which allowed me to double-check quotations when I was frustratingly distant from Harvard. He intended to write a book on the subject and it is tragic that he did not complete his work. All I can hope is that his widow and his friends will find some satisfaction in seeing the project carried further. Professor Irene Harris of Boston helped create the link for me with David Green's papers in the spirit of open encouragement, an appreciation of which is the greatest reward of working with scholars. Her own work on Keats and Shakespeare is important and I have gained much from her own thesis.

I owe another huge debt to Professor Ian Donaldson who took great pains to coax from me a more adequate book, expressing enthusiasm and reservations with impeccable timing. I owe it largely to him that the book is completed, and I wish for his sake it could have been better.

Others I must thank with brevity but sincerity: Professor Francis Berry, Dr Barrie Bullen, Dr John Casey, Professor John Colmer, Dr Christopher Cordner, Cathy Davidson, Barbara Everett, Dr Desmond Graham, Professor Ernst Honigmann, Dr Paul Hamilton, Claire Lamont, the late Dr Peter Laver, Dr David Norbrook, John McGahern, John Pellowe, Dr Peter Regan, Trude Schwab, Professor

Gary Waller, Jane Whiteley, John Willett. These and many others, extended to me the kind of sympathetic magic which is constantly displayed by John Keats himself; or those 'little, nameless, unremembered acts Of kindness and of love' celebrated by Wordsworth.

By no means finally, I recall with some gratitude but more awe the earliest contribution made by the late James Maxwell. When I was planning the book at a very early stage, I met him perambulating the cricket field at Oxford and showed him, with some smugness, what I considered an exhaustive list which I had compiled of things written on the subject. Apparently taking a split second to read it he curtly said, 'Apart from Chatterjee and *Notes and Queries*, 1952, I think you've got the main ones' and abruptly turned away. With characteristic modesty he had neglected to say the second was by himself, a tiny piece, but one whose implications helped me to think the job was worth doing. More recently, Brian Southam and the editors at The Athlone Press have demonstrated remarkable tolerance and patience in dealing with a text which involves many publishing problems. Jonathon Bates's *Shakespeare and the English Romantic Imagination* (Clarendon Press, Oxford, 1986) appeared too late for consideration.

October 1985   R.S. WHITE

Note On Quotations

For reasons of consistency, and to enable the reader to find quotations readily, I have decided to quote throughout from the Alexander text of Shakespeare's plays, rather than reproducing the respective texts which Keats himself read. When a textual point is relevant, I shall mention the wording in Keats's text. I attempt to indicate the nature of Keats's markings on his texts by underlining and by side-marking, although the printed result implies a neatness and regularity which Keats's own dashes do not have. Quotations from Keats's poems are taken from *The Poems of John Keats*, edited by Jack Stillinger (London, 1978), and the letters are quoted from *The Letters of John Keats*, edited by Hyder E. Rollins (two volumes, Cambridge, Mass, 1958). Frequent reference is made to *Keats: The Complete Poems*, edited by Miriam Allott (London, 1970) and to Caroline Spurgeon, *Keats's Shakespeare* (Oxford, 1929).

– and why should there not be another species with two rough edges like a Rat-trap? I hope you will find all my long letters of that species, and all will be well; for by merely touching the spring delicately and etherially, the rough edged will fly immediately into a proper compactness, and thus you may make a good wholesome loaf, with your own leven in it, of my fragments –

Keats to Reynolds, 3 May 1818

Introduction
Keats's Shakespeare: Shakespearean Keats

Shakespeare may never have had such an attentive, perceptive and creative reader as John Keats. The very representation of Shakespeare's face acted as a kind of talisman for the young poet. When he came across it on the Isle of Wight he found instant kinship:

> In the passage I found a head of Shakspeare which I had not before seen – It is most likely the same that George spoke so well of; for I like it extremely – Well – this head I have hung over my Books ...[1]

Two years later, the portrait continued to delight him, tassels and all:

> I am sitting opposite the Shakspeare I brought from the Isle of wight – and I never look at it but the silk tassels on it give me as much pleasure as the face of the Poet itself ...[2]

In 1817, when he first saw the face, Keats was saturating himself in the words of Shakespeare and by 1819, his enthusiasm tempered but not abated, he was writing his own greatest poetry which is often called 'Shakespearean'. By the latter stage he had absorbed the influence so deeply that the word 'sources' is inadequate to describe the omnipresent but transformed ghost of Shakespeare's poetry and language. In his formative period we may identify with a degree of precision what attracted Keats in Shakespeare's plays, but at the time of his own mature poetry we can speak only of a general spirit and mode of expression which, although intimately related to what he found in Shakespeare, emerges in his own unique voice. These are our twin subjects: the aspects of Shakespeare which Keats most valued upon systematically reading the plays in 1817, and the Shakespeare which obliquely emerges from Keats's own poetry.

There is quite a lot of evidence we can use in the enterprise. Keats's letters are packed with quotations from Shakespeare and comments upon his words. We also have two copies of Shakespeare's plays owned by Keats, which he has copiously marked and occasionally annotated.

The first is a seven-volume edition edited by Johnson and Steevens, which he acquired in April 1817.[3] The other is a 'facsimile' of the First Folio, which came into Keats's possession also sometime during 1817.[4] The markings lead us not only to the 'immortal scraps'[5] of passages in Shakespeare which are universally admired and often anthologized, but also to corners of the dramatist's writings which are not so often noticed, and which are equally evidence of Keats's own taste or interest. In addition, as temporary dramatic critic for *The Champion*, Keats wrote a short but pregnant piece published on 21 December 1817.[6] Although primarily in praise of Kean's acting, and journalistic in tone, the review provides valuable evidence of some of Keats's ideas on Shakespeare. Next, Keats shows himself to be knowledgeable about currents of critical thinking in an age dominated by Coleridge, Hazlitt and Lamb, and one which was reacting strongly against the approach of Doctor Johnson. In particular, we have Keats's copy of Hazlitt's *Characters of Shakespear's Plays* (1817) which he has marked and annotated,[7] and which deserves detailed attention in a later chapter since Hazlitt certainly influenced strongly Keats's way of thinking about Shakespeare. Finally, of course, there is Keats's own poetry which demonstrates how he absorbed and transmuted into his own poetic voice many of the aspects which interested him in Shakespeare. We can never forget that Keats is, in his own right 'among the English poets',[8] and that he cannot be placed in the pale beside even Shakespeare since his verse springs

> from so strange influence
> That we must ever wonder how, and whence
> It came.[9]

Keats's reading of Shakespeare started well before he owned the copies which we now have. Before 1817 he has quoted in his letters from *Macbeth* and *Hamlet*, he has mentioned Titania, Cordelia and (Shakespeare's?) Brutus in verse-letters, and as we shall see he draws on Shakespeare in 'I stood tip-toe' (December 1816). But there is little doubt that in 1817 Keats methodically saturated himself in Shakespeare. After April, when he acquired his copies of the plays, and up to December when he wrote his theatre review, his letters are peppered with allusions and quotations. By March 1818 he had quoted in letters or poems from all plays except *Titus Andronicus, 1 Henry VI, The Comedy of Errors* and *Pericles*. (Of these, only *1 Henry VI* is completely unmarked in his texts.) In this one year, from April to April, then, it is quite likely Keats had read the *Complete Works*. Whether or not the markings on his texts were made during this period we cannot tell, but it seems a fair assumption that most of them were. In the second half of 1818 and thereafter, the density of direct quotation in the letters decreases, although *King Lear* and *Hamlet* remain consistent points of reference. There is no reason to suppose, however, that Keats had retreated from his admiration of Shakespeare, since his poetry maintains a powerful Shakespearean presence, allusions and quotations fully absorbed into Keats's own poetic idiom but still traceable to their sources. *The Eve of St Agnes* and the great *Odes*, (February onwards, 1819) and *Otho the Great* (July-August 1819) are amongst the works which are most indebted to Shakespeare. The relative absence of quotation in the letters may simply mean that, having finished a first reading of the plays, Keats is not constantly encountering the words of the dramatist in an everyday fashion of noticing the precise wording, while his retentive, poet's memory has stored up what is creatively useful for his own work. John Middleton Murry in *Keats and Shakespeare*,[10] a book which remains helpful for its intuitive judgments rather than its scholarship, argues that Keats did lose interest in Shakespeare at the end of 1819 while he was composing the first version of *Hyperion* because 'Keats had fallen under the spell of Milton'.[11] I do not think the implicit conclusions drawn are inevitable. Certainly, Keats was reading and responding to Milton at this time as excitedly as he had to Shakespeare in 1817. Certainly the first *Hyperion* is a consciously Miltonic work. But it still contains enough Shakespearean allusion (as we shall see) for us to conclude that Keats was absorbing Milton into what he already knew about, rather than embracing Milton as a rejection of Shakespeare. The very evidence that Murry goes on to use, the fact that Keats returned shortly afterwards to a full employment of his Shakespearean resources in *The Eve of St Agnes* and the *Odes*, could be used to prove that he had never retreated from Shakespeare. None the less, Murry's overall thesis that *Hyperion: A Fragment* is less 'Shakespearean' than Keats's other great poetry, may not be wrong. However, when dealing with the revised though equally fragmentary *The Fall of Hyperion: A Dream*, the argument presented towards the end of this book is that, in its attitudes and expression, the second *Hyperion* is profoundly influenced by the Shakespearean vision of tragedy.

There is some evidence, however, that Keats's attitude to Shakespeare did change, and that it changed in line with his deepening scrutiny of the moral content of poetry itself. The development in his thinking can be traced as a kind of internal dialectic between March

1819 when he sends a long quotation from Hazlitt's defence of his critique on *Coriolanus* to his brother George's family in America, and July-August of this year when he composed *Lamia*. Before this period, it seems certain that Keats revelled in poetry as an expression of beauty, and although he was concerned about 'the lore of good and ill',[12] his general assumption was that the beautiful must also be true in a moral sense, that if something is said with poetic 'intensity' it must also be ethically acceptable. If anything, one could call this a Spenserian assumption, and we should remind ourselves of Keats's almost equal fondness in his youth for Spenser's poetry. But the reason explaining why the greatest expression of this idea at the end of 'Ode on a Grecian Urn' is so commented upon, may be that Keats by this time did not entirely believe the sentiment, and that he is in the middle of a personal debate about it. In the 'Ode' he can only put the phrase 'Beauty is truth, truth beauty' in inverted commas rather than in his own, narrator's voice,[13] as an indication that the Urn's limitations of perspective should be closely examined when its words are applied to the world of human passion. Hazlitt's argument, which Keats in the letter reproduces in full and without comment,[14] is that in *Coriolanus* Shakespeare is in fact misusing the rhetorical effects of poetry to reinforce an authoritarian and potentially evil principle that the needs of ordinary people are not so significant as the neuroses of 'great men'. When we come to *Lamia* we find Keats himself questioning the doctrine that 'beauty is truth', for the beautiful Lamia is merely a deceitful image while the 'truthful' Apollonius is far from beautiful in his capacity to destroy rainbows. The problems are not resolved in Keats's poem, but are instead left suspended in paradoxes, and it is quite likely that this uneasy resolution of the conflicts mirrors Keats's own worries about the relationship between an aesthetic surface and a moral message. The one thing we need to say at this stage is that Keats has retreated from an uncritical and idolatrous acceptance of a 'chameleon' Shakespeare and that, in a wary mood that rejects not Shakespeare but his own earlier image of Shakespeare, he is carrying on his own, independent enquiry into the 'truthfulness' of art, influenced as much by Milton as by Spenser, and no less 'Shakespearean' than ever.

Middleton Murry's book, *Keats and Shakespeare*, is conceived rather as literary biography and a study of the nature of poetry than as an examination of what Keats found, appreciated and used in Shakespeare. He sums up his scope and aim by saying,

Keats and Shakespeare are alike, because they are both pure poets, and pure poetry consists in the power so to express a perception that it appears at the same time to reveal a new aspect of beauty and a new aspect of truth.[15]

Caroline Spurgeon's *Keats's Shakespeare: A Descriptive Study Based on New Material*[16] is closer in its intention to the present enterprise. Spurgeon describes the two texts of Shakespeare marked by Keats, transcribes (mostly accurately) the markings on five plays, lists what she considers to be parallels between *The Tempest* and *Endymion*, and presents a fondly appreciative 'Introductory Essay' on the links between the writers. Her book is now difficult to obtain, and there are also reasons for producing a different kind of book using the material. Spurgeon reproduces only a small fraction of the markings, excluding the most interesting and important plays, *King Lear, Hamlet* and *Macbeth*, and her comments on these are necessarily brief. The interests of her generation of criticism are rather different from our own, and her approach is perhaps more anecdotal than truly exploratory. She does not attempt to place Keats's attitudes to literature and to Shakespeare in the context of contemporary concerns, such as the literary theory and criticism of Hazlitt who was undoubtedly crucial in helping Keats to formulate his own ideas. The present work is more comprehensive in its scope, more analytical in its approach.

Some criticisms of Spurgeon's book made by reviewers when it appeared focus the problems implicit in the task of analysing the markings on Keats's copies of Shakespeare. Nobody has ever challenged the supposition that they were made by Keats himself and inspection of the evidence reveals no reason to treat this as a problem. However, reviewers found more difficulty in accepting Caroline Spurgeon's general commentary. R.D. Havens made the following criticism:

She makes no study of the notable words, phrases, and passages that Keats did *not* mark and apparently has not considered the probability that reasons quite apart from esthetics or even Shakespeare may have been responsible for some of the markings.[17]

Helen Darbishire, a little less trenchant in her tone, was also worried:

Whilst most of her suggestions [about why Keats marked particular passages] are sound and she is never unduly dogmatic, yet the honest reader will protest that a number of other explanations would equally commend themselves.[18]

I have no magic solutions to these problems, and I must honestly admit them. There are, however, some things to be said in favour of the enterprise, and some caveats to be entered that might make an interpretation less vulnerable than was Spurgeon's. First, the existence of the markings in Keats's hand is in itself valuable evidence for any future study of the creative relationship between Keats and the words of Shakespeare. Even if there is room for many different interpretations from many different people, the evidence should be examined if we acknowledge the importance of Shakespeare to Keats. So long as we keep in mind the context of the letters and poems, the markings must at least give us valuable clues to Keats's mode of reading and his preferences. Secondly, to claim definitiveness in interpreting even the marks that are there, let alone (as Havens suggests) those that are not, would be unwise since the task is, frankly, impossible. There are too many unknowns and imponderables to make the attempt. The markings are not parts of a jigsaw that can be fitted together to give us a complete picture of what Keats found of value in Shakespeare, because often we discover important speeches (such as Hamlet's 'To be or not to be...') which are not marked but which are quoted in the letters. However, the body of material is a part of the evidence, and can contribute to our fuller (but never total) understanding of Keats's attitudes to Shakespeare. Thirdly, it is to be hoped that some things may be said which are not seeking speculatively for 'explanations' or reasons for the markings, but rather descriptive of the evidence. It may be of interest to know the *fact* that Keats chose to mark a phrase, since it may lead the reader to notice something in Shakespeare that one had never recognized before, or give a reason for linking up the information with something observed in Keats's own poetry. This is not the same as speculating upon why Keats marked a phrase, and in fact it is very rarely necessary to impute an intention on his part. For all these reasons, while admitting the theoretical difficulties, I believe it is worth proceeding with tact and imagination, in the knowledge that the intellectual dividends, in terms of our increased appreciation of both Shakespeare and Keats, are great enough in themselves. We can discover from the evidence of the letters and markings much of what Keats read, and what was significant to him. All this information often allows us to enhance our recognition of Shakespeare's poetic diversity since Keats is such a sensitive reader, and at other times it alerts us to words in Shakespeare which in some identifiable way have contributed towards his own poetry. In the final analysis the value of the enterprise lies in the amount of information which it makes available, and the stimulus it can provide other readers towards making their own general judgments.

The further problems encountered in defining the influence of Shakespeare upon Keats's poetry are perhaps even more delicate and difficult. I certainly do not wish to provide a host of verbal 'sources' and reminiscences which would run the risk of turning Keats into little more than a derivative poet leaning on Shakespeare, nor do I wish in a literal-minded way to trace Keats's 'Road to Xanadu' through his readings inevitably back to Shakespeare. Instead, I shall concentrate upon *kinds* of influence, general, 'Shakespearean' areas where Keats found a stimulus to his own creative imagination: areas such as a special use of language, a range of attitudes towards love and nature, and more comprehensively an awakening conception of tragic experience as exemplified in works of literature. It is, in fact, peculiarly difficult to speak of Keats's 'sources' without (in the words of Robert F. Gleckner) 'oversimplification of what is essentially an extraordinarily complex fabric of association, echo, and allusion (and hence indebtedness)'.[19] It may seem odd, for example, that at one point in the commentary I locate Hamlet's words behind Keats's, while at another I find Lear behind the same passage, in the belief that both plays contribute some verbal stimulus (perhaps, for the sake of argument, also in tandem with words by Milton or Wordsworth). What is happening in such examples, I suggest, apart from the unique alchemy by which Keats makes a phrase his own,[20] is often the much more mysterious process of Keats actually finding a point of imaginative contact between diverse passages which have struck his attention. To discover such a level of richly lateral associativeness is rewarding, but it is far too subtle and intricate a matter on which to make bold pronouncements.

The largest problem raised by the subject-matter as a whole is also the most exciting. By interpreting the evidence of the ways in which Keats understood Shakespeare, we find ourselves in some limited but real way recreating the mysterious process of reading itself, as carried out by an unusually alert and sensitive poet. We are at least catching a glimpse of what Proust describes as the nature of reading, 'that fruitful miracle of a communication in the midst of solitude'.[21] For Keats, reading is by its nature not a single thing, nor does it alternate between active and passive facets of a single activity. Reading provides, paradoxically, a simultaneous continuum between passivity and active creation, between self-annulment and self-absorption. The words Keats is reading begin as a kind of potential, to be activated by the reader's relationship with them, which may change from time to time even when the same reader reads the same text. Keats regards the relationship as a co-operative one, where reader and text become indissolubly united in a moment of creativity. In a wonderful image he implies that the experience may be shared mysteriously between like-minded readers of the same text. He writes to his brother George,

> You will remember me in the same manner – and the more when I tell you that I shall read a passage of Shakspeare every Sunday at ten o Clock – you read one at the same time and we shall be as near each other as blind bodies can be in the same room...[22]

In a comparable way, the unique relationship forged between Keats and the words of Shakespeare may in some measure extend to include us as we witness his experiences of reading.

I The importance of reading Shakespeare

One of Keats's readings of *King Lear* is well documented, enabling us to ascertain something of his attitude towards reading Shakespeare. In a letter to Bailey dated 23 January 1818, Keats describes how he began the reading:

> My Brother Tom is getting stronger but his Spitting of blood continues – I sat down to read King Lear yesterday, and felt the greatness of the thing up to the writing of a Sonnet preparatory thereto – in my next you shall have it There were some miserable reports of Rice's health...[1]

Earlier in the letter he had been brooding upon 'the deeps of good and evil', attempting to be philosophical about human suffering. The cluster of his concerns about misfortune and ill-health gathers around the act of reading *Lear*. He often comes to the play for understanding and for consolation or courage in times of mental pain suffered on behalf of others. In the special case of his brother's illness there is an added personal connection, for months later he is to return to the play and ring the words 'Poor Tom' in his Folio text, dating the mark 'Sunday Evening Oct. 4. 1818'. During this period and afterwards, Keats invariably refers to his brother in letters as 'Poor Tom'. It is also characteristic that Keats should find the reading of the play a creatively stimulating activity, 'up to the writing of a Sonnet'. On the same day as his letter to Bailey, he writes to his brothers George and Tom:

> I think a little change has taken place in my intellect lately – I cannot bear to be uninterested or unemployed, I, who for so long a time, have been addicted to passiveness – Nothing is finer for the purposes of great productions, than a very gradual ripening of the intellectual powers – As an instance of this – observe – I sat down yesterday to read King Lear once again the thing appeared to demand the prologue of a Sonnet, I wrote it & began to read – ...[2]

He then proceeds to transcribe a slightly revised version of the Sonnet that appears handwritten in the Hampstead Folio of Shakespeare's works, facing the first page of *King Lear*. The Folio version runs as follows:[3]

'On sitting down to read *King Lear* once again'

O Golden-tongued Romance, with serene Lute!
   Fair plumed Syren, Queen of far-away!
   Leave melodizing on this wintry day
Shut up thine olden Pages and be mute.
Adieu! for, once again, the fierce dispute,
   Betwixt Damnation and impassion'd clay
   Must I burn through; once more humbly assay
The bitter-sweet of this Shakespearean fruit.
Chief Poet! and ye Clouds of Albion,
   Begetters of our deep eternal theme!
When through the old oak forest I am gone,
   Let me not wander in a barren dream:
But, when I am consumed in the fire,
Give me new Phoenix wings to fly at my desire.
                        Jan. 22 1818

One would be hard pressed to decide whether the main subject of the Sonnet is *King Lear*, Shakespeare or the act of reading, but what is immediately noticeable is the tone of energetic optimism. The play represents for Keats some kind of personal purgation, and he must burn through the pain and suffering depicted in it to attain a new understanding and impetus towards action. The poet determines not to shy away from fiercely engaging with harsh truths. Rather than allowing himself to escape into a leisurely, far-away world of romance, he steels himself to live through severity and adversity. Shakespeare, 'Chief Poet', is the representative of the English poets who inherit 'our deep eternal theme' which may be misery and mortality. The experience is not, however, melancholy or depressing but exhilarating, a 'fierce dispute' which charges the reader with passion and energy, no matter how demanding the struggle. That Keats speaks of 'The bitter-sweet of this Shakespearean fruit' is significant, for it is the feeling for contrast, for light and shade, joy and melancholy, that Keats sometimes specifies as the quintessential, Shakespearean quality. When we come to examine the plays, we will notice that he often draws attention to oppositions, finding the undercurrent of sadness in a romantic comedy such as *As You Like It*, and the bright, lighthearted moments in the tragedies. In the epithet 'bitter-sweet', Keats is signalling his desire not to exclude any aspect of the Shakespearean experience, however disagreeble, uncomfortable or inharmonious.

The sonnet tells us a lot about Keats's habits of reading. He reads actively, energetically, involving himself totally in the concerns of the work. 'Must I burn through' is not only determined and positive but also holds a ring of passive submission, repeated in 'once more humbly assay'. He must be burned, as well as burn. 'Impassioned clay' has a wide reference to both reader and play. Perhaps invoking Lear's line as he wipes his hand, 'it smells of mortality' (IV.vi.133),[4] the phrase identifies the properties of both participants in the activity of reading. The reader is impassioned in at least two reciprocal ways: he is bringing his own feelings to bear on the play's actions, and in turn his feelings are modified or stirred by the words he is reading. Like clay, he is malleable under the influence of the dramatic action and the poetry, and after the violent modelling of his emotions has been carried out he is hardened as a fresh identity. Similarly, the play can be seen by the energetic reader as an almost living thing, projecting and eliciting emotion. It too is clay, under the hands of both playwright and reader in their respectively creative and re-creative functions. By a combination of active engagement and submissive receptivity, the reader finds himself present at the creative moment. As the play 'comes to life' in the mind and feelings of a reader, then the boundaries that are normally assumed to divide the writer, the play and the reader seem to dissolve, and this miracle may be repeated 'once again' at every new reading. Keats trusts and hopes that the experience of such a reading will not be a 'barren dream', divorced from his own personality and the reality in which he lives his own life. Instead, it will be a consuming fire which may destroy illusion, harden the clay, and allow the reader to emerge with a renewed spiritual wholeness, liberating him into a wider and more personal field of action: 'Give me new Phoenix wings to fly at *my* desire!' Keats, then, reads both actively and submissively, hoping to be changed by the experience, by approaching it with an accessibility which will enable him to live through it on his pulses. In another letter largely concerned with reading,[5] Keats draws a contrast between the energetic activity of the bee and the passive receptivity of the flower opening itself and there, as in the sonnet, he seeks to exemplify the properties of both. As a reader of *King Lear*, Keats risks the loss of one identity, in the hope that he will find another which will give him renewed hope in the face of destructive conflict. In the very act of writing a creative work of his own, Keats is asserting his own new identity, forged in the humility of succumbing to the play on past occasions. Self-annulment and self-assertion are equally important in Keats's view of the reader's activity, and hovering between the damnation of despairing self-forgetfulness and the impassioned clay of personal hope, the sonnet (presumably like Lear himself, in Keats's opinion, or the play as a whole) enacts the victory of the latter. The struggle was for the poet one he often had to face, and he was to write in May 1819, 'I must choose between despair & Energy – I choose the latter'.[6]

Implicit in the sonnet on *King Lear* is a mode of thought which appears to have been a personal archetype for Keats throughout his life, and however many metaphors he uses to describe his attitude towards the related subjects of reading, writing and living, he harps upon a single pattern. Complete submission to external impressions, complete immersion in the flux of experience, lead to a feeling awareness of the dark and light in human existence, and out of this knowledge, phoenix-like, emerges a fully responsible, compassionate and self-aware identity, able in its independence to 'do the world some good'[7] (a phrase which, ironically enough, Keats may have borrowed from the critic he most condemns, Dr Johnson[8]). The pattern runs consistently from self-annulment through self-assertive knowledge to the creation of an identity:

> Do you not see how necessary a World of Pains and troubles is to school an Intelligence and make it a soul? A Place where the heart must feel and suffer in a thousand diverse ways! Not merely is the Heart a Hornbook, It is the Minds Bible, it is the Minds experience, it is the teat from which the Mind or intelligence sucks its identity ...[9]

Even in such a generalized statement, the profound importance of reading is intimated by the image of the heart as a hornbook, and in developing the philosophy at different points of his life, Keats uses Shakespeare in particular as a touchstone and reference point for his thoughts. In the well known passages in the Letters concerning such ideas as 'negative capability', the 'egotistical sublime', and the 'vale of soul-making', Shakespeare is usually mentioned or quoted, and the dramatist's words are never far away when Keats's mind is working under full pressure. To the young poet, reading Shakespeare was an active pursuit of experience and self-knowledge, and the poetry was as 'real' as 'the existences of Sun Moon & Stars'.[10]

In repeating, and gradually developing, his ideas on the formation of the identity, Keats often works with antitheses to describe them. It is important, however, to realize that he is not setting up mutually exclusive opposites, but attempting to explain a process, a continuum of experience, lying between the poles of 'negative capability' and the assertion of the self as the 'egotistical sublime'. As a person grows through experience (of which reading is a part), he begins with an imaginative openness, a capacity for self-annulment in the fluctuations of things outside himself, and moves towards an integration of the self which emerges in full understanding and self-belief. On the way he should never lose the starting-point of sympathetic projection into the feelings of others, nor receptivity to new experience, but rather he should carry such things along as part of the process itself. This is why a play of Shakespeare may be fresh at each reading, and why the phrase 'once again' in the Sonnet should be emphasised,[11] for each reading may bring a renewed sense of self-identity. Keats's most analytical statement on the matter confides that there are three 'Materials' working simultaneously in the process of 'Spirit-creation':

> These three Materials are the Intelligence – the human heart (as distinguished from intelligence or Mind) and the World or Elemental space suited for the proper action of Mind and Heart on each other for the purpose of forming the Soul or Intelligence destined to possess the sense of Identity.[12]

In this concise formulation the capacity for feeling and receptivity is identified with the 'heart', and although quite distinct from rational thinking ('Mind'), the two are seen to be collaborative and mutually enriching. Whilst the one submits to external impressions, the other speculates more actively upon experience, and the result is a unique, continuously and continually evolving identity. In describing such a concept of individual identity, Keats is careful to avoid the opposing dangers of self-annihilation and egotism, and to eliminate what he sees as the false opposition of feeling and thinking. The most satisfying aspect of his theory is that it includes both aspects of the human mind, without denying the integrity of either. Even in his poetry, one feels that Keats, although worried about the occasional discrepancies between the reason and the feelings, prefers to encapsulate them both in a paradox, rather than deny, in binary fashion, the fact that each may have separate access to a single truth.[13] Each of the great Odes, in its individual way, generates its thought from this kind of paradox.

The importance of Shakespeare to Keats's thinking on these matters is profound, supplying both the example and the explanation. In the same letter, for instance, *King Lear* is close to his concerns, as he follows up an implication of his theory, the acknowledgment that suffering is not only instructive in forming the soul, but also inevitable to the innocent heart:

> The whole appears to resolve into this – that Man is originally 'a poor forked creature' subject to the same mischances as the beasts of the forest, destined to hardships and disquietude of some kind or other.[14]

So drenched in Shakespeare's language is Keats's mind by this time (April 1819) that, as one critic has pointed out, he is probably unconsciously but with 'effortless aptness' running together two Shakespearean references, one from *King Lear* and one from *Measure for Measure*.[15] In doing so, Keats is instructing us in an association made in Shakespeare's own mind when he contemplates the existence of suffering in the world. More than this, Keats's comment about the necessity of facing adversity as an inescapable responsibility involved in the creation of one's identity, is in part a gloss on *King Lear* as a whole, amplifying the thought in the Sonnet. Keats has forged his concept of life as a 'vale of soul-making' partly through reading *King Lear* and through examining his response to the experience. Although Lear himself must 'burn', 'bound upon a wheel of fire', through unmitigated mental suffering and unavoidable submission to emotional pain, the reader, first submerging himself in the painful feelings which are generated, may at last find his own identity again, as a cleansed and new person. There is a personal value to the reader (or the audience in the theatre) in burning through Lear's pain and suffering, as he emerges knowing his own separateness from the King, with an enhanced perception of the limitations of being human which also brings an awareness of its potential. More integrated, more self-aware by being imaginatively aware of the suffering of another, he may finally detach himself from vicarious experience and return to the limitations of personal existence, strengthened by the process:

> 'The oldest hath borne most; we that are young
> Shall never see so much nor live so long.'
>   (V.iii.325–6)

It may be a sobering and humble knowledge which is acquired through such a thought, but it is equally a comfort to know that somebody else has 'borne most' before us, allowing us the freedom of knowlege and of self-identification. The play itself is a 'vale of soul-making', enforcing upon the responsive reader a form of acceptance or understanding which is private and personal. Perhaps it is this strange power of the play to throw us back on our own resources which explains why there are so many differing critical interpretations, ranging from pessimism to optimism. The play may teach us as much about ourselves as about an external reality. If this should be so, then it is Keats who has led us to an intimate and profound secret.

Given his philosophy, it is no wonder that Keats should indicate, by underlining, an interest in the most important principle discovered by Hazlitt, his favourite critic, in reading *King Lear*:

> That poetry is an interesting study, for this reason, that it relates to whatever is most interesting in human life. Whoever therefore has a contempt for poetry, has a contempt for himself and humanity.[16]

Meanwhile, as the experience of the play is helping the reader to create his identity, the intensity of the reader in the activity is investing a new reality in the words of the work of literature. Keats says the following:

> As Tradesmen say every thing is worth what it will fetch, so probably every mental pursuit takes its reality and worth from the ardour of the pursuer – being in itself a nothing – Ethereal thing[s] may at least be thus real, divided under three heads – Things real – things semireal – and no things – Things real – such as existences of Sun Moon & Stars and passages of Shakspeare – Things semireal such as Love, the Clouds &c which require a greeting of the Spirit to make them wholly exist – and Nothings which are made Great and dignified by an ardent pursuit – Which by the by stamps the burgundy mark on the bottles of our Minds, insomuch as they are able to 'consec[r]ate whate'er they look upon'...[17]

The words of Shakespeare may be so immediate in their revelation that they are 'real' in themselves, requiring no greeting of the spirit, but reading in itself is a reciprocal activity, taking part of its value from the reader's creative energy. The quality of a reading, judged by its 'ardency' may 'consecrate' upon the words on a page an existence in the 'real' world. The writer's language is no more vital to the collaborative activity of realising a work of art than the perceiver's intensity of engagement. Reading depends as much on the existence of the reader as the text.[18]

For Keats, then, reading Shakespeare is an involved act of re-creation, allowing him to find a freshly renewed sense of his own personal identity. So much is present in the Sonnet on *King Lear*, and is consistently supported by comments in his letters. It is in the context of these ideas about the nature and value of reading that Keats's markings on his texts of Shakespeare's plays should be examined. He reads as a learned musician interprets a score of music, finding his own individual and personal sources of intense interest, manifesting the particular burgundy mark of his own mind in making his choices. Sometimes he marks isolated felicities of expression, and sometimes he records in his markings what he finds important in his reading of a whole play, identifying for us the passages, phrases and words that most immediately strike his attention in the act of reading. By doing so he is, in his own words, consecrating the text in a greeting of the spirit. When Keats asks Reynolds 'to pick out some lines from Hyperion and put a mark x to the false beauty proceeding from art, and one ‖ to the true voice of feeling',[19] he is saying something about his own practice in reading the works of other poets. In his copies of Shakespeare we find no crosses (except used as asterisks), but we find many side-markings and underlinings, presumably signifying those parts where Keats detected 'the true voice of feeling', whatever that should be in the particular context. In order to build up an impression of what kinds of literary qualities Keats may be finding in Shakespeare, we can now look at the well-formulated and public statements of critical method and practice made by the critic-philosopher whom Keats heard, read, admired, quoted and generally agreed with – William Hazlitt.

II Hazlitt and Keats's attitudes to Shakespeare

Keats always admired 'Hazlitt's depth of Taste',[1] and many commentators have pointed out how close are the two men in their thoughts on literature. Kenneth Muir, for example, argues that 'nearly all Keats's theories about poetry were developed from remarks of Hazlitt', although he adds a qualification:

> Because he accepted nothing on trust, but proved his axioms on his pulses, Keats's borrowings were all transformed and individualised, so that they came to express not merely his tastes but his deepest convictions.[2]

The purpose of this chapter is not to trace any specific indebtedness owed by Keats to Hazlitt, but to use Hazlitt's well-formulated precepts in order to build up some guidelines about Keats's central areas of interest in reading Shakespeare. Just as many of our own ideas on Shakespeare are partly conditioned by the teachers who inspired us or particular critical approaches with which we are acquainted, so Keats's thoughts do not come in a vacuum, and it is easy to prove that Hazlitt was a profound influence upon him. By reading Hazlitt, we can understand more about Keats's priorities. Since Keats's comments in his letters are often gnomic and opportunistic, and since he admired Hazlitt's criticism to a degree of idolatory, it seems reasonable to flesh out the cryptic words of the one with the more discursively expressed thoughts of the other. It is clear that the two men are like-minded in their ways of interpreting literature and of appreciating creativity in general, and so it does not much matter for our purposes whether Hazlitt is seen as a source for the younger poet, or as a public figure whose expressions of opinions, always incisive and firm, may have given Keats the confidence to believe in his own developing and half-formulated ideas. Whilst respecting differences in language, emphases and profundity, we can still recognize common preoccupations. The enterprise is also valuable for what we can discover about

Hazlitt as a serious critic who has until recently been underestimated. Keats's own trust in his critical taste and principles allows us to treat Hazlitt as an important and systematic thinker, neither undisciplined nor 'merely' impressionistic. (Indeed, he sought to turn impressionism into a disciplined mode of thinking.) The appearance of several recent books on Hazlitt should have begun to dispel any slighting evaluation of a critic who, in many ways, rivals Coleridge as the most coherent and serious critical thinker of his age.[3]

Keats had been reading Hazlitt's reviews from early in his own writing career, and when the two men eventually met (in winter, 1816–17[4]), they shared the dubious compliment of having both been vilified in the pages of *Blackwood's*, something which may have given them the basis for a friendship and mutual respect that lasted through several meetings. It was no mean feat to gain respect from Hazlitt, since he appears to have been a difficult and prickly person. Keats may have detected a rather lonely and melancholy man behind the tough, public exterior, for he was to jot on his copy of Hazlitt's book, beside the chapter on *The Tempest*, 'I cannot help seeing Hazlitt like Ferdinand – "in an odd angle of the Isle sitting" – his arms in this sad knot.' (In the context,[5] Ferdinand is grieving for his lost father.) Keats also generously expressed the wish that Hazlitt should know that he had more friends and admirers than he would acknowledge,[6] although his own near worship of the older critic did not prevent him from mischievously parodying his eccentricities.[7] Keats attended several of Hazlitt's lectures on poetry between January and March 1818, but he had to miss the lectures on the English comic writers at the end of 1818, despite his wish to go. Hazlitt was to give him a copy of the lectures in manuscript, when Keats called in December.[8] It is disputed exactly when Keats acquired his *Characters of Shakespear's Plays*, but it seems certain that he had read it by January 1818, which means that he was probably using it in 1817, the year when he was absorbing himself totally in Shakespeare. We need not go into more detail here about the timing of meetings between Keats and Hazlitt. Given the undoubted closeness of their opinions on literature, our task is to describe the ideas which they shared. Of course, Hazlitt cannot have been the only person who influenced Keats's ideas on Shakespeare. Although later to repudiate the taste of Leigh Hunt, some of that writer's dilettantish sentimentality must have rubbed off on Keats in the early days. It was when Keats came closer to Haydon that he began to back off from Hunt, and no doubt the painter's ebullient enthusiasm and energy were the qualities which encouraged Keats to read Shakespeare aloud in his presence, and talk animatedly about the poetry.[9] Keats must also have been aware of the few but influential essays on Shakespeare by Charles Lamb, whose extreme view on the matter must have given confidence to Keats that the reader's response to the text is just as valid as a particular performance in the theatre. (It should be added, however, that Keats was himself also an eager theatre-goer.) All these influences may one day claim attention, but at this stage the presence of Hazlitt is so impressively central to Keats that we must turn to his ideas in more detail. The account will proceed under general headings which are intended to reflect the important concepts shared by Hazlitt and Keats in their understandings of Shakespeare.

A philosophy of particularity

Hazlitt's refusal to be doctrinaire, or to generalize without considering particular details, was a mode of perception deeply congenial to Keats. He was to praise Kean's acting for precisely this quality:

> Other actors are continually thinking of their sum-total effect throughout a play. Kean delivers himself up to the instant feeling, without a shadow of a thought about any thing else.[10]

Every page of Keats's letters and poems demonstrates his trust in instantaneous, particularized responses through his feelings. Hazlitt provided a philosophical justification for Keats's instinctive method. Roy Park, working through Hazlitt's ideas on religion, philosophy, painting and poetry, insists that he devoted his life to counteracting what he saw as the pernicious tendency of the age towards abstractions, 'systems, theories, dogmas, creeds, doctrines and party-phrases',[11] and that in opposition he constantly asserted the importance of 'the individuality, complexity and diversity of "the truth of things"'. Whereas Coleridge, the other great critic of the age, tends to subordinate detail to general ideas (no matter how often he expresses himself in notes and cryptic ideas), the experiential to the constitutive, the poetic effect to the philosophical idea, Hazlitt argues that the general can only result from an 'aggregate of well-founded particulars...' not an 'abstract theory'.[12] Openness to the diversity of experience, non-assertive immersion in contrasts, fluctuations and complexity are qualities regarded as supremely important by Hazlitt and by Keats. Central to Hazlitt's thinking is a profound interest in painting, an interest also shared by Keats in a more amateur capacity. The painter must proceed by a careful and concentrated attention to detail, before the whole design is gradually built up through the revealed inter-relatedness of the the parts. Hazlitt describes his own writings as 'The thoughts of a metaphysician expressed by a painter'.[13] In his Shake-spearean criticism, the philosophy of the particular is very evident in the way Hazlitt so often allows quotations to stand in the place of lengthy description or commentary, a practice which, by and large, is reversed by Coleridge, where analysis far outweighs illustration. Although, as we shall see, Hazlitt finds equally important the overall impression of a play, he is at pains to quote many passages which he believes both constitute and qualify the general statement. Believing that a literary work, or a play on the stage, is an experience that occurs through time, where we encounter many specific and unique moments, he feels compelled to draw attention to the local felicities, the particular moment, which may or may not be consistent with other details. The 'immediate excitement or theatrical effect' is prim-ary, and only by recognizing it can we speak generally about a play as a whole. The poet 'seizes on the attention'[14] in a way which can be effective only if the reader allows himself to respond to the particular moment in the present. Of course, Hazlitt's emphasis here is the cor-nerstone of a philosophical structure which includes consideration of matters of religion and politics as well as aesthetics, but we are more concerned here to establish that Keats shared the assumption.

Keats repeats his own, independent belief in a philosophy of par-ticularity on many occasions. One of his most famous passages in the *Letters* demonstrates and also advocates the idea that general princi-ples should not be fretted after, but should be allowed to emerge after the encountering of experience in all its concrete detail:

> ...several things dovetailed in my mind, & at once it struck me, what quality went to form a Man of Achievement especially in Lit-erature & which Shakespeare possessed so enormously – I mean Negative Capability, that is when man is capable of being in uncer-tainties, Mysteries, doubts, without any irritable reaching after fact & reason – Coleridge, for instance, would let go by a fine iso-lated verisimilitude caught from the Penetralium of mystery, from being incapable of remaining content with half knowledge. This pursued through Volumes would perhaps take us no further than this, that with a great poet the sense of Beauty overcomes every other consideration, or rather obliterates all consideration.[15]

Keats is not arguing here that it is impossible ever to reach a level of general ideas, just as Hazlitt never makes such a claim. Indeed, the passage itself demonstrates how several disparate perceptions may 'dovetail' to form a statement of theory. He is, rather, emphasizing the point that we cannot reach further than our experience and knowledge will allow us, and that we should enjoy the wonder and mystery of the immediate and particular, without striving to generalize. He is implicitly rejecting the notion that there is some final, ultimate truth which will apply under all circumstances, since time is always bringing fresh sensations which will continually modify our ideas, and these must be rooted in the mystery of 'half knowledge' which the moment brings. When we come to examine Keats's markings on his own copies of Shakespeare, we shall be observing a reader in the process of encountering, and being overcome by, many 'fine, isolated verisimilitudes', particularly moments full of a 'Beauty' that takes the breath away by compelling the reader's whole attention. Through the experience of meeting such details in a coherent work of literature, Keats may trust that something whole and general is being built up, but the details never lose their primacy. Hazlitt speaks of the way in which he 'work[s] out some of [his] conclusions underground, before throwing them up on the surface', 'tracing any number of particular effects to a general principle'.[16] Although Keats rarely feels the need to formulate 'general principle' in a finished or polished form, as is necessary for the professional essayist and lecturer, yet the process of reasoning from a primary apprehension of 'particular effects' is one which is wholly his own.

Although Hazlitt and Keats sometimes express uneasiness about the critical procedure of Coleridge, whose interest lies more in the general truth than the particular detail, yet their real enemy is found to lie in the enterprise of Dr Johnson. In the Preface to his *Characters of Shakespear's Plays*, Hazlitt endorses Pope's comment that 'every single character in Shakespear, is as much an individual, as those in life itself; it is as impossible to find any two alike',[17] a sentiment which readily fits into Hazlitt's own philosophy of the particular, when applied to character. He uses Pope's words to berate Johnson:

> Dr Johnson's general powers of reasoning overlaid his critical susceptibility. All his ideas were cast in a given mould, in a set form: they were made out by rule and system, by climax, inference and antithesis: – Shakespear's were the reverse. Johnson's understanding dealt only in round numbers: the fractions were lost upon him. He reduced everything to the common standard of conventional propriety.[18]

Such a trenchant statement, of course, must be read in its historical context of an age in revolt against its grandfathers, and we should not use it to justify a dismissal of the fine perceptions of Johnson, particularly in the field of moral analysis, an area where the Romantics are at their most vulnerable. However, Hazlitt's comment is neatly symptomatic of his own preferences. Crucially, he asserts that Johnson saw only 'the average of things, not their striking differences'. The opposition Hazlitt sees between himself and Dr Johnson is much greater than disagreements he finds with Coleridge, but it is of the same kind. Johnson sees the plays and characters of Shakespeare as illustrations of general rules and universal truths, whereas Hazlitt celebrates the richness of particular detail, the variety and multifariousness. Coleridge admires the same qualities, but he too is drawn to see detail as part of a larger truth, rather than as an end in itself. Hazlitt can see that the accumulation of moments is creating a whole which lies in 'impression', but he is much more content to revel in the constantly shifting surface, preferring to remain in 'half knowledge' instead of reaching towards the general.

Needless to say, Keats shares entirely and intensely Hazlitt's dismissal of Johnson, perhaps even in a more prejudiced and less considered way. Time and again in his edition of the plays, Keats scores out the appended comments of Johnson, like a mischievous schoolboy mocking the headmaster, and in taking confidence from Hazlitt he is perhaps hiding behind a rebellious prefect. Sometimes Keats will use the words of Shakespeare as a rebuttal of Johnson's tone and procedure. For example, at the end of *The Merchant of Venice*, he writes beside Johnson's note '[this] pries not to the interior', quoting a line in the play. The comment crisply demonstrates the difference in critical perspectives. To Keats's admittedly biased eyes Johnson is concerned to judge, from above or outside the play, applying accepted rules of composition as his touchstone. Keats is intent upon living within the life and spirit of the play, enjoying the momentary fluctuations of feeling, the ebb and flow of the poetic surface, whilst recognizing that there is 'that within which passes show', a unifying principle which is spiritual rather than structural. Johnson is properly engaged in the business of criticism which, in a neo-classical ethos, involves judgment and the application of firm moral and aesthetic criteria. Keats is involved in reading, and when recording his responses he finds the mode of criticism to be irrelevant and sometimes destructive. We shall encounter more of Keats's comments on Johnson in later pages, but for the moment it is enough to say that he certainly agreed with Hazlitt that the primary enjoyment of the reader, and duty of the sensitive interpreter, *is* to number the streaks on the tulip, and to appreciate the diversity of Shakespeare's characters and language, by expressing an immediate and feeling response to each individually. Such a position need not strike us as hopelessly 'Romantic' or anachronistic in the more professional climate of twentieth century literary studies. To illustrate the continued currency of the ideas with which we are dealing, consider the distinction made by Wilson Knight, who in many ways may be seen as a successor to Hazlitt:

> At the start, I would draw a distinction between the terms 'criticism' and 'interpretation'.... 'Criticism' to me suggests a certain process of deliberately objectifying the work under consideration; the comparison of it with other similar works in order especially to show in what respects it surpasses, or falls short of, those works; the dividing its 'good' from its 'bad'; and, finally, a formal judgment as to its lasting validity. 'Interpretation', on the contrary, tends to merge into the work it analyses; it attempts, as far as possible, to understand its subject in the light of its own nature, employing external reference, if at all, only as a preliminary to understanding.... Criticism is a judgement of vision; interpretation a reconstruction of vision.[19]

Here we find a neat formulation of the differences of attitude towards literature between Johnson on the one hand, and Hazlitt on the other. The step from Hazlitt's 'interpretations' to Keats's 'readings' is but a short one, since an emphasis upon the particular is common and central to the thinking of both.

The primacy of feeling

In his important book, *John Keats's Dream of Truth*, John Jones makes the word 'feel' central to his argument, and he provides us with a 'Postscript on Romantic Feeling': 'The truth of feeling is the one universal persuasion of Romanticism'.[20] However, each writer and poet gives to the word his own unique range of meanings and connotations, and it is our job to investigate the usage of Hazlitt and Keats.

Hazlitt's word 'effects', which we have already met, is as loaded as 'feeling' in his vocabulary. He continually asserts that we are tied to the particular moment primarily through our feelings, and it is in this sense that art has its 'effect' on us. 'Poetry is the high-wrought enthusiasm of fancy and feeling',[21] he says, and he reiterates it many times in either more or less general terms:

> The best general notion which I can give of poetry is, that it is the
> natural impression of any object or event, by its vividness exciting
> an involuntary movement of imagination and passion, and produc-
> ing, by sympathy, a certain modulation of the voice, or sounds,
> expressing it.

> Poetry is the language of the imagination and the passions. It
> relates to whatever gives immediate pleasure or pain to the human
> mind.[22]

The words are those relating essentially to feeling. In order to amplify
and explain the notion of 'sympathy' between the work of art and its
recipient, Hazlitt borrows from the terminology of painting the word
'gusto':

> Gusto in art is power or passion defining any object ... and it is in
> giving this truth of character from the truth of feeling, whether in
> the highest or the lowest degree, but always in the highest degree of
> which the subject is capable, that gusto consists.[23]

John Kinnaird describes the term as 'one of those loose conversational
words brought back from Italy and France by connoisseurs',[24] and he
shows that Hazlitt's many uses of 'gusto' are not always consistent.
However, although the word may not stand up to the closest analysis,
Hazlitt's intention is to find a term to describe a complex idea, and in
this sense he is attempting to be precise. In fact, if Hazlitt's and
Keats's terms are seen as contributions to a study of the psychology of
art, rather than as terms of narrowly aesthetic application, then they
are actually more precise than they appear. He is referring to a quality
which is active at each stage of the whole *process* which brings together
the artist, the work of art, and the one who receives the work as reader
or observer. Therefore, at one moment he can speak of the lack of
gusto concerning the feelings of the artist with the objects depicted in
his work:

> Claude's landscapes, perfect as they are, want gusto ... they lay an
> equal stress on all visible impressions. They do not interpret one
> sense by another; they do not distinguish the character of different
> objects as we are taught, and can only be taught, to distinguish
> them by their effect on the different senses. That is, his eye wanted
> imagination: it did not strongly sympathise with his other faculties.
> He saw the atmosphere, but he did not feel it.[25]

No matter how accurate or imitative the depiction of his landscape, the artist has no emotional attitude towards his subject; he has no 'feeling' for it. At another time, Hazlitt uses the term to describe the attitude of the observer, when he is led to share with the artist an emotional point of reference when perceiving the picture: 'There is a gusto in the colouring of Titian. Not only do his heads seem to think – his bodies seem to feel ...'[26] An impression 'seems' to be one of thinking and feeling only when there is an observer who is responding to the picture with his imagination or emotions, in a way invited by the artist's presentation. Although the term 'gusto' cannot be closely defined because of the intangible concept it represents, yet the main point is that the quality links the creator, the work of art, and the observer in a continually re-creative process of emotional projection and sympathy. Co-operation in the mutual exercise of feelings is necessary at each point of the process.

The idea is more or less the same as the one we found in Keats's thinking about reading in the previous chapter. He does use the term 'gusto' himself. For example, when speaking of Kean's acting, he writes,

> There is an indescribable gusto in his voice, by which we feel that the utterer is thinking of the past and the future, while speaking of the instant. When he says in Othello 'put up your bright swords, for the dew will rust them,' we feel that this throat had commanded where swords were as thick as reeds.[27]

We 'feel' because the actor 'feels' because the character 'feels' because the dramatist 'felt' when he wrote the line. At each stage of the process, energetic, imaginative co-operation is required. Reading is the same process, except that one variable, the actor, is absent. A word more characteristic of Keats himself, describing the same quality as gusto, is 'intensity':

> I spent Friday evening with Wells & went the next morning to see *Death on the Pale horse*. It is a wonderful picture, when West's age is considered; But there is nothing to be intense upon; no women one feels mad to kiss; no face swelling into reality. the excellence of every Art is its intensity, capable of making all disagreeables evaporate, from their being in close relationship with Beauty and Truth – Examine King Lear & you will find this examplified throughout; but in this picture we have unpleasantness without any momentous depth of speculation excited, in which tó bury its repulsiveness ...[28]

The distinction Keats is making is very close to that made by Hazlitt in his comments on Claude's landscapes. The words he uses, such as 'feels mad to kiss', 'disagreeables', 'repulsiveness', are describing emotions which Keats thinks should be found in such a picture. Others, such as 'Beauty and Truth' and 'speculation' refer to a coherence or cohesiveness amongst the emotions and thoughts created in the observer or reader by a work of art which has true 'intensity'. Stuart Sperry's description of another familiar Keatsian concept, 'sensation', is equally applicable to 'intensity':

> ... the nature of our primary grasp over material reality, the way our sense impressions are channeled and combined in consciousness, and the way in which such states of perception assimilate with feeling and emotion.[29]

In other words, Keats is striving to find a word more precise than 'feelings' to include the sense impressions, and a word more personal than Hazlitt's 'gusto', but the thought is very similar in each case. For him, tactile immediacy, palpability of impression, are all connected with the feelings, which thus need not simply be states of emotion. In all his different attempts to convey the idea, Keats repeatedly refuses to rise above the level of participation in a process which is sub-rational and virtually instinctive. More than just emotion is required, for there must be a surface (of paint or of language) which is so convincing that it impresses one as a reality; and even more, in a great work of art 'speculation' is aroused when the process is truly co-operative, drawing on the thoughtful intellect of the perceiver to ponder upon the piece. But at the heart lies something as simple as feeling itself. Our vocabulary of aesthetics and psychology alike may not be ample enough to analyse closely the involvement of the emotions and the primal senses, both of which, commonsense tells us, are activated in the reading of great literature, even though what we are perceiving is a set of words on a page. But our own inadequacies of analysis should not lead us to dismiss as vague, insubstantial or non-existent the area which Hazlitt and Keats are attempting, somewhat in the dark, to affirm and explore. 'Feeling' with all its associated and related terms, is a word of crucial importance if we seek to co-operate and find ourselves within the process of relationship given to us by Keats in his own deep involvement with the words of Shakespeare.

The pictorial

It is not surprising that Hazlitt and Keats, with their insistence on the particular and their celebration of sensuousness and feeling in art, should be committed to the pictorial qualities they find in Shakespeare. It is significant that Keats can move in one sentence between West's painting and *King Lear*, and that Hazlitt in his essay 'On Gusto' can speak in one breath of Claude and Titian, Shakespeare, Milton and Pope. For both, the 'pictorial' is a central element in literary art, as it is the basis of painting. After all, among their 'set' (as Keats calls them), we find Benjamin Haydon the painter, and Leigh Hunt, who often enthused over painting as much as poetry. Hazlitt himself was a painter of some ability. Ian Jack has examined how art is important to Keats's poetry,[30] and it is necessary here merely to pick out what is relevant for an examination of his reading of Shakespeare. A contrast with Coleridge in particular is revealing, for it might be argued that the Lake poets in general centred their interests upon social and religious matters, upon ideas rather than images for their own sake, and upon the symbol.

These days our word for the use of the pictorial in literature is 'imagery', and this is one of the most difficult and disputable words in critical terminology. We find that everybody uses it in a subtly individual way. As a very rough generalization, it might be suggested that modern critics have shown interest especially in the *function* of images rather than in their vivid, pictorial immediacy, and in *patterns* of recurrent and related images, rather than in the isolated occurrence of one, powerful image. Coleridge is perhaps the father of this line of development, for many of his statements show that he is interested in images for their ability to communicate through themselves some figurative or non-discursive thought. Poetry must be sensuous, he agrees, but for a special reason, 'since it is only by sensuous images that we can elicit truth at a flash'.[31] It is truth or 'the Idea' which constitutes his main interest. He admits that 'passion' is necessary in order to make the image work effectively, but he usually adds the word 'thought' as the higher function of the writer: 'No man was ever yet a great poet without being at the same time a profound philosopher'.[32] Coleridge comes very close on occasions to saying that a literary work is essentially figurative, conveying meaning through external signs such as narrative, situations, images, all of which exist primarily to convey an idea. Particular moments become 'the clothing and manifestation of the spirit that is working within'. We need not make a sharp distinction between Coleridge and Hazlitt, for just as the former can stress the importance of sensuousness of imagery, at least as a prelude to the idea, so Hazlitt and Keats admire the capacity of language to act figuratively as 'hieroglyphics' leading us to a 'spirit that is working within'. There is, however, a difference of emphasis which is implied in Keats's suggestion that Coleridge reveals a limitation in not remaining content with half-knowledge. Whilst Coleridge attempts to understand the connection between language, the picture and the idea, Hazlitt and Keats take more for granted the strange phenomenon of language *as* picture, a capacity which allows us to 'see' things through the medium of words. Their trust in the physical, plastic nature of language to create immediate, mental pictures, gives them some advantages in reading Shakespeare, for they can appreciate the extraordinary diversity and the unresolved contrasts, that we find in Shakespeare's texts, without striving to find some single truth or idea behind them, and without deadening the use of imagery by emphasising only recurrent patterns.

In general terms, Hazlitt sees imagery as being more important for its surface, pictorial effects than for its capacity to give us access to some deeper truth. Indeed, as Keats was to emphasize, sensuous language can in itself be a deeper truth, for it taps an intuitive, sense-based knowledge of the world, rather than one that depends on rational thought. But Hazlitt does recognize that the main point of examining images in poetry is to discover a function in the play itself. He says of *Antony and Cleopatra*, for example,

> It is worth while to observe that Shakespear has contrasted the extreme magnificence of the descriptions in this play with pictures of extreme suffering and physical horror.[33]

This, he implies, has a function in creating a set of moral contrasts. But primarily, he speaks of images as being effective in the immediate accuracy and picturesqueness of their impression, and the main function they have is to set up contrasts in the audience's mind. If presented and greeted with gusto, the image can appeal directly to an emotion or mood; or it can vividly project the mood of the speaker who uses it in the dramatic situation. To Hazlitt, there can be little interest in the mere repetition of a particular image, unless it is repeated each time with powerful effect. A single, momentarily arresting image is more significant to him than the recurrence of images presented without vigour or pictorial immediacy but with some form of intellectual linking.

Keats is not so systematic in his comments on pictorial language, and his early attitude at least may owe more to the kind of 'florilegia' approach of Leigh Hunt than to Hazlitt. That he is closer to Hazlitt than to Coleridge, however, might be exemplified by his description when he speaks of the 'fine things said unintentionally' in Shakespeare's Sonnets. He probably means that Shakespeare does not use images 'with an intention', or with an intellectual design, but because they are intrinsically striking. He continues:

> He has left nothing to say about nothing or any thing: for look at Snails, you know what he says about ... 'cockled snails' – well, in one of these sonnets, he says – the chap slips into – no! I lie! this is in the Venus and Adonis: the Simile brought it to my Mind.[34]

And he goes on to quote lines 1033–38 of *Venus and Adonis*. 'In the intensity of working out conceits', Shakespeare attends so closely to the image itself that it becomes a thought, its own *raison d'être*. The very fact that Keats can confuse the contexts between the Sonnets and *Venus and Adonis*, and also throw in the phrase 'cockled snails' from *Love's Labour's Lost*, shows that he makes association through images himself, rather than having a rooted sense of literal context. His letter is full of fine things remembered unintentionally, with the same loosely associative and self-generative power of the Sonnets themselves. He is also interested in the vividness of the isolated image, taken out of context, and in the complex relationship between the picture which is evoked ('cockled snails') and the language used to create the picture. Elsewhere, Keats admires the way that an image may be used to define the emotional state of a character at a certain moment, as when he recalls the reported vignette of Antony kicking at the rushes in anger.[35] In his markings of the texts, the explanation for his finding some phrase noteworthy is probably quite often that the image strikes him as effective in isolation for its immediate appeal to the senses. Or sometimes the image may be important for what it tells us about the speaker, or what it conveys in terms of atmosphere or mood. All these functions of the image are appropriate also in the field of visual art, for both Keats and Hazlitt see these arts as closely connected. In this sense, the best gloss on Keats's attitude to pictorial language is his own poetry. When for example, he delicately taps the sources of each of the five senses in 'To Autumn', it might be thought that the visual is primary, and that painting is its artistic analogy: 'Somehow a stubble plain looks warm – in the same way that some pictures look warm ...'[36]

Contrast

Already we have noticed Hazlitt emphasizing contrast in imagery, and the general notion is another shared by Keats. Although contrast may be seen clearly on the level of imagery, it is a symptom of a more comprehensive, structural matter. Indeed, to Hazlitt, 'the principle of poetry exists...by contrast'.[37] He often couches the principle in a discussion of large antitheses of moralities and moods. He notes the conflicting passions displayed by Othello, who swings 'from the fondest love and most unbounded confidence to the tortures of jealousy and the madness of hatred'.[38] He speaks of *Macbeth* as being a quintessential tragedy, built upon contrast at every level:

> *Macbeth* (generally speaking) is done upon a stronger and more systematic principle of contrast than any other of Shakespear's plays.... It is a huddling together of fierce extremes.[39]

We need not spend time over more examples of Hazlitt's belief in contrast in Shakespeare, for it is demonstrated in every essay he writes on the plays. Again, his acuteness on this subject no doubt proceeded from his interest in painting.

Keats sees contrast as essential not only to the design of Shakespeare's plays and to his use of imagery, but to the vision of the dramatist himself. It is in thinking along these lines that he lifts the plays from the momentary impressions of single occasions to an awareness of a thinking presence behind the play, holding the details together on a steady plane. The principle of contrast provides Keats with a stabilizing factor in his excited appreciation of the detail of Shakespeare's poetry. Whilst celebrating the amorality of the chameleon poet, relishing the dark side of things as much as the light, creating an Imogen as readily as an Iago,[40] he also recognizes the existence of a higher 'knowledge' which does not allow momentary sensations merely to overwhelm, confuse, or morally corrupt the reader and audience. Knowing his own fluctuating moods, Keats yearns for such stability himself:

> The difference of high Sensations with and without knowledge appears to me this – in the latter case we are falling continually ten thousand fathoms deep and being blown up again without wings and with all [the] horror of a [bare] shoulderd Creature – in the former case, our shoulders are fledge[d], and we go thro' the same [air] and space without fear.[41]

The passage is loaded with Shakespeare, not only in Lear's 'poor, bare fork'd animal', not only in Polonius's 'New-hatch'd unfledg'd courage',[42] nor only in the distant bells of the Duke's speech on death in *Measure for Measure*.[43] Shakespeare is present also in the 'knowledge' which Keats found so pre-eminently in the dramatist, an almost god-like capacity to hold together diverse and conflicting points of view in the single focus of one play. It is the capacity which Keats is to associate with the truly 'disinterested' and compassionate person.[44] In his last letter, Keats is to show in moving fashion his own awareness of contrast, not as a literary phenomenon alone, but as a mode of perceiving the world. It may prove a torture to the dying poet:

> ... and now – the knowledge of contrast, feeling for light and shade, all that information (primitive sense) necessary for a poem are great enemies to the recovery of the stomach.[45]

It may be the single most important contribution Keats makes to our knowledge of Shakespeare, that in his markings on the texts, as we shall see, he shows recognition of the many contrasts to be found in each play. In the comedies he concentrates equally upon the melancholy and anti-romantic sentiments as upon the happy expressions of love and joy. Indeed, his markings of *As You Like It*, coupled with his comments in letters, make that play something less than 'festive'. By concentrating equally upon passages of lyrical poetry and abrasive prose in a play like *The Merry Wives of Windsor*, Keats incidentally points us towards contrasts of characterization, modes of speech and moments of dramatic intensity. By noting the extraordinary range of reference used in the creation of images in any single play, he is tacitly acknowledging the fact that diversity and multiplicity are just as important as consistency of observation in building 'the world of the play'. Examined in the light of their shared belief that the plays are made up of a set of arresting particulars rather than consistent, schematic patterns, Hazlitt and Keats see contrast as holding within itself a unifying principle of organisation, creating the stable sense of 'knowledge' or controlling consciousness, about which the oppositions and diversities move like stars in a galaxy around their sun. Philosophically, Keats's trust in some such notion of 'knowledge of light and shade' may have provided the fuel for his own immense capacity to 'say yes to life',[46] to combine his absolute delight in the uniqueness of every living thing with a sanity that can retain a centre when the world around him seemed so disturbingly inconstant and fluctuating. For a faith in contrast is a faith in the autonomy and yet connectedness of all impressions, and a faith in movement and change, cycle and repetition, for the sake of their own inner consistency.

Movement and impression

Despite their concentration upon images and contrast, we should not conclude that Hazlitt and Keats regard a play as a progression from one static picture to another, or a simple oscillation between balanced opposites. On the contrary, since drama is unlike painting in moving through time, it is the existence of process and change from moment to moment that engages their attention as much as the arresting quality of individual details. Roy Park speaks of Hazlitt's 'kinetic vocabulary' in the following way:

> a vast network of synonymous and cognate terms all expressive of the need for action and movement: motion, life, workings, fluctuations, play, flexibility, wrestling, writhing, yielding, varying, transient, evanescent, fleeting, momentary, passing. These terms, in turn, are related to others which emphasized the infinite variety and complexity of life: a complexity and variety which must on no account be diminished by the imposition of a conceptual framework or indeed any form of abstraction.[47]

Hazlitt himself puts this eloquently: 'Poetry puts a spirit of life and motion into the universe. It describes the flowing, not the fixed.'[48]

It follows that Hazlitt, seeing a play as a dynamic, volatile creation, regards the unifying power not as an imposed structure or completeness of the narrative, but as the overall impression on the feelings. He sees the play as an experience, not as an artefact, and his general comments are invariably directed at the feelings which the play raises in the spectator or reader, rather than at the dramatist's skill in subordinating parts to the whole in the fashion of a craftsman:

> [*The Tempest* is] full of grace and grandeur.[49]

> *Timon of Athens* always appeared to us to be written with as intense a feeling of his subject as any one play of Shakespear.[50]

> *Lear* stands first for the profound intensity of the passion; *Macbeth* for the wildness of the imagination and the rapidity of the action; *Othello* for the progressive interest and powerful alternations of feeling; *Hamlet* for the refined development of thought and sentiment.[51]

We should be careful to acknowledge that Hazlitt does not make such impressionistic judgments in isolation, but in the context of the accumulated evidence of detail and quotation; we should constantly remember his philosophy of particularity. Sometimes, too, Hazlitt's relative lack.of interest in structure as a formal or consciously patterned matter, rather as a spirit of the play, leads him close to espousing the Romantic belief that a fragment can be just as complete as a finished, rounded work. Even when he finds a play to be structurally imperfect, he does not regard this deficiency as especially destructive, although he is quite capable of perceiving the inadequacies in a thoroughly professional manner. On *Troilus and Cressida*, he begins his essay this way:

> This is one of the most loose and desultory of our author's plays: it rambles on just as it happens, but it overtakes, together with some indifferent matter, a prodigious number of fine things in its way.[52]

What is seen as the 'rambling' quality is built into the total impression of the action, and thus turned into something positive. Keats is even more consistent in the belief that 'a prodigious number of fine things' may override structural flaws, thematic inconsistencies or philosophical contradictions. Again, he sees these positively as a part of the 'feeling for light and shade' which characterizes Shakespeare's vision.

In some of his annotations on his text of Shakespeare, Keats displays his tacit agreement with Hazlitt that movement and action are important. For example, in his Folio copy of *King Lear*, beside Goneril's speech which begins, 'You see how full of changes his age is' (I.i.287), he writes, picking up the notion of 'changes':

> How finely is the brief of Lear's character sketched in this conference – from this point does Shakspeare spur him out to the mighty grapple – "the seeded pride that hath to this maturity blowne up" Shakspeare doth scatter abroad on the winds of Passion, where the germs take b[u]oyant root in stormy Air, suck lightning sap, and become voiced dragons – self-will and pride and wrath are taken at a rebound by his giant hand and mounted to the Clouds – there to remain and thunder eve[r]more.

The piece shows us a lot about the spirit in which Keats read Shakespeare. He uses Shakespeare's own language, quoting from *Troilus and Cressida*[53] to make a point, demonstrating his desire to 'pry to the interior' and be faithful to the spirit of the play as he sees it. The note is strikingly full of 'kinetic' words of action and turbulent movement:

spur, grapple, scatter, suck, mounted, thunder. These convey the sense of the play as a continually mobile, dynamic and changing experience in Keats's excited reading. The passage also purports to be a statement about the whole play, drawing attention to the central character, 'full of changes' as he is, the violently eruptive quality of action throughout the play right from the first scene, and the mingling of moral weakness (self-will and pride and wrath) with a momentous and exhilarating significance. The statement, one must conclude, is clearly not intended to be analytical in its language nor judiciously balanced in its account of the play; but remembering the terms of Hazlitt's philosophies of literary interpretation, Keats's swift impressionism, expressed in a personal, poetic vocabulary, conveys an acute and comprehensive insight as effectively as more discursive treatments of the play. The note shows Keats gathering up many details of momentary interest, and creatively binding them into an excited, personal and involved impression of the play.

Both Hazlitt and Keats believe in the importance of finding a personal 'impression' of a play, for this is a test of the 'gusto' or 'sensation' with which it is presented, but when we speak of an emphasis on movement, we need to make a qualification. Keats's poetry gives ample evidence that he is equally interested in stasis, or rather, the fluctuations between activity and stillness. This marks a difference from Hazlitt in temperament. One could not readily imagine the impatient, quick-witted intellect of Hazlitt remaining content in the kind of initially passive absorption in a text or a phrase which Keats finds so congenial. When he speaks of the 'delicious diligent Indolence' of spending a whole morning reading just a page of poetry, the 'voyage of conception' which may be launched by simply recalling in leisure the words of a single passage, the 'ethereal finger-pointings' of a beautiful phrase, Keats is speaking for himself, although also, it should be said, for many another lover of poetry.

Despite Hazlitt's desire to work from detail to the whole, his description of the 'impression' of a play generally comes in the form of an overall 'spirit' pervading the dramatic piece. Given the descriptive, synthetic nature of the critical enterprise, this is virtually inevitable. Keats, however, unconstrained by the form of the short essay, is truer to the creed, and time and again he shows a delicate awareness of the momentary, tonal and atmospheric touches which may have little to do with the overall design of the play. We shall see that he does so constantly in his markings.

In casual allusions in his letters, too, Keats shows a deft grasp of the impression of a moment he has observed in Shakespeare. His memory may sometimes deceive him as to the exact words, but rarely over the context. For example, forced to babysit for a morning, Keats compares his lot with that of Caliban, through his use of a quotation:

> The servant has come for the little Browns this morning – they have been a toothache to me which I shall enjoy the riddance of – Their little voices are like wasps stings – 'Some times am I all wound with Browns.'[54]

The allusion acquires a certain bizarre aptness when we compare the original (with Keats's underlinings):

> Sometime like apes that mow and chatter at me,
> And after bite me; then like hedgehogs which
> Lie tumbling in my barefoot way, and mount
> Their pricks at my footfall; sometime am I
> All wound with adders, who with cloven tongues
> Do hiss me into madness.
>
> (The Tempest, II.ii.9–14)

Keats has humorously placed himself in Caliban's position, and he playfully reproduces the feelings of annoyance and pain, and also the sense of being a larger, lumbering person, persecuted by agile, small creatures. The quotation, in a minor way admittedly, illuminates Keats's feelings better than a direct description, and it also gives a certain quality of dignity to the persecuted Caliban, by showing that we can find fellow-feeling with him. Another example might be taken from *The Tempest*. When Keats suggests to Reynolds in a letter that the 'common taste and fellowship' learned through sharing art, will turn the world from a threatening place into a happy republic, he is again using words from the play:

> … every human might become great, and Humanity instead of being a wide heath of Furse and Briars with here and there a remote Oak or Pine, would become a grand democracy of Forest Trees.[55]

Three separate quotations are run together here, in such a way that we can recognize cross-references in the play. Gonzalo is the one who in the storm would give anything for dry land 'long heath, brown furze, any thing' (I.i.64), and it is he who later extols the virtues of a Utopian democracy. Caliban, the character who is excluded from fellowship and democracy, is afraid of 'Tooth'd briers, sharp furzes, pricking goss, and thorns' (IV.i.180). Prospero, the benevolent despot on the island, has 'rifted Jove's stout oak' and 'by the spurs pluck'd up The pine and cedar' (V.i.45 and 47–8). It is remarkable how tightly the association has worked in Keats's mind. Speaking of political democracy and republicanism (things which he believed in as strongly as Hazlitt), he has chosen apparently casually quotations which lead us to political issues in *The Tempest*, and they are all concerned with landscape. He has, in fact, discovered an association in Shakespeare's own mind. Very often we find that Keats's quotations illuminate not only his own feelings but also the dramatic context from which he takes the words. It is a two-way relationship between quotation and source. These examples may not be highly significant in themselves, but we find similar ones on virtually every page of Keats's letters, especially in the 'Shakespearean' year, 1817. He proves himself to be a snapper-up of unconsidered trifles, recalling snippets of Shakespeare's language in almost any situation, but (unlike the bore who uses quotations to show off) Keats's imagination is always beautifully accurate to the moment in which the words are used in a play. When he says 'The great beauty of Poetry is, that it makes every thing every place interesting',[56] he is speaking really of his own capacity, partly learned from Shakespeare and fostered by the plays, to grasp and value every moment of existence as potentially 'poetical', celebrating and immortalizing the tiny, insignificant detail. He is also recognizing that in his mind the 'poetical' may be real.

Character

Harking back to Keats's note on *King Lear*, it is of interest to examine the implications of his use of the word 'character'. Lear is not represented as a confined representation of a fixed identity who exists only in a work of literature. He has an existence outside the play. Shakespeare sets the seeds for a character, he creates a potential, and then tests this potential by spurring the character out to encounter experience. There is a curious independence between the creator and his creation, as if the character has taken on an identity of his own, which may surprise even the dramatist. This is a highly idiosyncratic attitude to character-presentation in drama, but it is one that Keats adopted throughout his life, for some characters take on a full and independent life of their own in his mind, separate from the dramatic context and from the dramatist.

In finding the freedom to hold this idea, Keats is again indebted to the more theoretical reflections of Hazlitt who, although he does not go to the same radical extreme, helped to make respectable the notion that Shakespeare's characters may be as vital and individual as people who exist in our world. The very title of Hazlitt's book, *Characters of Shakespear's Plays*, published in 1817, although not unprecedented, marks an important step in bringing the concept of character to the centre of the English critical tradition, where it remained at least until the early twentieth century. Hazlitt pays the highest respect to Schlegel who is said to have recognised Shakespeare's comprehensive genius 'for the delineation of character',[57] and he quotes the German scholar at length on the truth and diversity of the playwright's characters. In English, Hazlitt mentions that he has come across only two works on the subject. One is William Richardson's various volumes.[58] On reading Richardson, one cannot imagine Hazlitt gaining much inspiration for his own enterprise, since the essays are, in the words of Nichol Smith, 'the dull effusions of a clever man'.[59] The main purpose of Richardson's work, as proclaimed in his title, is to present *A Philosophical Analysis and Illustration...* and he unashamedly proposes 'to make poetry subservient to philosophy, and to employ it in tracing the principles of human conduct'. Richardson is interested in Shakespeare's characters only as examples of moral conduct. He speaks of the general rather than the particular, the ideas rather than the feelings or dramatic life. All these things imply that Hazlitt took little from him, and his acknowledgment is merely lip-service. Richardson does, however, make one forceful statement which may be the first occurrence in English of the word 'protean' as applied to Shakespeare: '[Shakespeare] the Proteus of the drama, changes himself into every character, and enters into every condition of human nature.'[60] Hazlitt uses the term 'protean',[61] and so does Coleridge when he speaks of Shakespeare's capacity 'to become by power of imagination another thing'.[62] Hazlitt, in an essay which probably contributed to Keats's idea of 'negative capability', writes of Shakespeare:

> ... he revelled in the world of observation and of fancy:...He seemed scarcely to have an individual existence of his own, but to borrow that of others at will, and to pass successively through 'every variety of untried being', to be now *Hamlet*, now *Othello*, now *Lear*, now *Falstaff*, now *Ariel*. In the mingled interests and feelings belonging to this wide range of imaginary reality, in the tumult and rapid transitions of this waking dream, the author could not easily find time to think of himself, nor wish to embody that personal identity in idle reputation after death, of which he was so little tenacious while living.[63]

The idea of Shakespeare's protean qualities of characterization was one of the Romantic commonplaces, and it is no use looking for any particular figure who initiates it, since it originates much earlier in the eighteenth century. Hazlitt, however, was the one to write a whole set of lectures based on it. Keats, with a typical gesture of giving the god a local habitation, uses the image of Shakespeare as chameleon, changing his colour to suit the landscape, or the character he is presenting.

The other critic mentioned by Hazlitt is Thomas Whately (whom he confuses with one George Mason, presumably because they both wrote books on gardening, the only thing they seem to have in common). Whately writes only on Macbeth and Richard III, and Hazlitt's account of these characters owes something to the comparison drawn by Whately. But again, the earlier book is too limited in its scope and intelligence to have given much help or inspiration to the Romantic critic. Whately's importance is that he is one of several who points a finger towards the development on systematic lines of a study of Shakespearean characterization. Noting that criticism has confined itself to 'the fable' and to 'rules' of composition, Whately suggests that there is a more worthy subject for attention, 'the distinction and presentation of *character*'.[64] It seems unlikely that Hazlitt knew Maurice Morgann's *An Essay on the Dramatic Character of Sir John Falstaff* (1777), which is a pity since this essay is a far more searching, rigorous and sensitive exploration of dramatic character than the other pieces mentioned.

Keats displays his own personal understanding of the living autonomy of Shakespeare's characters by often slipping into a close identification with one character or another. For example, as he neared the end of his life, his feelings about death tend to gather not around a grand tragic hero, but around Falstaff. He writes in September 1820, four months before his death:

> The time has not yet come for a pleasant Letter from me. I have delayed writing to you from time to time because I felt how impossible it was to enliven you with one heartening hope of my recovery; this morning in bed the matter struck me in a different manner; I thought I would write 'while I was in some liking' or I might become too ill to write at all and then if the desire to have written should become strong it would be a great affliction to me.[65]

The words he quotes deftly recall the context of Falstaff's melancholy in Act III of *I Henry IV*:

Bardolph, am I not fall'n away vilely since this last action? Do I not bate? Do I not dwindle? ... Well, I'll repent, and that suddenly, while I am in some liking; I shall be out of heart shortly, and then I shall have no strength to repent ...[66]

When the whole passage is recalled, there is something very poignant in Keats's apt allusion. It turns on Falstaff's last sentiments in the passage, for at this time of his life Keats found himself out of heart often, and his strength was ebbing away by the day. It is a consolation that comes as 'a different manner' of seeing things, that a robustly comic character can feel the burden of melancholy, and one detects Keats's self-demeaning sense of humour in choosing to associate himself with the feelings of the fat knight. It is also characteristic that he changes 'I'll repent' to 'I'll write', as if his own salvation depends upon his links with a close friend. At the same time, the allusion refreshes a perception into the play which is easily forgotten; that, in Hazlitt's words, 'Sir John is old as well as fat, which gives a melancholy retrospective tinge to the character'.[67] It is interesting to notice that the real association with Falstaff in Keats's mind comes through the notion of health rather than illness or death. In an early letter to J.H.Reynolds he jovially remarks,

> Banish money – Banish sofas – Banish Wine – Banish Music – But right Jack Health – honest Jack Health, true Jack Health – banish health and banish all the world.[68]

Keats is, of course, adapting Falstaff's own words in reference to himself. After admitting that he is fat and old, Falstaff continues,

> No, my good lord: banish Peto, banish Bardolph, banish Poins; but, for sweet Jack Falstaff, kind Jack Falstaff, true Jack Falstaff, valiant Jack Falstaff – and therefore more valiant, being, as he is, old Jack Falstaff – banish not him thy Harry's company, banish not him thy Harry's company. Banish plump Jack, and banish all the world.
>
> (*I Henry IV*, II.iv.455–63)

Perhaps the association with health is picked up from the word 'plump', a more charitable reconstruction of 'fat', but what is later to become so tragically ironic is that just as Jack Falstaff is eventually banished from Harry's company, so Keats and Jack Health must part company. Once again, the unobtrusive aptness of the reference acts on

several levels, and turns us equally towards understanding Keats's
feelings and emphasizing an important aspect of the dramatic irony in
the text. Even on his deathbed Keats can find fellow-feeling with the
figure of Falstaff, again with a moving appropriateness, since he refers
to Falstaff's dying moments:

> How astonishingly does the chance of leaving the world impress a
> sense of its natural beauties on us. Like poor Falstaff, though I do
> not babble, I think of green fields.[69]

He even has his own moment of sublime babbling just before the end,
if we can trust the report of his companion Severn:

> I shall soon be laid in the quiet grave – thank God for the quiet
> grave – O! I can feel the cold earth upon me – the daisies growing
> over me.[70]

Quite inadvertently, Severn is playing exactly the role of Mistress
Quickly reporting in grief-stricken fashion the death of Falstaff to his
friends. The reported words of Keats take on even more resonance
when we recall that Falstaff's feet are 'as cold as any stone' even while
he speaks, and that he plays with flowers in his fingers.[71] It would, of
course, be quite insensitive to suggest that Keats is consciously creat-
ing a dramatic scenario in which he plays the leading part; even if such
a thought could occur to his modest personality, one would not think
the comically bombastic character would appeal as a model for high
tragic emotion. (There is a comic twist even in the diminutive Keats's
semi-identification with the corpulent Falstaff.) Instead, the refer-
ences show us that the reality of Shakespeare's character was so
immediate for Keats that he feels on the pulses experiences which
Shakespeare depicts Falstaff going through, and the words come as
fluently and appositely as his own.

Keats does not consider as a fallacy what many post-Bradleyan cri-
tics have deplored: the tendency to regard characters in Shakespeare
as 'real' in the sense that our friends are, people whom we remember,
feel for, and quote as if their words are our own. He enters their experi-
ences with the fullness and gusto of a Kean, sometimes to the point of
self-identification. When he jokingly says he would rather follow
Juliet into Pandemonium than Imogen into Paradise, 'heartily wish-
ing myself a Romeo to be worthy of her',[72] he is unashamedly regard-
ing the characters to be as much creatures of flesh and blood as the
Reynolds sisters to whom he is writing. Hazlitt quotes Schlegel as say-
ing of Shakespeare, 'He gives us the history of minds; he lays open to

us, in a single word, a whole series of preceding conditions.'[73] Hazlitt himself can maintain some academic distance from the characters he deals with, but Keats does not feel this need. He speculates upon the 'preceding conditions' and the impression or spirit of a character as if there were no confining limits between the play-world and his own. In another person this would be a mere self-indulgence, but so acute is Keats's memory for dramatic context, so unerring is his eye for the apt reference, that we can be grateful for his freedom to illuminate the plays in this genial way.

Armed with the knowledge that Keats agreed with Hazlitt on many major assumptions about reading Shakespeare, and with some of these common concerns fresh in mind, we may approach the evidence of Keats's own ideas about Shakespeare with a little more self-assurance. As we do so, it might be useful to keep in mind a general statement made by Coleridge about the keen faculties of a poet:

> a great Poet must be, implicité if not explicité, a profound Metaphysician. He may not have it in logical coherence, in his Brain & Tongue; but he must have it by Tact for all sounds, & forms of human nature he must have the ear of a wild Arab listening in the silent Desert, the eye of a North American Indian tracing the footsteps of an Enemy upon the Leaves that strew the Forest – ; the Touch of a Blind Man feeling the face of a darling child –[74]

In attempting to recapture something of the spirit with which Keats read Shakespeare, we are made aware that Keats himself is just such a poet, exercising just such Tact. So far as possible, we should strive to do the same.

III Keats's readings of Shakespeare's comedies

'I look upon fine Phrases like a Lover'
(To Bailey, 14 August 1819)

We are now in a position to examine the evidence of Keats's readings of Shakespeare's plays, in the light of comments in his letters and markings on the texts. The subject of this chapter will be the Comedies in general, and in the next chapter we shall look more closely at the two that Keats regarded most highly, *A Midsummer Night's Dream* and *The Tempest*.

What, then, did Keats read amongst the plays classified by the First Folio as Comedies? The evidence of his texts suggests that the answer is virtually everything. Every play is marked to a greater or lesser extent. *Pericles* is the one play where he may not have got past Act II in a particular reading, for the scarce markings end at II.v.44–6. On *The Comedy of Errors*, *Love's Labour's Lost* and *The Taming of the Shrew*, the markings are few but they extend throughout the five Acts in each. Of the three, *Love's Labour's Lost* was important enough for him to quote several times in his letters. In particular, he quotes in full the first seven lines of the play in a letter to Haydon:

My dear Haydon,

> Let Fame, which all hunt after in their Lives,
> Live register'd upon our brazen tombs,
> And so grace us in the disgrace of death:
> When spite of cormorant devouring time
> The endeavour of this present breath may buy
> That Honor which shall bate his Scythe's keen edge
> And make us heirs of all eternity.

To think that I have no right to couple myself with you in this speech would be death to me so I have e'en written it – and I pray God that our brazen Tombs be nigh neighbours ...[1]

Keats was to write two sonnets himself on the subject of Fame,[2] and in both the message is basically the same as that shown by the ironic action of *Love's Labour's Lost*, that fame cannot be directly pursued as a goal. Keats echoes Shakespeare's linking of 'grace' and 'fame' in the final lines of one of the sonnets:

> Why then should man, teasing the world for grace,
> Spoil his salvation for a fierce miscreed?

The idea that fame is, for young men, a 'fierce miscreed' is the same as Berowne's in the play, and in fact Keats's other markings (not surprisingly, in the light of the poetic quality) are upon that character's speeches about 'study' and about love, One of Berowne's images clearly stuck firmly enough in the poet's memory to be quoted in the letters:

> Love's feeling is more soft and sensible
> Than are the tender horns of cockled snails.
>   (IV.iii.333–4)

'Snailhorn touch' is the quality selected by John Jones in his book *John Keats's Dream of Truth*[3] as central to Keats's poetic vision, and if Shakespeare provided the image it is a significant legacy of this play. In fact, the passage in which it occurs, and which Keats has marked, seems very close to the Keatsian concept of sensation and poetry, for Berowne is saying that the power of love is to heighten each of the senses in turn, and that it is intrinsically the stuff of poetry, 'as sweet and musical, As bright Apollo's lute' (IV.iii.338–9). *The Two Gentlemen of Verona* is another play with few markings which are scattered throughout. Keats picks out the poignant poetry of love, and at least one passage, Julia's haunting description of herself in the third person

> The air hath starv'd the roses in her cheeks
> And pinch'd the lily-tincture of her face,
>   (IV.iv.150–1)

may have contributed to the description of Keats's own comparably love-lorn knight in 'La Belle Dame Sans Merci':

> I see a lily on thy brow
>   With anguish moist and fever dew,
> And on thy cheeks a fading rose
>   Fast withereth too.

When Valentine says

> Love hath chas'd sleep from my enthralled eyes
> And made them watchers of mine own heart's sorrow
>   (II.iv.130–1)

we may again detect a forecast of La Belle Dame with her enthralling powers over knights who brood upon their sorrows. On a lighter note, Keats appreciates Launce's role, and especially the image for his sister, 'as white as a lily and as small as a wand' (II.iii.20), for he directly quotes it to describe the trees in a little wood he saw on the way to Southampton in April 1817.[4] But primarily it is lines which express 'The inly touch of love' (II.vii.18) that he chooses to mark in this play.

The language of lovers, of course, bulks large in most of the comedies, and Keats shows himself consistently susceptible to Shakespeare's lyricism. In *Twelfth Night*, a play which Hazlitt describes as a 'sentimental' comedy, Keats picks out for underlining all the notable pronouncements on love made by Orsino, Olivia and Viola, for example:

> Away before me to sweet beds of flow'rs;
> Love-thoughts lie rich when canopied with bow'rs.
>
> (I.i.40–1)

At least one of Feste's songs, 'Come away, come away, death' (II.iv.50ff.), attracted his notice in the reading, since he side-marks it. On the other hand, this is a good play to exemplify the fact that it is not only the romantic poetry of love which interests Keats. he catches at striking images and uses of language, such as 'When time hath sow'd a grizzle on thy case' (V.i.159), and the description of the captain's face:

> it was besmear'd
> As black as Vulcan in the smoke of war.
> A baubling vessel was he captain of,
>
> (V.i.46–8)

He appreciates the colourful language of Sir Toby, such as his phrase 'so much blood in his liver as will clog the foot of a flea' (III.ii.58–9), and he side-marks quite a few lines of Maria, the Clown, Sir Andrew and Fabian, most of which seem to be distinguished by a comic use of imagery:

> CLOWN. O, he's drunk, Sir Toby, an hour agone; his eyes were set at eight i'th'morning.
>
> (V.i.190)

Keats even quotes in a letter a line by Maria (III.ii.66) which he also underlines in his text) as evidence against 'Shakespeare's Christianity',[5] as part of a debate in which Keats implicitly maintains Shakes-

peare's impartiality. The general point to be made is that the evidence
of Keats's markings on a relatively copiously marked play like *Twelfth
Night* shows that his interest is dispersed and opportunistic, and it
would be misleading to suggest any consistency. Here he is displaying
pre-eminently the capacity to appreciate many different kinds of lan-
guage and centres of interest in Shakespeare's play.

The same is true of Keats's markings of *The Merchant of Venice*,
which point us to several areas of interest in the play. Many of
Shylock's scenes are marked, and some of his phrases which some-
times reveal character (such as the craftiness in 'How many months
Do you desire' at I.iii. 53–4 and 'I had forgot' at I.iii.61) and some-
times provide striking verbal effects: 'the vile squeaking of the wry-
neck'd fife' (II.v.29). Since Keats, like Hazlitt, had seen Kean play the
role, his interest in the character is topical. Kean's interpretation was
to influence generations of critics, by presumably confirming Lamb's
view in seeing the play largely from Shylock's point of view. More
unusual is the attention paid by Keats to the part of Launcelot Gobbo.
Whole passages are side-marked: II.ii, where he meets his father, in
which almost all the lines are noted; II.iii, a short scene in which he
speaks to Jessica. Although other scenes in which he appears are not
marked, there is enough evidence to say that this bemused simpleton
interested Keats. It may be significant that Hazlitt writes apprecia-
tively of Gobbo in his account of the play, and we remember that Keats
uses a phrase from this character to describe Hazlitt himself on the
title-page of his copy of the *Characters*. It might well have been Haz-
litt's interest that directed Keats's attention to the pathos in the role.
However, the lyrical poetry of lovers in the play is more likely to have
influenced Keats's own work. There is quite a lot of reference to music
and Keats is quick to pick it up:

> Then, if he lose, he makes a swan-like end,
> Fading in music.
>
> (III.ii.44–5)

> He may win;
> And what is music then? Then music is
> Even as the flourish when true subjects bow
> To a new-crowned monarch;...
>
> (III.ii.47–50)

> The crow doth sing as sweetly as the lark
> When neither is attended; and I think

> The nightingale, if she should sing by day,
> When every goose is cackling, would be thought
> No better a musician than the wren.
> How many things by season season'd are
> To their right praise and true perfection!
> Peace, ho! the moon sleeps with Endymion,
> And would not be awak'd.
>
> (V.i.102–11)

Particularly in the last of these passages, we can detect several premonitions of Keats. Since he almost certainly read the play whilst he was planning to write *Endymion*, the final reference must have held some personal value for him. Furthermore, Portia's passage, in its advocacy of appreciating the beauty of 'seasonable' sounds could very well be seen as an amplification of the philosophy implicit in the final stanza of 'To Autumn' when the poem is dealing with sounds:

> Where are the songs of spring? Ay, where are they?
> Think not of them, thou hast thy music too, –

Endymion's

> Let me have music dying, and I seek
> No more delight –
>
> (IV,139–40)

borrows not only from Orsino's 'dying fall' in the opening lines of *Twelfth Night* but also Portia's words quoted above. When, in the same portion on music in *Endymion*, Keats allows his hero to describe himself as 'giddy at that cheek so fair and smooth' (IV, 311) and to speak of 'the giddy air' (IV, 355), he is verbally recalling Bassanio, 'Giddy in spirit' (III.ii. 144, side-marked) at the sight of Portia. When Endymion experiences his rapturous unions with Cynthia his feelings are similar to those of Bassanio,

> Where every something, being blent together,
> Turns to a wild of nothing, save of joy
> Express'd and not express'd.
>
> (III.ii.182–4)

If Portia's music and Bassanio's rapture bring us close to *Endymion*, Lorenzo draws together all the appropriate associations. As he sits on the bank with Jessica, admiring the moon, he invokes the classical world to describe the beauty and harmony which was to enrapture Endymion:

The moon shines bright. <u>In such a night as this,</u>
<u>When the sweet wind did gently kiss the trees,</u>
<u>And they did make no noise – in such a night,</u>
<u>Troilus methinks mounted the Troyan walls,</u>
<u>And sigh'd his soul toward the Grecian tents,</u>
<u>Where Cressid lay that night.</u>
...
      <u>In such a night,</u>
<u>Stood Dido with a willow in her hand</u>
<u>Upon the wild sea-banks, and waft her love</u>
<u>To come again to Carthage.</u>
...
<u>How sweet the moonlight sleeps upon this bank!</u>
<u>Here will we sit and let the sounds of music</u>
<u>Creep in our ears; soft stillness and the night</u>
<u>Become the touches of sweet harmony.</u>
<u>Sit, Jessica. Look how the floor of heaven</u>
<u>Is thick inlaid with patines of bright gold;</u>
<u>There's not the smallest orb which thou behold'st</u>
<u>But in his motion like an angel sings,</u>
<u>Still quiring to the young-ey'd cherubins.</u>
                              (V.i.1–62 *passim*)

Music, the subject of these lines, provides a thematic link which is supported by verbal echo with Keats's own great celebration of the immortal harmony of beautiful sound, 'Ode to a Nightingale'. Just as 'In such a night as this' the Trojan War was being fought, so in Keats's words the voice he hears 'this passing night' was heard in Ruth's biblical times. The sense, sound and images of Lorenzo's words (subliminally associated with Portia's reference to a nightingale), look forward to

tender is the night,
And haply the Queen-Moon is on her throne,
Cluster'd around by all her starry Fays;
      But here there is no light,
Save what from heaven is with the breezes blown
Through verdurous glooms and winding mossy ways.

The imaginative world of the Ode, far from the sole self of the poet, is in a specific way a Shakespearean world, created by the imagination and by language. Lorenzo's attention comes to rest on the power of music and beautiful sound and the harmonious numbers of the poet:

> …
> You shall perceive them make a mutual stand,
> Their savage eyes turn'd to a modest gaze
> By the sweet power of music. Therefore the poet
> Did feign that Orpheus drew trees, stones, and floods;
> Since nought so stockish, hard, and full of rage,
> But music for the time doth change his nature;
>
> (V.i.77–82)

The terms of the discussion are Elizabethan and neo-platonic, but the central concern with 'concord of sweet sounds' is a steady preoccupation of both Shakespeare and Keats. The fact that we can find the 'ethereal finger-pointings' of these passages beckoning towards *Endymion* and the Odes suggests that they provided a memory which acts as a reference point throughout the poet's writing career.

As usual, there are some lines picked out by Keats as particularly interesting, irrespective of their contexts, and these may simply be listed for interest:

> To wind about my love with circumstance
> (I.i.154; quoted by Keats in a letter,
> appropriately enough, asking for
> money.)[6]

> The shadowed livery of the burnish'd sun
> (II.i.2)

> To allay with some cold drops of modesty
> Thy skipping spirit
> (II.ii.171–2)

> …as lying a gossip in that as ever knapp'd ginger
> (III.i.9)

> Why dost thou whet thy knife so earnestly?
> (IV.i.121; admittedly, this takes its force
> from the context.)

> Fair ladies, you drop manna in the way
> Of starved people.
> (V.i.293–4)

> Sit like his grandsire cut in alabaster?
> (I.i.84)

> There are a sort of men whose visages
> <u>Do cream and mantle like a standing pond</u>
> (I.i.89)

> <u>Some that will evermore peep through their eyes,</u>
> <u>And laugh like parrots at a bag-piper</u>
> (I.i.52–3)

Keats's markings of *The Merchant of Venice* are unclassifiable, and it is impossible to say that any one aspect interested him. They illustrate his eclectic interest in the Shakespearean text, as he opens himself to appreciate strikingly bizarre images just as readily as the beautiful poetry of love and romanticism which influence *Endymion*.

In his marking of *As You Like It*, however, it is possible to detect a fairly consistent interest lying behind the markings, and it is quite a significant one in the light of Keats's own temperament. It is possible, of course, that by the time he came to mark the play Keats may have already read it, and is returning to confirm a strain which he had formerly detected. Or perhaps he was in a certain mood when he made the reading recorded in the Johnson-Steevens text. The fact is, that under Keats's hand *As You Like It*, apparently one of the most unequivocally romantic and joyful comedies without truly felt conflict after the first Act, becomes something of an ode to melancholy. In the same way, we remember, Keats recalls Falstaff when he thinks of his own death. Whatever Keats's intentions in marking this play as he does, he is showing us that even in the most lighthearted and infectious of Shakespeare's comedies, there are 'disagreeables', such as melancholy, old age and adversity:

> Ay, in the very temple of Delight
> Veil'd Melancholy has her sovran shrine.

It is a lesson Keats teaches through his markings in several of the comedies, and in his own letters and poetry.

Keats regarded Jaques as a fine creation. In a letter, he concludes a barrage of quotations which show his taste in poetry, with a reference to the character:

> Why should we be owls, when we can be Eagles? Why be teased with 'nice Eyed wagtails' [Hunt], when we have in sight 'the Cherub Contemplation' [Milton]? – Why with Wordsworths 'Matthew with a bough of wilding in his hand' when we can have Jacques 'under an oak &c.'[7]

His contrasts are between a merely pictorial prettiness and a contemplative seriousness, and he cites the latter as showing a 'grandeur and merit' which is 'uncontaminated and unobtrusive'. Always in his thoughts and practice of poetry, Keats is reaching through a joy in sensuous immediacy to the 'eagle's' high seriousness, and awareness of dark areas of experience. He even identifies with Jaques to some extent:

> I wish I knew always the humour my friends would be in at opening a letter of mine, to suit it to them as nearly as possible I could always find an egg shell for Melancholy – and as for Merriment a Witty humour will turn any thing to Account...[8]

Incidentally, this comment is a piece of evidence in the argument that Keats sees reading as a co-operative activity, where both the reader and the document meet in the 'gusto' of a mood. Keats underlines in his edition Jaques' line, 'I can suck melancholy out of a song, as a weasel sucks eggs' (II.v.12–13), and the sentence can stand as a description of the spirit of Keats's markings of *As You Like It*. Keats speaks many times of his congenital melancholy which he, like Jaques, can accept as a form of enjoyment:

> I will not spoil my love of gloom by writing an ode to darkness.[9]

> You tell me never to despair – I wish it was as easy for me to observe the saying – truth is I have a horrid Morbidity of Temperament which has shown itself at intervals... How ever every ill has its share of good – this very bane would at any time enable me to look with an obstinate eye on the Devil Himself...[10]

His brother George speaks of John's 'nervous morbid temperament',[11] and Keats was so self-knowing and frank that he probably gave this information himself. The 'Ode on Melancholy' is an attempt to suck joy out of melancholy, and perhaps in the strange sonnet, 'Why did I laugh tonight?' Keats is brooding upon a melancholy which is suddenly perceived to be a form of ecstasy.

Keats marks down the side the touching description of Jaques grieving over the wounded deer (II.i.25–43), and he underlines much of it as well. He side-marks the character's delight at meeting the fool in the forest (II.vii.12–34), underlining the striking coinage 'lack-lustre eye'. When the Duke offers Jaques the opportunity of wearing motley himself, Keats marks Jaques' enthusiastic reply (II.vii.44–61), underlining

I must have liberty
Withal, as large a charter as the wind,
To blow on whom I please, for so fools have.

At this point, the Duke launches an oddly savage attack on Jaques, suggesting that he is hypocritical to chide sin in others when he has himself been a libertine (II.vii.64–9, side-marked). Jaques replies haughtily that sin is universal, hinting in a tone thinly disguised as courtesy that anybody angered by his ideas cannot be free of vice himself (II.vii.70–87, side-marked). Keats, not surprisingly, marks down the side one of the most quoted, and most pessimistic passages in Shakespeare, Jaques' 'seven ages of man' speech (II.vii.139–66), underlining only the phrase about the schoolboy's 'shining morning face'. Of course, Keats did not need to be pessimistic himself to notice this famous passage. III.ii.238–77 is an inconspicuous but lengthy dialogue side-marked by Keats, and it shows that the older, jaded melancholic has no affinity with Orlando who is posing as the love-sick melancholic. Their dislike is immediate and mutual. One exchange deserves quotation, since it concerns the subject of poetry:

> JAQ. I pray you mar no more trees with writing love songs in their barks.
> ORL. I pray you mar no more of my verses with reading them ill-favouredly.

> (III.ii.245–6)

Orlando is voicing a plea which Touchstone will also make, and which Keats would certainly endorse in general terms: that poetry should be read in a spirit of co-operation and generosity. At the same time, there is at least a quiet irony at the expense of Keats, for if he is so determined to note the melancholy aspects of a play which most readers find exuberant, then perhaps he is reading somewhat 'ill-favouredly'.

Jaques later gives us his own description of the particular brand of melancholy which he possesses. Running through the Burtonian categories, he says it is not the scholar's melancholy, nor the musician's, nor the courtier's, nor the soldier's, nor the lawyers,

> nor the lady's, which is nice; nor the lover's, which is all these; but it is a melancholy of mine own, compounded of many simples, extracted from many objects, and, indeed, the sundry contemplation of my travels; in which my often rumination wraps me in a most humorous sadness.

> (IV.1.14–18)

Even in such an idiosyncratically expressive phrase as 'a most humorous sadness', not to mention the general sentiment, the passage is rather similar to Keats's own brand of humour as revealed in the letters.

The rest of the markings support the melancholy keynote struck by Jaques. Duke Senior, although philosophizing away the physical discomforts of the outdoor life, eloquently describes them:

> Now, my co-mates and brothers in exile,
> Hath not old custom made this life more sweet
> Than that of painted pomp? Are not these woods
> More free from peril than the envious court?
> Here feel we not the penalty of Adam,
> The seasons' difference; as the icy fang
> And churlish chiding of the winter's wind,
> Which when it bites and blows upon my body,
> Even till I shrink with cold, I smile and say,
> 'This is no flattery; these are counsellors
> That feelingly persuade me what I am.'
> Sweet are the uses of adversity;
> Which, like the toad, ugly and venomous,
> Wears yet a precious jewel in his head;
> And this our life, exempt from public haunt,
> Finds tongues in trees, books in the running brooks,
> Sermons in stones, and good in everything.
>
> (II.i.1–17)

The passage is close to Keats's constant emphasis upon 'feelingly' encountering experience with the naked senses. The Duke's ideas have at least an oblique connection with Keats's concept of life as a 'vale of soul-making', where we grow in response to the pressures of pain and adversity. The Duke has almost succeeded in achieving an enviable equanimity described by Keats:

> ...the inhabitants of the world will correspond to itself – Let the fish philosophise the ice away from the Rivers in winter time and they shall be at continual play in the tepid delight of summer.[12]

If man can come to terms with the unavoidable physical circumstances and reconcile himself to them, then happiness, although relative, is possible. The Duke's speech looks forward to the songs later in the play, one with a refrain that indicates life is better lived in the harshness of the elements than in the court:

> Come hither, come hither, come hither.
>   Here shall he see
>   No enemy
> But winter and rough weather.
>
> (II.v.5–8)

and the other, linked by the winter's wind, expands this sentiment by comparing man's moral deficiencies to the relative harmlessness of natural adversity:

> Blow, blow, thou winter wind,
> Thou art not so unkind
>   As man's ingratitude;
>   ...
>
> (II.vii.174–90; all
> side-marked)

One might feel that the Duke does not show much sign of actually encountering hardship, since he has transplanted most of the good company and comforts of the court into this alfresco setting. Apart from a stray moment of pity for the deer, 'poor dappled fools', his relationship with nature seems more a matter of philosophy than feeling, and in its patrician way quite unlike Keats's earnest emphasis upon natural adversity as educative.

The character who most often and feelingly expresses the pain caused by 'man's ingratitude' is old Adam. The oak whose antique root peeps out, providing shade for the melancholic, could be Adam himself, who is called a representative of an 'antique' age (II.iii.57). (The oak is described as 'antique' twice[13].) Keats marks the passage in which Adam, like a choric commentator on society, says that Orlando's virtues 'Are sanctified and holy traitors', because they attract other people's viciousness:

> O, what a world is this, when what is comely
> Envenoms him that bears it!
>
> (II.iii.14–15)

Adam has always been aware that some day he will grow old and useless:

> When service should in my old limbs lie lame,
> And unregarded age in corners thrown;
>
> (II.iii.41–2)

and the lines hold an irresistible connection with those in *The Eve of St Agnes* when the Beadsman, 'For aye unsought for slept among his ashes cold'. Other lines from this kindly old man are marked by Keats, until the character disappears in the middle of the play, 'unsought for' in a world of young lovers fleeting the time carelessly as they did in the golden age.

The shepherd, Corin, is another example of old age, 'frosty but kindly', and in a comic but poignant exchange with the young Silvius he confesses he was once in love, but has forgotten much of the experience (II.iv.21–6, side-marked). Love is for the young, and Corin, like Adam, represents a different ethic, a firm, old-fashioned loyalty and generosity, not complaining even of his unpleasant master (II.iv.75–9, side-marked). Keats marks down the side the passages of conversation between the acerbic Touchstone and Corin (III.ii.13–20 and 69–75), and distributing his interests evenly he notes Corin's sharp answer establishing the hardship of country-living (III.ii.22–8). In this exchange, Touchstone's sophistication shows up Corin's untutored simplicity, but the shepherd's close relationship with the elements and his necessary recognition of sickness, poverty and discomfort expose the shallow selfishness of the court-dweller. Keats, loving such paradoxes in experience, surely appreciated the blend of witty scepticism and harsh living represented in the two characters here.

As the play goes on, Keats shows growing interest in Touchstone's words, and one passage in particular holds great importance for the poet. It is almost certainly marked primarily not for the way it reveals personality or explains the context, but for its ideas about poetry. Touchstone is peeved that the rustic Audrey cannot understand his classical allusion to Ovid:

> ... When a man's verses cannot be understood, nor a man's good wit seconded with the forward child understanding, it strikes a man more dead than a great reckoning in a little room. Truly, I would the gods had made thee poetical.
>
> (III.iii.9–13)

The necessity for 'understanding', a 'greeting of the spirit'[14] to be extended by the reader of poetry is one of Keats's central concerns. He regards reading as a collaborative activity, in which the writer supplies potential meanings embodied in a text, and the reader brings a receptive, open ear. It is a sad irony that Keats's own poems were greeted with little understanding by contemporary reviewers, and the experience no doubt contributed to what may be a heartfelt endorsement of

Touchstone's statement. The result of an unco-operative reading is that the great treasures enclosed in the writing are deadened and constricted by being locked up in 'a little room'. Keats uses the quotation, slightly re-phrased, against Dr Johnson, accusing the critic in effect of an unsympathetic reading. Keats vigorously scribbles out Johnson's comments at the end of the text of the play, and writes first, 'Is <u>Criticism</u> a true thing?' and then:

> When a man's verses cannot be understood, nor a man's good wit seconded by the forward child, understanding, it strikes a man more dead than a great reckoning in a [line cut]

Keats's harshness does not on this occasion seem just, because Johnson's comments are appreciative, although perhaps not enthusiastic enough for the liking of the young poet. Johnson also laments the fact that

> By hastening to the end of this work. Shakespeare suppressed the dialogue between the usurper and the hermit, and lost an opportunity of exhibiting a moral lesson, in which he might have found matter worthy of his highest powers.

– a moral lesson that others must be relieved to have been spared. A further irony, at the expense of Keats himself, is that, judging alone from the nature of his markings, it seems that on at least one occasion he himself has become engrossed in what Johnson calls 'the graver parts', although we cannot use this evidence to suggest that he did not enjoy the lighter love interest as well.

The only words marked in the fifth Act are again passages from Touchstone, who this time is scoring off the hapless William. He exercises his wit rather superciliously and with a cruel superiority in V.i, passages which Keats side-marks. Perhaps he simply enjoyed Touchstone for his more attractive side, his intellectual vitality, directness and inventiveness of language.

We may safely assume that other passages marked by Keats and not already mentioned, are poetically attractive, irrespective of character or context, and they are very 'Keatsian' in language, for example,

> <u>West of this place, down in the neighbour bottom</u>
> <u>The rank of osiers by the murmuring stream</u>
> <u>Left on your right hand brings you to the place.</u>
>   (IV.iii.77–9)

which mirrors the poetic strategy of 'Ode to Psyche' circling in upon its flowers, brooklet, and lovers. Phebe's description of the disguised Rosalind,

> There was a pretty redness in his lip,
> A little riper and more lusty red
> Than that mix'd in his cheek; 'twas just the difference
> Betwixt the constant red and mingled damask.
>
> (III.v.119–22)

feeds into Keats's words when Lamia 'Blush'd a live damask'. It is also likely that Keats's embellished description of the snake in *Lamia* has a prototype in Shakespeare's passage on the snake, entirely underlined (IV.iii.106–14).

And what of romantic love, the overriding subject of the play? Keats pays virtually no attention to it in his markings. He marks only passages that present passion ironically, such as Orlando's sentimentality which is punctured by Jaques, Silvius's statement to Corin, Phebe's haughty revelation that she is attracted to the peevish, pretty 'boy' (III.v.108–34), and one of Touchstone's many reductive statements about sexuality (II.iv.43–52). Without Rosalind, and without her many passages of exhilarating indulgence in feeling, we would expect the play to be quite a different experience. And so it is, but what Keats's markings have led us to recognize is that the joy and optimism of the romantic comedy are built upon a substratum of adversity and 'disagreeables'. Paradoxically, the information helps to enhance much of the humour in the play, which springs from excessive sentimentality of lovers, and an observation by Keats himself could well have been voiced by Rosalind or Touchstone witnessing Orlando:

> Nothing strikes me so forcibly with a sense of the rediculous as love – A Man in love I do think cuts the sorryest figure in the world – Even when I know a poor fool to be really in pain about it, I could burst out laughing in his face – His pathetic visage becomes irrisistable.[15]

Is it really wise, faced with such a case, to ask the question whether Keats is illuminating a strand of the play which has escaped critical attention *or* whether he is using the play to reveal his own temperament? Surely he is doing both, and it may be true that every acute reader and sensitive critic, no matter how much he may strive for 'disinterestedness' or 'negative capability' is in fact doing the same. It may even be a curious paradox that applies equally to both poets and readers, that the more subjectively engaged in their activities they are (so long as they do not literally see more than is before them), the more they may activate some potential aspect of their subject-matter or the text. However this may be, the markings of *As You Like It* are evidence of a symbiotic relationship between Keats and Shakespeare's text.

It is not so surprising, in the light of what recent critics have said about *All's Well That Ends Well* that a collection of the lines marked by Keats reveals an element which, if not quite melancholy, is at least 'mixed' in mode. Hazlitt had said of the play that it is 'one of the most pleasing of our author's comedies' with the qualification that 'the interest is however more of a serious than of a comic nature'.[16] Keats firmly underlines the words of the First Lord, an otherwise insignificant character:

The web of our life is of a mingled yarn, good and ill together:
(IV.iii.67)

and in a letter he quotes as 'exquisite' the description of the King's condition, 'Nature and sickness Debate it at their leisure' (I.ii.74–5).[17] Taken together, the quotations are consistent with others marked by Keats, and the general theme is one we have observed in the concentration of Keats upon 'contrast' in literature and life. Just as there is a fool in *King Lear*, so there is a dying king in *All's Well*. Several passages marked by Keats present us with conflicting feelings and qualities such as virtue and vice (I.i.96–9, IV.iii.67ff), inner virtue and outward title (II.iii.115ff), virginity and increase (I.i.117–52 *passim*), joy and grief (III.ii.47–9, V.iii.37–41). Again, simply because we find a thread of consistency that links many of the passages marked by Keats, and one which we know from other contexts contains attitudes held independently by him, there is no need to question whether the notion of contrast is more in his mind than in the play. Nor do we need to assume that his predisposition to appreciate contrast in a play is the *reason* for the markings. It is quite plausible to suggest that Keats was picking out what, for him, were the best lines of poetry or the most linguistically interesting passages of prose. We cannot fail, however, to sense something particularly creative and mutually illuminating in this meeting of a unique reader with a particular text.

In other ways, the words of *All's Well* may have provided Keats with either confirmation or inspiration for his own creative efforts. When, in his famous passage, he describes Negative Capability as 'when man is capable of being in uncertainties, Mysteries, doubts, without any irritable reaching after fact and reason...'[18] and Coleridge as 'incapable of remaining content with half knowledge', just how much is he unconsciously recalling of Lafeu's speech?

> They say miracles are past; and we have our philosophical persons to make modern and familiar things supernatural and causeless. Hence is it that we make trifles of terrors, ensconcing ourselves into seeming knowledge when we should submit ourselves to an unknown fear.
>
> (II.iii.1–6)

One could not confidently claim the passage in *All's Well* as a source, or even necessarily an influence upon Keats, not least because the respective distinctions are somewhat different. But the similarities of thought and expression are worth noticing. Similarly, it is not possible to ignore a creative connection between Keats's resonant line, 'Bright star, would I were stedfast as thou art–' and on the one hand the phrase of the undoubtedly 'stedfast' character, Helena,

> 'Twere all one,
> That I should love a bright particular star,
>
> (I.i.79–80)

and on the other, although the play is not marked, Julius Caesar's more ironic 'But I am constant as the northern star' (*Julius Caesar*, III.i.60). Such echoes, whether intended, unconscious or even coincidental, display vividly the special compatibility between the language and thought of Keats and the parts of Shakespeare which he appreciated and assimilated so thoroughly. In another, indirect way, *All's Well*, through the mediation of Hazlitt, may have guided Keats's poetic output. It was Hazlitt in his essay on this play (and again in his lecture 'On Dryden and Pope' which Keats attended on 3 February 1818) who praised the underrated qualities of Boccaccio. The joint venture between Keats and Reynolds to versify tales by Boccaccio was, of course, to give us *Isabella* and *The Eve of St Agnes*.

Upon *The Merry Wives of Windsor* and *Much Ado About Nothing*, there is a moderate sprinkling of markings which show that Keats read with a discriminating eye for language. He clearly enjoyed the eccentric idioms of the characters in Windsor such as the Welshman, Evans, and Slender in particular as well as Falstaff's indignant fustian upon being tricked. Ford's 'Hum! ha! Is this a vision? Is this a dream? Do I sleep?' (III.v.123; sidemarked) is one of several Shakespearean quotations which inform the last lines of the 'Ode to a Nightingale': 'Was it a vision, or a waking dream... – Do I wake or sleep?' Keats quotes several times in his letters snatches from Windsor's life and language, for example in making a jocular reference to Parson Evan's 'I will make an end of my dinner; there's pippins and cheese to come' (I.ii.10):

> for I do not see why a Mind like yours is not capable of harbouring and digesting the whole Mystery of Law as easily as Parson Hugh does Pepins – which did not hinder him from his poetic Canary...[19]

he amusingly appropriates Falstaff's description of eggs as 'pullet sperm' (III.v.26) to describe bad poems.[20] The spirit of these and other quotations seems to indicate Keats's enjoyment of the play, and in particular its verbal inventiveness. It is interesting that some other quotations demonstrate Keats's unique value as a guide to Shakespeare. One is, in fact, a mistake, but a revealing one. He wrote to Reynolds, 'As to the Matter I hope I can say with Sir Andrew "I have matter enough in my head" in your favor ...'[21] Keats's memory has slipped up. It is not Sir Andrew Aguecheek in *Twelfth Night* but Slender speaking to Falstaff in *The Merry Wives*: 'I have matter in my head against you' (I.i.112). What is somewhat 'elegant' about this error is that not only are the two characters similar in their roles as easily manipulable lovers, but also the respective situations in each play deserve comparison, for in both the gullible character is being unwittingly steered by a dubious friend towards a duel. By unconsciously conflating the characters, Keats is inadvertently discovering a repetition in Shakespeare involving a particular kind of character in a similar situation. In a more conscious way, Keats provides us with a genuine critical insight, when he links two speeches by Falstaff with a note of his own. 'Now, Master Shallow, you'll complain of me to the king?' (I.i.99; sidemarked) and 'Now, Master Brook, you come to know what hath passed between me and Ford's wife?' (III.v.55) are both marked with a cross in Keats's text, and his note runs '*This is a way of Falstaff's – vid "Hen 4th" Mastr Shallow I owe͞ you a thousand pound" '. He annotates the second with 'Another instance of Falstaff's peculiar way'. By noticing Falstaff's tone of imperious affirmativeness when on the defensive, Keats has quietly contributed to our knowledge of the ways in which Shakespeare characterizes his people through individuated speech habits. There is not much poetry in this play, although what there is, Keats notices:

> In em'rald tufts, flow'rs purple, blue and white;
> Like sapphire, pearl, and rich embroidery,
> Buckled below fair knighthood's bending knee.
> Fairies use flow'rs for their charactery.
>
> (V.v.68–71)

By the relative frequency with which he marks many of the prose passages, however, Keats demonstrates that it is not only the consciously poetical language of Shakespeare which he respects. He is alive to arresting language of any kind, particularly in this play when it is comically revealing of character.

Much Ado About Nothing is another play predominantly in prose, but characters break into verse under the pressure of emotion, and this time Keats's markings are most frequent in Act III when the poetry starts. He underlines the kinds of phrases and lines that Hazlitt calls 'picturesque' – literally painting in words – such as 'the woodbine coverture' (III.i.30), 'her spirits are as coy and wild As haggards of the rock' (III.i.35–6) and the beautiful description of Beatrice in her 'pleached bower' (III.i.7–11; all underlined). Keats was clearly so struck by the word 'pleached' that he was to use it himself.[22] He also marks the atmospherically significant and haunting couplets beginning 'The wolves have prey'd...' in Act V (V.iii.25–7). He is most interested in Hero's expressive but ambiguous blush at the broken wedding, a piece of evidence that would no doubt interest Professor Ricks who finds blushing throughout Keats's poetry.[23] Amongst several descriptions of her blush which are marked, we have the Friar's interpretation:

> I have mark'd
> A thousand blushing apparitions
> To start into her face, a thousand innocent shames
> In angel whiteness bear away those blushes.
>
> (IV.i.158–61)

The only character whose words are marked at any length in the play is Leonato, and although we cannot say whether it is the words or the character which interested Keats primarily, we can at least acknowledge that when he bursts into savage denunciation of his daughter, the moment marks the point when poetry emerges from prose and the atmosphere intensifies. One phrase, 'with grey hairs and bruise of many days' (V.i.65) may have been stored away in Keats's memory to inform distantly his description of Saturn in the second *Hyperion*, and it is possible also that his own stated inability to 'philosophise away' natural adversity in the world made him sympathetic to Leonato's idea:

> For there was never yet philosopher
> That could endure the toothache patiently,
> However they have writ the style of gods,
> And made a push at chance and sufferance.
> (V.i.35–8)

In his copy of the play, Keats marks only one sentence from the part of Dogberry (V.i.300–2), but this should not lead us to believe he did not appreciate this memorable character. Indeed, Dogberry is one who is given the privilege of quotation in the letters on two occasions. Writing about the manager of the Drury Lane Theatre, to whom Keats had submitted *Otho the Great* for consideration, Keats says:

> As he has not rejected our Tragedy I shall not venture to call him directly a fool; but as he wishes to put it off till next season I cant help thinking him little better than a Knave.[24]

He is referring to Dogberry's indictment against Borachio and Conrade:

> Masters, it is proved already that you are little better than false knaves, and it will go near to be thought so shortly.   (IV.ii.19-20)

Keats's fine distinction is somewhat more meaningful than Dogberry's, but the tone is the same in both passages. The second comment Keats picks out is Dogberry's 'merciful' instruction to his redoubtable watchmen:

> the most peaceable way for you, if you do take a thief, is to let him show himself what he is, and steal out of your company.
> (III.iii.53–5)

Writing to his good friend Charles Brown, Keats applies this sentiment to the rain:

> I hope the weather will give you the slip; let it show itself, and steal out of your company.[25]

As well as the obvious, amusing aptness (rain is like a criminal whom one would rather not apprehend but allow to slip away), there is another associational link which shows Keats's grasp of the context. Dogberry and his men are standing in the drizzling rain (III.iii.97), and for shelter they go to sit upon the church-bench. Keats has picked up every detail visualized in the scene, and has enhanced by clarifying the full humour of his own quip and the play's scene. *Much Ado About Nothing* was then, like *The Merry Wives of Windsor*, a play which Keats evidently read with enjoyment and intentness, and although it may not have provided him with any deep source for creativity, there are points at which the ideas and language are compatible with his own, and there are also ways in which his own quotation can light up corners in the play that perhaps he was peculiarly equipped to notice. Once again, our subject points both ways, backwards to Shakespeare and forwards to Keats, with mutually enlightening results.

Measure for Measure is another play which many readers have thought 'bitter to sweet end' (IV.vi.8; Keats's underlining), and Keats marks it judiciously (transcribed by Spurgeon). With the great anthology pieces about death and power, he picks out striking images such as 'with idle spiders' strings' (III.ii.257), 'warped slip of wilderness' (III.i.143), 'bite the law by th' nose' (III.i.110), and

> … as blossoming time
> That from the seedness the bare fallow brings
> To teeming foison; even so her plenteous womb
> Expresseth his full tilth and husbandry.
> (I.iv.41–4)

He is arrested by Barnardine described in 'drunken sleep' and 'desperately mortal' (IV.ii.138), and caught at the moment when he is most defiantly alive: 'He is coming, sir, he is coming; I hear his straw rustle' (IV.iii.32). Keats was to take over Shakespeare's coinage in describing Isabella as 'a thing enskied and sainted' (I.iv.34) when Endymion is 'Ensky'd' (Book IV, 772). Many another 'fine isolated verisimilitude' chosen by Keats to mark could be quoted, but rather than illustrate Keats's taste we can be more selective, for in this play he does follow through one interest. At the end of the play, Keats decisively scores out Johnson's comment that 'the time of the action is indefinite', and he also turns the words of the play against what he sees as the limitations of Johnson's general remarks, by writing:

> 'But Man! Proud Man!
> Drest in a little brief authority
> Plays such fantastic tricks before high heaven
> As makes the Angels weep'!!!

It seems fairly definite that some of his markings in the second half of the play are designed to refute Johnson on the specific matter of the time-scale:

To-morrow you set on (III.i.62)

Upon the heavy middle of the night (IV.i.33)

The vaporous night approaches (IV.i.56)

'Tis now dead midnight, and by eight to-morrow
Thou must be made immortal...
(IV.ii.59–60)

None, since the curfew rung (IV.ii.70)

As near the dawning, Provost, as it is (IV.ii.90)

it is almost day (IV.ii.101)

Look, th' unfolding star calls up the shepherd (IV.ii.190)

Come away: it is almost clear dawn (IV.ii.206)

Ere twice the sun hath made his journal greeting
To the under generation...
(IV.iii.84–5)

Keats is literally underlining Shakespeare's precise and atmospheric presentation of the dragging time during the tense night which passes during Act IV. It may even have been the wording of the Song which opens the Act that alerted Keats to the idea that the characters are looking forward to break of day as a time when problems will be solved and anxiety will evaporate, although the singer in the context prefers to remain in the dark:

Take, O, take those lips away,
   That so sweetly were forsworn;
And those eyes, the break of day,
   Lights that do mislead the morn.
(IV.i.1–4)

However this may be, the evidence of Keats's markings leads us to recognize Shakespeare's careful planning and control in the sequence of events that occur in the darkness and murky half-light. The critical mind of a practising poet lies behind Keats's markings on this occasion. He is observing his own trade in Shakespeare the master-craftsman. A reading of *Isabella*, for example, reveals a careful specificity about details of time. The love affair is conceived in May, spoken on 'one fair morning' in June (stanzas IV and VI), Lorenzo is murdered on a journey which should have taken three hours on a hot summer morning; Isabella mourns through autumn and winter (stanza XXXII), her trip into the forest with the nurse takes from morning till evening (XLIII and XLIV) after the night on which she dreams of the ghost of her lover, and they dig up his body after three hours' toil (XLVIII). Thereafter, the time becomes appropriately indeterminate, for Isabella loses track of its passing, but her grieving over the basil pot lasts at least until the following autumn (LIII). Keats keeps control of a lengthy time-scheme in this poem for the benefit of the reader, whilst also demonstrating that the pace at which time moves for an individual is subjective. Even more analogous to *Measure for Measure* is the time of the action in *The Eve of St Agnes*, for here Keats keeps us continuously aware that one night is passing, from the winter's evening heralding a noisy feast, through the 'tranced midnight' of a moonlit night which turns to a storm of sleet, to the moment before dawn. It is the strictness of the time-scheme here which makes so bewildering and effective the sudden switch in the final stanza: 'And they are gone: ay, ages long ago'. An event which the consciousnesses of lovers experience over one intense night suddenly becomes in the myth-making of the poet the *kind* of night which has always and always will exist in the mind. The paradox is surprisingly close to that contained by the idea of the 'Ode to a Nightingale', where continuing present tense is merged with past to create an eternal present. In fact this Ode is verbally influenced by the speeches on death by the Duke (III.i.5–42) and Claudio (III.i.118), both heavily marked by Keats, and one critic has cited the influence to argue that there is a close and special relationship between *Measure for Measure* and the 'Ode to a Nightingale'.[26] However, since others have located important sources in other Shakespearean works and elsewhere, it seems more accurate and interesting to analyse the 'Ode' as partly a clever celebration of the seductive powers of poetry in general, and Shakespeare in particular.

In Keats's time, *Cymbeline* was undergoing something like a resurrection from the grave of 'unresisting imbecility' to which Dr Johnson had consigned it. Both Coleridge and Hazlitt found the play attractive, the latter calling it 'one of the most delightful of Shakespear's historical plays', and classifying it as 'a dramatic romance'.[27] One can account for this new attitude in terms of the priorities of the age. Not being over-bothered by concerns of structure, moral complexity or credibility, they were free to enjoy the poetry for its own sake. Keats's markings are evidence for this conclusion. He marks the play copiously, drawing attention to the considerable amount of 'romantic' and pastoral poetry. He ignores the cloddish character of Cloten, much of the dialogue at court except for speeches involving Imogen and Posthumus and the patriotic words about England, and he largely neglects the unravelling of the plot in the long final scene, although unerringly he finds the few conscious poeticisms in the scene, such as 'Hang there like fruit, my soul, Till the tree die!' (V.v.263–45 and

> See,
> Posthumus anchors upon Imogen;
> And she, like harmless lightning, throws her eye
> On him, her brothers, me, her master, hitting
> Each object with a joy; the counterchange
> Is severally in all.
>
> (V.v.393–8)

Like Hazlitt, Keats has a special admiration for Imogen, seeing her as the prime example of one kind of Shakespearean womanhood. Hazlitt positively worships her, and he sets the pace for such 'Imogen-idolators' as Swinburne and Dowden later in the century:

> We have almost as great an affection for Imogen as she had for Posthumus; and she deserves it better. Of all Shakespear's women she is perhaps the most tender and the most artless.[28]

Keats shows his interest by marking many of her lines, and by a comment in a letter which shows that he was aware she is only one kind of ideal:

> Imprimis – I sincerely believe that Imogen is the finest Creature; and that I should have been disappointed at hearing you prefer Juliet. Item Yet I feel such a yearning towards Juliet and that I would rather follow her into Pandemonium than Imogen into Paradize – heartily wishing myself a Romeo to be worthy of her ...[29]

Whereas Juliet has an adolescent spontaneity and employs a language of impetuous excitement, Imogen, married from the start, demonstrates a mature, moral firmness and patient fidelity. She can be quietly tender, domestically practical (even cutting the roots she is to cook into special shapes at IV.ii.49–51, a passage underlined by Keats), spirited and mischievous, and brutally frank in her rejection of Cloten. Keats shows that he appreciates all these sides of her character. It is Imogen, we recall, who provides Keats with his touchstone of moral virtue, to be contrasted with Iago in illustration of Shakespeare's chameleon-like capacities.[30] In claiming this ethical versatility for Shakespeare, Keats could well have mentioned Iachimo, many of whose lines he marked, since he is a rather chameleon-like figure himself. The plot makes him a villain, but it is Iachimo who speaks some of the most beautiful poetry, in the scene in which he rhapsodizes over the sleeping Imogen. He is enthralled into a virtuous state of mind by the appearance of Imogen, and describes his feelings in a language close to Keats's own on occasions:

> Had I this cheek
> To bathe my lips upon; this hand, whose touch,
> Whose every touch, would force the feeler's soul
> To th' oath of loyalty; this object, which
> Takes prisoner the wild motion of mine eye,
> Fixing it only here; ...
>
> (I.vi.98–103)

The way 'touch' and sensation in general lead him later into a genuinely virtuous state of mind, might well have helped to confirm Keats in his early belief that beauty is truth. A rather more surprising aspect of the markings is the interest they display in the words of Posthumus. Hazlitt almost completely ignores this character, saying he is 'only interesting from the interest [Imogen] takes in him',[31] but Keats marks many of his lines, even his angry outburst 'I'll do something' (II.iv.149) and other lines in the same scene, revealing violent jealousy:

> O vengeance, vengeance!
> Me of my lawful pleasure she restrain'd,
> And pray'd me oft forbearance; did it with
> A pudency so rosy, the sweet view on't
> Might well have warm'd old Saturn; that I thought her
> As chaste as unsunn'd snow:-
>
> (II.v.8–13)

Admittedly such passages have dramatic force, and they reveal much of this rather unpleasant man's character, but it is fruitless to speculate upon Keats's attitude. He side-marks the Gaoler's down-to-earth speech on death in V.iv delivered to Posthumus, a passage which introduces a note of roughness in prose into an essentially poetic play. We find, as we would expect, that Keats shows close interest in the language of the pastoral scenes (III.iii and IV.ii), and more generally the occasional images from the natural world:

> The benediction of these covering heavens
> Fall on their heads like dew!
>
> (V.v.350–1)

Since there are so many markings on *Cymbeline*, it is not possible to attempt an overall interpretation, except to say that Keats is always susceptible to fine language and touches of unusual imagery, both of which he finds in abundance. Instead, we can explore more broadly how important the play was to Keats's own creativity. It seems, in fact to have contributed substantially to his poetry. For example, these two passages remained in his memory, both referring to the gods:

> our crooked smokes climb to their nostrils
>
> (V.v.475)

and the exchange between Jupiter and Sicilius:

> JUPITER   Mount, eagle, to my palace crystalline.
> SICILIUS.   He came in thunder; his celestial breath
> Was sulphurous to smell; the holy eagle
> Stoop'd, as to foot us. His ascension is
> More sweet than our blest fields. His royal bird
> Prunes the immortal wing, and cloys his beak,
> As when his god is pleas'd.
>   …
> SICILIUS.   The marble pavement closes, he is enter'd
> His radiant roof.
>
> (V.iv.113–21)

Keats is merging the two quotations together when he comes to write this:

> But one of our whole eagle-brood still keeps
> His sov'reignty, and rule, and majesty;
> Blazing Hyperion on his orbed fire
> Still sits, still snuffs the incense teeming up
> From man to Sun's God –[32]

The influence shows that Keats did not require first-rate poetry to stimulate his own imagination, for ironically the scene is often nowadays considered to be inferior in quality and perhaps non-Shakespearean. Another line, ' 'Tis still a dream, or else such stuff as madmen Tongue, and brain not' (V.iv.144–5) is one of several Shakespearean passages that feed into Keats's thoughts on poetry in *The Fall of Hyperion* as he broods on dreamers and fanatics. Given the dramatic similarity between the scene in which Iachimo observes the sleeping Imogen and the episode in *The Eve of St Agnes* in which Porphyro watches Madeline, it is not surprising that there is a general atmospheric similarity and some verbal echoes, such as the sleeper's eyes, described in the play as 'White and azure' whilst Madeline 'slept an azure-lidded sleep'. Before sleeping, Imogen is reading the story of Philomel, and Madeline is likened to 'a tongueless nightingale'. There is a taper in both accounts and the sleeping woman's breathing is closely studied by the man in each case. None of these details in itself is strong enough to claim the play as a 'source' in any narrow, direct way, but the overall similarity in the hushed, reverential tone and delicacy of description in the play and in the poem generate a sense that the one is a creative influence upon the other. There is a similarly oblique relationship between Isabella weeping over the corpse and Imogen in IV.ii.290 ff. It is rare for Keats to be obvious in his poetic echoes, for even when clearly derivative he always makes something original and unique. Finally, I cannot help wondering, however fancifully, whether Keats's reported last words about hearing the daisies growing above him might hold an association from the play:

> let us
> Find out the prettiest daisied plot we can,
> And make him with our pikes and partisans
> A grave.   (IV.ii.400–3)

'The swoon of Imogen' mentioned by Keats in *Endymion* (II,31) was the event which led to her apparent death. Taking all the evidence together, it would appear that *Cymbeline*, held in higher esteem by the Romantics than by recent critics, was admired by Keats and was a creative influence throughout his writing life. Hazlitt, in describing the play, says of Shakespeare: 'If he was equal to the greatest things, he was not above an attention to the smallest.'[33] Much the same could be said of Keats's own critical temperament in reading through Shakespeare's text, and if he showed little interest in matters of structure or unity, he reaped a rich harvest in seeing the play as a marvellous collection of intense, poetic language.

The Winter's Tale is marked moderately throughout, although it is a little surprising that Keats does not mark the 'resurrection' of Hermione, perhaps because as an event its theatrical significance is greater than its poetic. He underlines heavily much of the passages by

Leontes in his jealousy, passages which are compressed in their imagery to such an extent that Hazlitt was drawn to describe them in this way:

> Even the crabbed and tortuous style of the speeches of Leontes, reasoning on his own jealousy, beset with doubts and fears, and entangled more and more in the thorny labyrinth, bears every mark of Shakespear's peculiar manner of conveying the painful struggle of different thoughts and feelings, labouring for utterance, and almost strangled in the birth.[34]

Whether Keats would agree with this analysis can only be surmised, but he certainly pays much attention to the language of Leontes, and it is at least possible that his interest was aroused by Hazlitt's incisive comments. Some markings on the play we can, by now, claim as special interests of Keats. He underlines Perdita's charming expression, 'I'll blush you thanks' (IV.iv.575), and we are reminded that the blush is as characteristic a gesture of Perdita (see IV.iv.12, 67,160; V.ii.89) as it is of Hero in *Much Ado* and other Shakespearean heroines in whom Keats shows interest. He also underlines the name of 'that rare Italian master, Julio Romano' (V.ii.94) who was well known to the Keats circle through his paintings. He was a favourite of the painter Benjamin Haydon who was in close contact with Keats, and Leigh Hunt compares Romano's pictures with the literary style of Spenser in a passage from *The Faerie Queene* described as 'a picture of the supernatural… wonderfully fine and ghastly'.[35] Ian Jack has detected Romano's influence behind passages in *Hyperion*, 'Ode to Psyche' and 'To Autumn'.[36] Given this background, it is logical that Keats would be interested in the Shakespearean invocation of the painter. He sidemarks quite a lot of the racy, colourful prose of Autolycus, who takes his place beside Launce in *The Two Gentlemen of Verona* and Launcelot Gobbo in *The Merchant of Venice* as a character-type whose language engages Keats's interest. Other phrases are almost certainly marked for the vividness of imagery, such as, 'Still virginalling Upon his palm?' (I.ii.125–6); 'imprison't not In ignorant concealment' (I.ii.396–7) 'welkin eye' (I.ii.136); 'a weather-bitten conduit of many kings' reigns' (V.ii.50). 'The fire-rob'd god, Golden Apollo' (IV.iv. 29–30) is a reference which would attract Keats's interest because Apollo was an important figure in his own use of mythology, from the early 'Ode to Apollo' through to *The Fall of Hyperion* in which he wears 'flaming robes', gives a roar 'as if of earthly fire' and 'on he flared'.[37]

There is evidence that one passage struck Keats as very typical of the language of Shakespearean lovers. On his text of *Antony and Cleopatra* he notes beside an exchange between the lovers ('Fie, wrangling queen!') the following:

> How much more Shakespeare delights in dwelling upon the romantic and wildly natural than upon the monumental. see Winter's Tale, 'When you do dance, &c.'

When we turn up the passage, we find it is underlined in an interesting way:

FLORIZEL.   When you speak, sweet
        I'd have you do it ever. When you sing,
        I'd have you buy and sell so; so give alms;
        Pray so; and, for the ord'ring your affairs,
        To sing them too. When you do dance, I wish you
        A wave o' th' sea, that you might ever do
        Nothing but that; move still, still so,
        And own no other function. Each your doing,
        So singular in each particular,
        Crowns what you are doing in the present deeds,
        That all your acts are queens.

(IV.iv.136–46)

The broken underlining is perhaps Keats's way of recording the movement of the verse as it echoes the ebb and flow of the sea by the combination of run-on lines and *caesurae*. Interpretations of Keats's marginal note may differ since his words are characteristically suggestive, but the implication is that Keats believes the greatest Shakespearean poetry is reserved for lovers and perhaps also for using imagery from the natural world. Both 'the romantic' and 'the wildly natural' are illustrated by Florizel's passage. It is possible also that Keats recognized the functional ambiguity of the word 'still' in 'move still, still so' and uses it with precision himself in 'Ode on a Grecian Urn': 'Thou still unravish'd bride of quietness' and 'For ever warm and still to be enjoy'd'. Despite the elusiveness of identifiable verbal reminiscence, there are associational links between Keats's poem and this play. In both we find pipes and timbrels or their equivalent playing upon a festival occasion in dales of Arcady and Bohemia respectively. Sheep-shearing is the occasion of the one, sacrificing a heifer of the other, and in the classical ethos of both there is a sense that 'deities and mortals' overlap, for Perdita's language is full of references to the gods (Proserpina, Dis, Juno, Cytherea, and Phoebus all in one passage at IV.iv.116–

25 which is underlined). She also expresses 'a flowery tale' in describing the rosemary, rue and marigold (IV.iv. 74–5; IV.iv. 105–6, both partially underlined) as she disperses them. If the lovers in *The Winter's Tale* speak verse that is 'romantic and wildly natural', the images of lovers on the urn are full of 'wild ecstasy' in their happy love. Furthermore, both the play and the Ode turn on a very particular ambivalence of attitude towards art and reality. A statue comes to life, leaving spectators in a dazed state of mind at the end of *The Winter's Tale*, whilst 'On a Grecian Urn' presents a work of art that is both living and not living, teasing us out of thought by its life-like representation and even coming to life long enough to leave us with tantalizing words. The Ode sets chiming distant bells which can be traced back delicately to *The Winter's Tale*, even in tones of indulgent humour and rationality mingled teasingly with wonder.

Shakespearean comedy gave Keats a poetic vision, a cluster of subjects which are 'Full of sweet desolation – balmy pain',[38] as much art as 'life', treated with imagery which dwells upon the 'romantic and wildly natural'. The natural outcome of the vision is the composition of the great Odes to which our analysis has often led. But the story began earlier in Keats's career, even before he had acquired the copies of Shakespeare which we now have. At the end of 1816 he wrote 'Sleep and Poetry' and 'I stood tip-toe upon a little hill', and already Shakespeare's presence is potent. In the former the 'musk-rose blowing' conflates phrases from *A Midsummer Night's Dream* (II.i.249–52), Oberon's description of flowers which all find their way into Keats's poem; the 'puling infant's force' (line 185) gives a clever portmanteau word from Jaques' 'infant, Mewling and puking' while 'whining boyhood' comes from the same passage (*As You Like It*, II.vii.139 ff.), and the general theme of time's fragility comes time and again in the Sonnets and in songs in the comedies. In 'I stood tip-toe' the word 'quaint' to describe the 'curious bending Of a fresh woodland alley' (lines 19–20) comes from the unusual usage in Titania's 'quaint mazes in the wanton green' (*A Midsummer Night's Dream* II.i.99, used in its more normal sense at II.ii.7, and repeated by Keats at line 40); 'A natural sermon o'er their pebbly beds' (line 71) comes from 'sermons in stones' (*As You Like It*, II.i.17); the harps strung by Apollo (line 50) are no doubt

> as sweet and musical
> As bright Apollo's lute, strung with his hair...
> (*Love's Labour's Lost*, IV.iii.338)

and more generally the young men and maidens who learn love in each other's eyes 'Until their tongues were loos'd in poesy' (lines 231–5) are precisely following the fortunes of the young men and women in *Love's Labour's Lost.* (All these lines are underlined in Keats's edition but since the poems were written earlier this fact is evidence of no more than a consistency in Keats's taste.) What really matters is not the existence of verbal sources but a comprehensive, imaginative similarity. Keats's two poems, and particularly the latter, add up to an equation: nature plus love equals poetry, at least for the poet conscious of his youth. The kind of poetry which results from the combination is akin to an alternative, more pure and sensuous world which is intimately related to sleep and dream. All these concerns point back as a coherent group to the dominant themes and subjects of *A Midsummer Night's Dream, As You Like It* and *Love's Labour's Lost,* and they also point forward just as coherently and consistently to 'Ode to Psyche', 'Ode to a Nightingale', 'Ode on a Grecian Urn' and 'Ode on Melancholy'. It would be absurd to claim Shakespeare as the only source for either the earlier poems or the Odes, since Keats's poetic memory is extraordinarily capacious, and equally it cannot be argued that Shakespeare inhibits Keats's originality – rather he enhances it in many ways. But to find in common a group of central subjects, a shared way of dealing with these themes, and a clearly comparable attitude to poetry and art itself, with in addition a deeply related technique of making images and poetic language – is all too much to be coincidental, and no trivial or peripheral legacy from the dramatist to the young Romantic poet.[39]

At the very least, we may conclude that Keats read through all of Shakespeare's comedies with a discriminating care that is apparent from his many markings. By and large, they lead us to passages and phrases which stand out for their poetic effects and use of language. The influence upon his own poetry is difficult to assess with any precision, although it must be seen as generally pervasive. Annotated editions of his poems cite many more verbal reminiscences from the comedies in addition to those suggested here, although Keats invariably produces his own, unique style which may be 'Shakespearean' but is never merely quotation. Although he wrote a body of comic verse which is impressively large, he wrote no poem that could be claimed to bear structural resemblance to a Shakespearean comedy, and so on this aspect we must remain silent. However, it seems certain from many of his markings that he must have regarded comedy as a 'mixed mode' (in Hazlitt's phrase), embracing elements of melancholy and distress as well as joy, and this accords with his belief that art is grounded in a sense of contrast. It might be possible also to argue that his heroines, Isabella and Madeline, owe something to Shakespearean heroines such as Imogen, Helena and Hero rather than the more actively assertive women in Shakespeare, and even that the general conception of love in *Endymion* and *The Eve of St Agnes* as an idealizing, ardent and transient experience activating all the senses, owes much to Shakespeare's presentation in plays from *Love's Labour's Lost* to *The Winter's Tale*.

IV 'Shakespearean hieroglyphics' in
The Tempest *and* A Midsummer Night's Dream

A Midsummer Night's Dream and *The Tempest* meant more to Keats as a reader and creative artist than any of the other comedies, and together with *King Lear* they form for him the triumvirate of Shakespeare's greatest plays. The texts of the plays are profusely marked in his Johnson-Steevens edition, and in addition some passages from the *Dream* are marked in the Folio. His letters are full of quotations from these plays, especially in 1817 and early 1818 when he is talking about poetry in general, forming his own aesthetic. *Endymion*, at least, is heavily influenced by both plays.[1] Later on tragedies, together with Milton and Wordsworth, may have been his poetic touchstones, but in his early poetry at least, these two comedies (together with Spenser) gave him his fill of poetic 'intensity' and verbal inventiveness.

It is essentially the plays' language which held Keats under a spell. There is little point in trying to be thorough in presenting the evidence of what attracted his interest amongst the words, phrases and passages because, although still discriminating, he has marked more than 600 lines in each play.[2] While attempting to be generous in quotation, I shall here be both more general and more specific than elsewhere, in attempting to assess broadly the principles behind the kinds of language which attracted Keats, and selecting some areas of detail for closer inspection. These two plays give us an opportunity to explore Keats's attitudes to Shakespearean language in a way which will illuminate his readings of all the others. But it is impossible, needless to say, for an analytical critic to be definitive on the matter, because a reader's receptivity to language is unique, and too private to be closely inspected. Keats himself says so much, in calling poetic language 'hieroglyphics'.

It is likely that every person who hears or reads the words of Shakespeare with attentiveness will have a uniquely personal, and ultimately incommunicable, understanding of Shakespeare's language. When one suddenly notices a 'secret' meaning in a pun or an oblique expression, one feels either alone with the mind that created the work, or at least an initiate amongst the elect. Merely to say this is in itself an act of interpretation. It is a description of one of the most abiding qualities of Shakespeare's works to say that new meanings may be elicited at each reading or viewing, that old meanings may slip away into irrelevance, and that all potential meanings can never be held simultaneously in the mind of any one person, no matter how learned. Shakespeare seems to express himself in a complex system of 'codes' which can never be fully cracked. The dangers and difficulties involved in trying to explain analytically how this phenomenon works are fully recognized by both Hazlitt and Keats, for they both prefer simply to quote, speaking of the 'fineness' or 'beauty' of the words, leaving it up to the reader to discover his own sense of mystery. Matthew Arnold, in his idea of the 'touchstone', is a later exponent of the method. Schlegel, in a passage quoted by Hazlitt, contents himself with generalizing that in Shakespeare, 'energetical passions electrify the whole of the mental powers, and will, consequently, in highly favoured natures, express themselves in an ingenious and figurative manner'.[3] Hazlitt in his essays attempts to illustrate the generalization, by quoting as much as he can, keeping his critical commentaries to a minimum, and constantly stressing a 'spirit' which he detects behind the statements of a character in a context, hoping that by this method he will draw his readers into a frame of mind capable of sharing an understanding of the code.

Although Keats is generally unwilling to attempt analysis of the effects of Shakespeare's language, preferring to keep 'the penetralium of mystery' intact, he does make one suggestive statement on his notion of the general function of poetic language in Shakespeare. Speaking of what he regards as Kean's fidelity to the spirit of Shakespeare's characters and words, Keats writes in his review:

> A melodious passage in poetry is full of pleasures both sensual and spiritual. The spiritual is felt when the very letters and prints of charactered language show like the hieroglyphics of beauty; – 'the mysterious signs of an immortal freemasonry'. 'A thing to dream of, not to tell'. 'The sensual life of verse springs warm from the lips of Kean, and to one learned in Shakespearian hieroglyphics, – learned in the spiritual portion of those lines to which Kean adds a sensual grandeur: his tongue must seem to have robbed 'the Hybla bees, and left them honeyless' [*Julius Caesar*, V.i.34–5].[4]

The passage is not so vague and impressionistic as it might seem on first glance, for Keats is making concisely a fine and clear distinction. He is explaining his own attitude to the strange relationship in Shakespeare's language between the sound and the sense, the 'sensual and spiritual' properties which are simultaneously exclusive and inseparable. The actor may reproduce the sounds of the words, but unless he can also be fully inward with the sense and spirit 'behind' the words, he is doing only half his job. A great actor in Keats's opinion must be close in understanding to the creator of the words and an audience must be acquainted with Shakespeare's 'code' in order to observe fully the fitness of sound and spirit which together create the meaning. All the participants in the co-operative process of re-creating Shakespeare's text must be able to hear the language both in its melodious self-sufficiency of sound as something beautiful in its own 'sensual' splendour, and also as a set of 'hieroglyphics' whose sense needs to be sensitively interpreted. Through an understanding of the 'mysterious signs' we can enter 'an immortal freemasonry'.[5]

Although Keats is using the word 'hieroglyphics' in a personal (although cogently explained) way, he found it as usual in other writers. Since Sir Thomas Browne the word had carried associations of a sacred text, as well as a language difficult to translate, and Keats is certainly invoking both connotations. Coleridge, however, when he uses the word, is criticizing Hamlet as a personality, for his habit of not paying attention equally to outward objects and inner thoughts. In his state of morbid intellectualism, Hamlet 'beholds external objects as hieroglyphics',[6] and is unwilling to treat any statement at face value. Hazlitt is alleged to have heard Coleridge lecturing on *Hamlet* early in Coleridge's career, and he may have picked up the notion from his lips (although it is tempting to think the word may have been 'in the news' because the Rosetta Stone was brought to France in 1798 and eventually deciphered in 1824.) Hazlitt moves towards Keats's more general notion, after using Coleridge's specific idea of *Hamlet* as his starting-point:

> But here we are more than spectators. We have not only 'the outward pageants and the signs of grief'; but 'we have that within which passes shew'. We read the thoughts of the heart, we catch the passions living as they rise.[7]

Keats himself, in his own understanding of the word 'hieroglyphics', finds in Hazlitt, as in Kean, a person with the skill to decode Shakespeare's words. In his copy of Hazlitt's *Characters* Keats underlines the following statement on *King Lear*:

> We see the ebb and flow of the feeling, its pauses and feverish
> starts... <u>the manner in which it avails itself of every passing word</u>
> <u>or gesture, its haste to repel insinuation, the alternate contraction</u>
> <u>and dilation of the soul.</u>[8]

Keats annotates with the words, 'This passage has to a great degree the
hieroglyphic visnomy'. The word 'has' surely bears various meanings,
from 'captures' or 'explains' to 'exemplifies' or 'contains', while the
odd 'visnomy' probably means 'form'.[9] When we look back at the pas-
sage itself, we can presume that Keats is admiring an analytical qual-
ity, not just a descriptive vigour, for Hazlitt is seeking to define a gen-
eral principle, or set of principles, which lie beneath the linguistic
'manner' of the words in the play. In giving equal weight to 'word or
gesture' and 'the soul', Hazlitt is giving a specific illustration of
Keats's notion that the 'sensual' – the physical properties of sound
itself – acts as a code which embodies the spiritual – the feelings and
the soul of a character and the play as a whole. By apprehending with
our sense of hearing the special rhythms ('contraction and dilation') in
the words of *Lear*, we are initiated into a corresponding *feeling* of con-
traction and dilation of the soul, which operates on a sub-verbal or
spiritual level to determine our understanding of the play.

Throughout his essays, Hazlitt provides many examples of the
theory that language is a hieroglyph for the soul of a character. In
speaking generally of Shakespeare's 'ideal beings' who, 'if we suppose
such beings to exist at all, they could not act, speak, or feel otherwise
than he makes them', Hazlitt goes on to give examples:

> He has invented for them a language, manners, and sentiments of
> their own, from the tremendous imprecations of the Witches in
> *Macbeth*, when they do 'a deed without a name', to the sylph-like
> expressions of Ariel, who 'does his spiriting gently'; the mischiev-
> ous tricks and gossiping of Robin Goodfellow, or the uncouth
> gabbling and emphatic gesticulations of Caliban in this play.[10]

Such a statement presupposes that there is a close connection between
the outer and the inner, the language and the character, the mode of
expression and the personality of the speaker, the words and the feel-
ings, the code and the referent.

Keats's use of the word 'hieroglyphics' in application to Shakes-
peare's language is pregnant and suggestive, but not vague or undis-
ciplined. He is reaching towards a way of explaining the apparently
spontaneous aptness in Shakespeare's way of using language to

express feelings, and Keats is attempting to take account of both the sound and the sense. In the area of sound we should include not simply words but rhythms and cadences which may flow through a whole play. The notion also includes some idea of the way sense itself may be expressed with a 'darker purpose', by way of 'a sort of riddling terms' as we find, for example, in the utterances of the Fool in *King Lear*. Ultimately, Keats's is a poet's interest in such a matter, rather than an analytical critic's, although he can often help us towards new interpretations of the text. A later poet, Edmund Blunden, in an elegant essay on 'Shakespeare's Significances', has made his own attempt to demonstrate the 'oracular and laconic' in Shakespeare's art, suggesting that we must all be 'cryptographers' in finding the various purposes of Shakespeare's language, and he argues that the sound may operate on both a superficial and a more deeply complex level. For both Keats and Hazlitt poetic language has a double nature; it is significant for its immediate sense impression, and also for the whole range of meanings and concepts which it encodes.

The sheer excitement which Keats felt on reading or recalling lines from *The Tempest* is expressed in a letter to Reynolds:

> Whenever you write say a Word or two on some Passage in Shakespeare that may have come rather new to you; which must be continually happening, notwithstanding that we read the same Play forty times – for instance, the following, from the Tempest, never struck me so forcibly as at present,
>
> > 'Urchins
> > Shall, for that vast of Night that they may work,
> > All exercise on thee –'
> > How can I help bringing to your mind the Line –
> > In the dark backward and abysm of time –
>
> I find that I cannot exist without poetry – without eternal poetry – half the day will not do – the whole of it – I began with a little, but habit has made me a Leviathan …[11]

We shall return to the phrases quoted, and others like them, for their syntactical construction reveals a specific and individual aspect of the 'hieroglyphics' of this play. For the time being, we may notice the insatiable appetite of Keats for the language of *The Tempest*. At the same time he can jocularly compare his delight in unpacking a copy of Shakespeare with Stephano's sense of relief on finding his bottle after the shipwreck: 'I felt rather lonely this Morning at breakfast so I went and unbox'd a Shakespeare – "There's my Comfort"' –[12]   There is a characteristic joke here at Keats's own expense in recognizing that his own enjoyment of Shakespeare's poetic expression is as heady and intoxicating as alcohol to the sodden character in the play who is also trying to cheer himself up: 'This is a very scurvy tune to sing at a man's funeral; well, here's my comfort.' (II.ii.45–6; unmarked)

Keats is exceptionally interested in the stage-directions in *The Tempest*, and indeed, they are unique in Shakespeare for their degree of detail. They dwell upon the magical illusions of the island, its 'solemn and strange music' and thunder, its dances, its 'Spirits in the shape of dogs and hounds', and they refer to the invisibility of Ariel, a character who particularly fascinates Keats, along with Prospero's ability to charm people. One might account for such stage-directions in the play by recollecting that *The Tempest* was written in the heyday of the Jacobean masque, when there was elaborate emphasis upon stage illusion which had to be described in some detail. A centre-piece of the play, of course, is Prospero's masque to celebrate the nuptials between Ferdinand and Miranda. Since Keats, however, is more interested in reading than in theatrical presentation, we might account for his interest (signalled by frequent markings) by suggesting that the directions make *The Tempest* into a satisfactory 'closet' play, since they give the reader enough information to visualize the action for himself. Being so detailed and evocative with a strange dignity of their own, they allow the reader to create in his mind's eye events and illusions in a much more smooth and delicate way than could possibly have been achieved by creaking machinery in the Jacobean theatre. The directions are, in fact essential to the play's imaginative world, and they have the same status as the poetry itself in terms of the reader's response. We need not go to the lengths of one ingenious critic who suggests that Keats's underscorings 'may have been the result of a conversation in which a new theory – possibly concerning the Elizabethan stage – was propounded'.[13] At no time does Keats show any scholarly or antiquarian interest in the dynamics of the stage.

Keats was far too sensitive to language, and too craftsmanlike in his attitude to his own use of words in poetry, to allow us to assume that he took no more than an uncritical and excited interest in Shakespeare's practice. It is possible to be a little more analytical in dealing with the varieties of language which he appreciated, and in doing so we discover more about the linguistic mode of *The Tempest*. For a start, when looking at Keats's text of the play in the Johnson-Steevens edition, it is convenient to distinguish between two categories of markings. One is the marking of a whole passage, paragraph or speech, and these may indicate various interests ranging from language to character and context. We shall return to these. The second group includes words and short phrases which he marked, and it may be assumed that Keats's interest here lay in the language itself, the 'hieroglyphics'. As Caroline Spurgeon argues, it is 'images and epithets' which chiefly enchant [Keats]',[14] and in the phrases below it is easy to appreciate the vividness of the words in creating images. However, it is also possible to detect an interesting consistency in the linguistic habits of Shakespeare in this play, and although Keats may not consciously have noticed it, his choice of the phrases which he found most arresting allows us to make an interpretation. To the phrase doubly underlined in his letter to Reynolds 'vast of night', we can add others marked in the text, all of which share a syntactical similarity in that they give us possessive phrases, where nouns rock upon a fulcrum which is the word 'of':

last of our sea-sorrow (I.ii.170)

The washing of ten tides (I.i.54)

The very virtue of compassion (I.ii.27)

In the dark backward and abysm of time (I.ii.50)

heavy offer of it (II.i.185)

dregs of the storm (II.ii.39)

brimful of sorrow (V.i.14)

a chronicle of day by day (V.i.163)

Other isolated phrases which are marked might be described linguistically as adjectival phrases:

Absolute Milan (I.ii.109)

crying self (I.ii.132)

Dull thing (I.ii.285)

Hag-seed (I.ii.365)

subtle, tender and delicate temperance (II.i.41)

My strong imagination (II.i.199)

To the perpetual wink (II.i.276)

Ling'ring perdition (III.iii.77)

Sour-ey'd disdain (IV.i.20)

temperate nymphs (IV.i.132)

fellowly drops (V.i.64)

My tricksy spirit (V.i.226)

It is noteworthy that such a group of apparently isolated and random phrases simply 'left over' from the longer passages marked by Keats should display such a consistency, and the fact can show us something interesting about the language employed by Shakespeare in *The Tempest*. Moreover, if we follow up the clue and examine the longer passages as well, we find they are full of the same adjectival phrases and the possessive construction using 'of'. Using the descriptive capacities of the literary critic to interpret this linguistic observation, we might conclude that such constructions demonstrate at a verbal level an essentially static yet richly detailed impression conveyed by the play as a whole in its action. The possessive phrases allow us to detect in the rhythms of the syntax a verbal equivalent of the tidal rhythm of the sea, ebbing and flowing, waves that rock backwards and forwards, a central image of the play. By examining closely a group of Keats's markings, we may possibly have found ourselves in possession of one understanding of the 'hieroglyphics' of language in *The Tempest*, although our act of decoding must necessarily be as cumbersomely analytical as Keats's was quick, instinctual and apparently random.

Of the longer passages and sections, those spoken by Ariel clearly fascinated Keats, for almost all the lines by or about this character have some sort of marking. Ariel appears to represent for Keats an aspect of Shakespeare's poetry which is quintessential, since echoes spring to mind when he is dealing with general matters:

> The poetry of Shakespeare is generally free as is the wind – a perfect thing of the elements, winged and sweetly coloured. Poetry must be free! It is of the air, not of the earth; and the higher it soars the nearer it gets to its home …[15]

In words like 'winged' and 'of the air' we detect the conception of Ariel, (called 'my bird' by Prospero at IV.i.184) and we recall that his desire for freedom is central. Prospero, perhaps confirming an image for Keats, tells Ariel, 'Thou shalt be free As mountain winds' (I.ii.498) Many readers have regarded Ariel as a character peculiarly in

touch with the spirit of poetry, a personification of Shakespeare's crea-
tive imagination as it reaches for the communion of the dance upon the
yellow sands which embraces actors and audience and, in the act of
reading, text and reader. In his song, 'Full fathom five...' (I.ii.398–
403; underlined), Ariel is contemplating the capacity of art to make
something as static and beautiful as pearls out of once-living eyes.
Ariel is 'but air' with only 'a touch, a feeling' (V.i.21) for the emotions
of others, and he displays an exuberant delight in his own skimming
power:

> Before you can say 'come' and 'go',
> And breathe twice and cry, 'so, so',
> Each one, tripping on his toe,
> Will be here with mop and mow.
> Do you love me, master? No?
>
> (IV.i.43–8)

If any character in Shakespeare represents 'the viewless wings of
Poesy', the deceiving elf of Fancy, it is (with a nod towards Puck),
Ariel. Interestingly, Keats also appreciates Caliban for his language,
and he presumably would agree with Hazlitt's assessment of the
'eloquent poetry of the senses' of this character. Attempting to answer
the charge that the language of *Endymion* is 'unnatural and too high-
flown', Keats points to the context in which the poetry occurs, and
adds: 'He must first prove that Caliban's poetry is unnatural, – This
with me completely overturns his objections ...'[16] Whatever particular
facet of Caliban's poetry Keats has in mind, it is certain that he
appreciates virtually all of his lines. Caliban can be 'high-flown' and
lyrical in his utterances:

> I prithee, let me bring thee where crabs grow;
> And I with my long nails will dig thee pig-nuts;
> Show thee a jay's nest, and instruct thee how
> To snare the nimble marmoset; I'll bring thee
> To clust'ring filberts, and sometimes I'll get thee
> Young scamells from the rock.
>
> (II.ii.180–5)

The precise quality which Keats finds duplicated in *Endymion* can be
a matter for speculation only, but we can be fairly sure that there is an
exemplary echo in Endymion's promises:

Honey from out the gnarled hive I'll bring,
And apples, wan with sweetness, gather thee, –
Cresses that grow where no man may them see,
And sorrel untorn by the dew-claw'd stag:
Pipes will I fashion of the syrinx flag,
That thou mayst always know whither I roam,
When it shall please thee in our quiet home
To listen and think of love.

(IV, 682–9)

The passage goes on in the same vein. Another of Caliban's speeches reveals a pattern of experience repeated many times by Keats:

Be not afeard. The isle is full of noises,
Sounds, and sweet airs, that give delight, and hurt not.
Sometimes a thousand twangling instruments
Will hum about mine ears; and sometime voices,
That, if I then had wak'd after long sleep,
Will make me sleep again; and then, in dreaming,
The clouds methought would open, and show riches
Ready to drop upon me, that, when I wak'd,
I cried to dream again.

(III.ii.129–38)

The intense dream, followed by a dismayed awakening into reality is a recurrent motif in Keats's poetry, to be found several times in *Endymion*, most famously in 'Ode to a Nightingale', 'La Belle Dame Sans Merci' and *The Eve of St Agnes*, while *The Fall of Hyperion* is subtitled 'A Dream'. Caliban's speech is certainly not the only time Shakespeare describes the experience of the 'waking dream' (there are other instances in *The Tempest* itself), but Keats's heavy marking on this occasion must indicate a recognition that the passage itself is a powerful statement of one of his own poetic obsessions. This is ample evidence for his admiration for the 'high-flown' poetry of Caliban. If he thinks also that Caliban's language is not 'unnatural', perhaps he means that it can be literally close to nature in its delicate observation:

'Pray you, tread softly, that the blind mole may not
Hear a foot fall.'

(IV.ii.196–7)

On the other hand, Keats equally marks Caliban's frequent notes of cursing and grumbling, so he can hardly have noticed only the appealing poetry of grace and nature. One trick of speech occurs so often that it is a linguistic trade-mark which can hardly be called lyrical. Caliban begins many speeches with exclamations such as 'O ho, O ho!' (I.ii.349) and 'Lo, now, lo!' (II.ii.14), he often shouts 'Ho!' and he greets farcical enjoyment with 'ha, ha, ha!' (III.ii.78). Keats marks these ejaculations, sometimes independently of the speeches in which they occur, leaving the rest unmarked. As in the case of Falstaff, he may well have been interested in Shakespeare's way of defining a character through some trick of speech.

In many of his markings of lengthy passages, it is less likely that Keats is registering interest in 'character-as-personality' than that he is admiring the poetic expressiveness. Therefore, he did not need to be especially interested in Prospero to be attracted by such celebrated passages as those beginning 'Our revels now are ended...' (IV.i.148ff.) and 'Ye elves of hills...' (V.i.34), as well as many sententious or reflective phrases: 'The rarer action is In virtue than in vengeance' (V.i.28) and 'Every third thought shall be my grave' (V.i.311). When Keats quotes in a letter the words of Prospero, at a time when he was most under the spell of *The Tempest*, he gives an oblique indication of his thoughts on the tone of the speech:

> I feel that I am not in the Mood to write any to day; and it appears that the loss of it is the beginning of all sorts of irregularities. I am extremely glad that a time must come when every thing will leave not a wrack behind. You tell me never to despair – I wish it was as easy for me to observe the saying – truth is I have a horrid Morbidity of Temperament which has shown itself at intervals...[17]

The context reveals that Keats is associating Prospero's speech delivered after the masque ('Leave not a rack behind') not with any celebration of theatrical illusion but with melancholy and 'despair', a word perhaps called to mind by recollection of Prospero's 'despair' in the Epilogue to the play. Striking a quite different note as a critical reader, Keats even turns his hand to textual detail. He places an asterisk beside Ferdinand's lines,

> 'This is a most majestic vision, and
> *Harmonious charmingly...'
> (IV.i.118–19)

and in the margin makes the suggestion '*Harmonises?' The emendation has all the advantages and disadvantages of normalizing the language, and on the principle that the more difficult reading is the more likely in such cases, editors from Johnson onwards have chosen to retain the Folio reading. This fact, however, should not detract from the evidence that Keats is never so sentimentally in awe of Shakespeare's 'hieroglyphics' that he is not alert to textual difficulties, at least to the extent of checking one text against his other.

Enough has been said, I hope, to indicate Keats's general areas of interest in *The Tempest*. The semi-conscious way in which his memory used the play as a quarry for expressing his own thoughts may now be illustrated by looking at an early letter written to Reynolds on 19 February 1818.[18] It is a delightfully relaxed letter, prompted by the fine weather and by a lazy morning spent napping on the sofa. A very characteristic Keatsian pattern which we have already observed is followed in the development of the letter: from reading to thinking to writing. The letter begins by suggesting the profits of letting some passage of 'full Poesy, or distilled Prose' inhabit our mind for a day, it continues by creating a distinction between two kinds of 'readerly' minds, imaged in the flower and the bee, and it ends with an original sonnet composed on the day. Always, for Keats, reading, thinking and writing are interrelated and mutually collaborative activities. He also believes in some form of co-operation between reader and writer, or at least between reader and text, even in the contemplation of a single passage:

> Nor will this sparing touch of noble Books be any irreverance to their Writers – for perhaps the honors paid by Man to Man are trifles in comparison to the Benefit done by great Works to the 'Spirit and pulse of good' by their mere passive existence.[19]

Keats is here reiterating a common literary doctrine, that great writing, by its very existence, is an active inducement towards good actions, and in his cryptic way he is contributing towards the genre of 'Defences of Poetry', stretching from Sidney and Dryden to Shelley and beyond.

Although Keats confesses that he has read no books on this morning, there is one work which lies behind his language and observations. That work is *The Tempest*. There are phrases from other writers and from Shakespeare dotted about: 'a girdle round the earth' from *A Midsummer Night's Dream*, 'Journey's end' from *Twelfth Night*, and the face that 'hath felt the Winter's wind' from *As You Like It*, but these are opportune flashes. *The Tempest* is more pervasive in lending both images and a line of thought. Some references are clear. 'A strain of musick conducts to "an odd angle of the Isle"' conjures up the picture of Ferdinand (I.ii.223), and Keats is accurate to the context, for Ferdinand is lured on by Ariel's music. Similarly, when speaking of democracy, Keats's memory recalls Gonzalo's prayer for 'long heath, brown furze' (I.i.63):

> Man should not dispute or assert but whisper results to his neighbour, and thus by every germ of Spirit sucking the Sap from mould ethereal every human might become great, and Humanity instead of being a wide heath of Furse and Briars with here and there a remote Oak or Pine, would become a grand democracy of Forest Trees.[20]

The appropriateness here lies in the fact that it is Gonzalo who later creates a vision of an egalitarian society akin to Keats's 'democracy'. It is possible also that he is recalling Prospero's words about 'Jove's stout oak' (particularly since Keats goes on to mention Jove) and the 'pine and cedar' (V.i.33–57 *passim*). For an instant we catch a glimpse of Prospero instructing Miranda, in Keats's description of the transmission of wisdom: 'A old man' (is Keats's cockneyism showing here?) 'and a child would talk together and the old Man be led on his Path, and the child left thinking'. And there is an echo in grammar and rhythm as well as sense that links Keats's 'the Morning said I was right – I had no idea but of the Morning and the Thrush said I was right …' and Shakespeare's

> Methought the billows spoke, and told me of it;
> The winds did sing it me.
>
> (III.iii.96)

In the sonnet which Keats appends to the letter we find more echoes:

> Whose eye has seen the Snow clouds hung in Mist
> And the black-elm tops 'mong the freezing Stars[21]

recalls Prospero's 'cloud-capp'd towers', and the line

> To thee the Spring will be a harvest-time –

crams into its iambic pentameter Ceres' couplet in the masque:

> Spring come to you at the farthest,
> In the very end of harvest!
>
> (IV.i.114–15)

The last line of the sonnet, 'And he's awake who thinks himself asleep' refers to a state of mind common in importance to Keats and to

Shakespeare, and specific precedent can be found in *The Tempest*:

> SEBASTIAN. ... and surely
> It is a sleepy language, and thou speak'st
> Out of thy sleep. What is it thou didst say?
> This is a strange repose, to be asleep
> With eyes wide open; standing, speaking, moving,
> And yet so fast asleep.
>
> (II.i.201–6)

So pervasive is the presence of the play in this letter that we find a hint from *The Tempest* informing Keats's central distinction:

> ... it seems to me that we should rather be the flower than the Bee
> – for it is a false notion that more is gained by receiving than giving
> – no the receiver and the giver are equal in their benefits – The
> flower I doubt not receives a fair guerdon from the Bee – its leaves
> blush deeper in the next spring – and who shall say between Man
> and Woman which is the most delighted? Now it is more noble to
> sit like Jove that [*sic*] to fly like Mercury – let us not therefore go
> hurrying about and collecting honey-bee like, buzzing here and
> there impatiently from a knowledge of what is to be arrived at: but
> let us open our leaves like a flower and be passive and receptive ...[22]

Ariel, the character who most of all represents the 'common taste and fellowship' of art which is the subject of the letter, associates himself with both the bee and the flower:

> Where the bee sucks, there suck I;
> In a cowslip's bell I lie;
> ...
> Merrily, merrily shall I live now
> Under the blossom that hangs on the bough.
>
> (V.i.88–94 *passim*)

Ariel, whose significance in the play and in Keats's mind is closely associated with the freedom of art, is not the bee though he sucks where the bee sucks; he is not the flower but he lies passively in the cowslip's bell. The power of Ariel partakes of the nature of both bee and flower. He is the Shakespearean character who embodies the combination of 'whispering' tact in his non-assertiveness, the 'spiritual touch' of open receptivity, and the ability to effect the artist's intentions. Just as Ariel is the invisible agent of magical changes in the play, so is he an invisible guiding spirit in a letter so full of *The Tempest*.

A Midsummer Night's Dream is undoubtedly the other play which most enchanted the young Keats in 1817–18. His letters are full of playful allusions. We find him invoking in comic contexts such passages as those by Bottom warning his fellow-actors not to bring a lion amongst the ladies[23] and expressing a preference for the tongs and bones.[24] Keats lightheartedly encourages either of his brothers to take his own part in company while he is absent, again quoting Bottom and the Artisans:

> – you need only agravate your voices a little and mind not to speak Cues and all – when you have said Rum-ti-ti – you must not rum any more or else another will take up the ti-ti alone and then he might be taken God shield us for little better than a Titmouse.[25]

In such a pastiche of quotations, Keats is setting and preserving the tone of Shakespeare's presentation of Bottom's theatrical enterprise. There are many snatches of phrases from other characters momentarily lifted into the letters. Keats quotes one of Hermia's exclamations, 'of all loves',[26] he changes Puck's 'roasted crab' to 'coasted' since he is at Margate,[27] he recalls Theseus's appreciation of the 'gallant chiding' of hounds when he is himself beset by creditors, and ironically they are 'untuneable' rather than 'tuneable'.[28] He quotes Puck's 'I'll put a girdle round about the earth' in connection with the transport of the imagination in the activity of reading, and he picks out one of the images in the play to convey his enthusiasm for Shakespeare's poetry of the sea, which he often equates with Shakespeare himself:

> Which is the best of Shakspeare's Plays? – I mean in what mood and with what accompenament do you like the Sea best? It is very fine in the morning when the Sun
>
> > 'opening on Neptune with fair blessed beams
> > Turns into yellow gold his salt sea streams'[29]

Keats seems to be trusting his memory for the quotation, for his 'salt sea' is actually 'salt green' (II.ii.392–3). By associating Shakespeare himself with the moods of the sea, Keats is perhaps conveying something of his notion of the dramatist's development, implying that after the morning of this play the sea will become rougher as the day goes on. Shakespeare's sea-music informs Keats's poetry as well, particularly in the sonnets 'On the Sea' and 'Bright Star'. The *Dream* itself heavily influenced Keats's early poetry, particularly *Endymion*. Much later in his career, in *The Jealousies* (or *The Cap and Bells*) Keats was to return to the plot of the *Dream* for 'the criss-cross loves of fairies and mortals', as C.L. Finney demonstrates.[30]

So detailed is Keats's knowledge of the *Dream* that it would not be profitable to examine in detail his markings on the texts. Instead, it is interesting to concentrate on two matters: a lengthy note he appends to one of Titania's speeches, and the fact that he marks one section in both his copies, presumably on different occasions. The passages which he marks twice make an interesting comparison, since they show that his taste and interests have hardly changed from one reading to another. The whole section occurs at II.i.81–164. The most striking similarity is that on both occasions Keats heavily marks the rather curious phrase 'human mortals' (II.i.101). A phrase which other readers may not notice, or which they may be inclined to condemn as a tautology, struck Keats on two occasions forcibly enough to mark in this way. We can only guess at the nature of his attention to this detail, but at least we may notice that it is consistent with his own emphatic concentration upon 'men and women' rather than 'wonders'.[31] We recall that in several of his own poems he mingles gods and mortals in much the same way as Shakespeare mixes fairies and people, and on each occasion it is the experiences of the 'human mortals' which Keats stresses. Endymion must constantly be reminded of the beauties of nature and of humanity around him by his sister, and he must be recalled to his 'human mortality' after his moments of love for the immortal goddess. Both versions of *Hyperion*, and particularly the later, turn on the co-existence of human feeling and a divine condition of Oberon-like overview. Finally, in considering the 'deities or mortals', 'men or gods' on the Grecian Urn, we realize that they are not mortal for they can never die, and yet they are human in the passions which they so clearly express. We suddenly realize a crucial ambiguity in the word 'above' in Keats's line, 'All breathing passion far above', and wonder whether the figures are above human passion, or whether passion is above them. In this Ode, 'human mortals' becomes a functional distinction. Apart from this intriguing detail of consistency in his markings of the respective texts, there are also some differences which might indicate how Keats's attention changes subtly. In the Folio, he attends closely to the words of Titania, 'If you will patiently dance in our Round' (II.i.140) which he does not mark in the other reading. Again, he marks in the Folio reading a different passage:

PUCK.   I remember.
OBERON. That very time I saw (but thou couldst not)
         Flying betweene the cold Moon and the earth,
         Cupid all arm'd; a certaine aime he tooke
         At a faire Vestall, throned by the West,
         ...

                                        (II.i.154–8)

The next four lines are marked in both copies. Then the Folio continues:

And the imperiall Votresse passed on,
In maiden meditation, fancy free.
                                        (II.i.163)

On the other hand, Keats does not mark in the Folio the lines about 'big-bellied sails', a parenthesis in Titania's speech which he marks in the Johnson-Steevens text. There is so much detail of extraordinary beauty in all the fairies' speeches in this section, that such variations in the markings, assuming that Keats is on both occasions being consciously selective, are only marginal. What the comparison shows is that Keats's taste in poetry is generally consistent from one occasion to another, a fact which can be used to justify the assumption that the markings taken as a whole on his copies of Shakespeare do show something individual and revealing about his poetic tastes. On the other hand, the differences of detail prevent us from being in any way dogmatic on this point. Like anybody else, Keats could find different sources of interest each time he read a text, within broad areas of similarity. Generally speaking, the attraction which the passage held for Keats is not difficult to understand. The lyrical poetry of nature, conducted on the most minute level of perception, lies at the heart of the fairies' utterances. Employing a wide range of verse forms, Shakespeare's eye reaches the tininess of dewdrops, the enamelled skin of a snake, acorn cups and a bewildering variety of summer flowers. Almost all of Keats's own early poetry is saturated in such imagery, and it would be impossible to assess the particular debts. *A Midsummer Night's Dream* has given to Keats not just a language but a special way of looking, an imaginative vision.

To the whole of Titania's speech on the upsetting of the seasons in the mortal world, Keats appends a note in his Folio, and it shows well how he prefers to dwell on local detail, finding a world of imaginative fullness, rather than examine too closely the overall logic. Whereas Dr

Johnson (in a note which Keats probably did not see) finds the whole passage 'unintelligible' and worries about its logic, Keats dives upon a phrase, 'since the middle summer's spring', and his mind plays delightedly with the idea:

> There is something exquisitely rich and luxurious in Titania's saying 'since the middle summer's spring' as if Bowers were not exuberant and covert enough for fairy sports untill their second sprouting – which is surely the most bounteous overwhelming of all Nature's goodnesses. She steps forth benignly in the spring and her conduct is so gracious that by degrees all things are becoming happy under her wings and nestle against her bosom: she feels this love and gratitude too much to remain selfsame, and unable to contain herself buds forth the overflowings of her heart about the middle summer. O Shakespeare thy ways are but just searchable! The thing is a piece of profound verdure.

Such a note reveals clearly all the dangers involved in claiming Keats as a 'critic' of Shakespeare in any professional sense, but on the other hand it shows what an acute reader he is, and how valuably his perceptions can enhance our own understanding. By allowing his imagination to create the concept behind a phrase which, it is safe to say, few professional critics would spend time over, he conveys a striking inwardness with the principle of lush growth in nature which is at the heart of a play profoundly concerned with the subject of change and creativity. By concluding with the words 'profound verdure' (instead of a blander 'profound poetry', for example), Keats shows that he is attentive to the verse primarily as an expression of a meaning which has to be imaginatively apprehended, rather than as an artefact that can be admired from the outside. In this note, which could stand as a prose poem by Keats himself, we recognize the significance of his notion of Shakespeare's language as 'hieroglyphics' which a skilled reader can translate by being faithful to the sound and to the sense, to what is implied as lying behind the words as much as to the literal meaning. The phrase 'but just searchable' captures the spirit of Keats as a reader of Shakespeare's poetry, and reveals a commitment which is both intellectual and imaginative at the same time.

So complete was Keats's knowledge and affection for the *Dream* that he can hardly have learned much from Hazlitt on the play. However, it is interesting to note that Hazlitt felt that the play is too much of a piece of fanciful poetry to be effective on the stage. Judging from a performance he has seen, starring as Bottom the incomparable

Kean, he adjudges it a failure: 'All that is finest in the play is lost in the representation....Poetry and the stage do not agree well together.'[32] Ironically enough, he gives for the play's unwieldy theatrical presence a reason which is exactly the fault exhibited by Peter Quince's play, that the literal presence of props and actors is too obtrusive to allow the imagination free play:

> That which was merely an airy shape, a dream, a passing thought, immediately becomes an unmanageable reality. Where all is left to the imagination (as is the case in reading) every circumstance, near or remote, has an equal chance of being kept in mind, and tells according to the mixed impression of all that has been suggested. But the imagination cannot sufficiently qualify the actual impressions of the senses.[33]

Keats enjoyed the theatre, but we can assume that he would agree with Hazlitt on the general distinction between reading and watching a play, since the reader's mind, alive in all its 'senses' can without hindrance apprehend 'the mixed impression of all that has been suggested'. In the speedy business of the stage, the delighted *frisson* revealed in Keats's note on 'since the middle summer's spring' would have no time to operate, and the phrases he apparently so lovingly pored over in marking his texts would be over in the twinkling of an eye.

Caroline Spurgeon has helpfully tabulated as 'parallel passages' many points in *Endymion* where she detects the influence of *The Tempest* and *A Midsummer Night's Dream*, 'illustrating various kinds of reminiscence of thought or verbal likeness...'[34] Not all the parallels she finds fulfil the stringent requirements of a 'source' but those that are self-evidently related are revealing of the process by which Keats turns Shakespeare's 'hieroglyphics' into the idiom which marks his own unique style. We find 'Full fathom five thy father lies; Of his bones are coral made' (I.ii.396–7) informing 'Who dives three fathoms where the waters run Gurgling in beds of coral' (*Endymion*, I, 639), and we appreciate that 'run Gurgling' marks a change from classical aloofness to romantic nature-poetry. Sometimes Keats uses the same word and image to evoke a scene, while being more metaphorical than Shakespeare. 'Midnight mushrooms' (V.i.39) becomes 'Nightswollen mushrooms' (I, 21) and 'Thy turfy mountains, where live nibbling sheep' (IV.i.62) is made more allusive in *Endymion*:

> ...ye, whose precious charge
> Nibble their fill at ocean's very marge...'
>   (I, 203)

Once we have noticed the source-passages, we realize that Keats is not simply echoing but interpreting (mushrooms are 'midnight' because they are 'Night-swollen', or maturing overnight), or, as in the second example, amplifying the scope of an image from a single word to a more comprehensively visualized scene. He is building upon Shakespeare, rather than just invoking the dramatist's words. At other points it is clear that the associational link is a combination of words and a guiding idea. Shakespeare writes:

> ... I'll break my staff,
> Bury it certain fathoms in the earth,
> And deeper than did ever plummet sound
> I'll drown my book.
>
> (V.i.54–7)

and 'I'll seek him deeper than e'er plummet sounded' (III.iii.101). Just as 'plummet' seems to be the word linked in Shakespeare's creative mind with downward movement, so Keats draws on the same association, tying it up also with the Shakespearean use of 'fathom' in various contexts:

> Down, down, uncertain to what pleasant doom,
> Swift as a fathoming plummet down he fell
> through unknown things...
>
> (II, 661)

A similar range of creative borrowings from *A Midsummer Night's Dream* feeds into *Endymion*. Keats obviously liked Shakespeare's 'spangled starlight sheen' (II.i.29) since he uses it twice in new forms – perhaps unfortunately in 'spangly light' (I, 569) (compare 'spangly gloom' in *Isabella*, line 326), and in 'over-spangled' (I, 629). A beautiful example of Keats's ability to build creatively upon a Shakespearean image comes when he makes functional the apparently random collocation of butterflies and eyes in Titania's

> And pluck the wings from painted butterflies,
> To fan the moonbeams from his sleeping eyes
>
> (III.i.158–9)

by directly making 'fans' into a noun instead of a verb:

> ...yet, his eyelids
> Widened a little, as when Zephyr bids
> A little breeze to creep between the fans
> Of careless butterflies ...   (I, 762–5)

Other examples show the inherent difficulties involved in identifying Keats's echoes from Shakespeare. One can feel sure that there is a connection between Shakespeare's reference to glow-worms as 'night-tapers' (III.i.155) and Keats's 'Glow-worms began to trim their starry lamps' (II, 141), and yet the link is not so much verbal but visual, in the sense that Keats has retraced the metaphor-making process of Shakespeare to create his own image. Anybody who works on Keats's sources will encounter the problem of where to draw a line between something prompted by Shakespeare's vision but verbally unconnected, and a literally verbal similarity which actually disguises a different thought. The problem is really one of distinguishing Shakespeare's hieroglyphics from Keats's own verbal codes. The one thing certain is that they are intimately and mysteriously related.

The legacy which Keats may be said to have derived from his reading of Shakespearean comedy is certainly comprehensive, but miscellaneous. He shows little sign of attempting to reproduce structural characteristics of the comedies, nor of consciously building into his poetry any overtly Shakespearean concepts of wit or low-life comedy. On the other hand, Keats clearly treasured Shakespeare's language, the unique 'hieroglyphics' which are at once so sensuously immediate and so packed with levels of meaning. Of course, this generalization holds true for the tragedies as well, but there is a difference in the areas of application. The comedies employ language in the service of love and detailed observation of nature, and in a contemplation of the nature of art itself. It is not surprising, given the content of *Endymion* and the other poems in Keats's first volume of verse, that we find the influence of Shakespearean comedy at its greatest in the earlier verse. *The Eve of St Agnes* is something of a watershed, for it amalgamates the language of the comedies with tones closer to *Romeo and Juliet* and even *Hamlet*, but one can say that it stays on the side of love comedy in its reverence for the intense experience of young love as a quasi-mystical experience rooted in a deeply humanist context. Like the comedies and romances, it is washed with the precious sense of the vitality of youth challenging the restrictive and corrupt social world around Madeline. Thereafter, however, it becomes clear that it is a tragic awareness of sadness in love, and death in life that begins to haunt Keats, and although he retained the comic sense of valuing energy and the sensuous immediacy of closely observed nature, yet the presence of Shakespearean tragedy looms larger as an informing principle.

V Hamlet *and* Macbeth

Although it is *King Lear* which draws out many of Keats's most important ideas and which has a considerable effect on his own poetry, he also records comments, allusions to, and markings upon, other tragedies. Some, such as *Othello* and *Julius Caesar*, he clearly read since he quotes from them, and as is the case with the comedies, the evidence is that he read all the tragedies. However, some were more significant than others in the development of Keats's ideas and poetry, and these happen also to be ones that he marked. *Antony and Cleopatra* may have been, at least on one occasion, his favourite play,[1] *Hamlet* deeply influenced some of his most celebrated ideas in the letters, while *Macbeth* became a potent infuence on his poetry from the time of *The Eve of St Agnes*. He marked *Troilus and Cressida*, providing also careful and illuminating annotations, some of a textual nature, which reveal a kind of scholarly interest behind Keats's generally impressionistic enthusiasm for Shakespeare's text. For reasons which are slightly more than ones of convenience, the three marked tragedies of love, *Antony and Cleopatra*, *Romeo and Juliet* and *Troilus and Cressida*, will be grouped together. Since *Hamlet* and *Macbeth* may be seen as paramount in Keats's intellectual and poetic development respectively, they complement each other. In examining the markings on each, however, a slightly paradoxical strategy is necessary. Because there are so many markings on the text of *Macbeth* there is little point in conducting a thorough examination of them, and by and large we may concentrate on what the play meant to Keats's own poetry. On the other hand, the relatively sparse marking on *Hamlet* in itself gives us the opportunity to look more closely at what interested Keats on the occasion of what may have been a single reading. In dealing with this play, we also find much of significance in the letters, in contexts where we see Keats developing many of his own most original and thoughtful attitudes to the place of art in life and to the tragic experience which lies behind his own later poetry, a subject which will be dealt with more fully in the final chapter.

Keats's markings of his copy of *Hamlet* are scanty, but from the evidence of his letters, it is clear that the play is profoundly important to him. He mentions it and quotes from it more than any other, often in developing some of his most central and personal ideas. When he mentions the play, it is usually during a consideration of human affairs rather than aesthetic theories, and it seems to stand for him on some borderline between art and life. At a certain point, *Hamlet* seems to have become so much a part of the tissue of his own experiences that it is close to his own real life:

> ... axioms in philosophy are not axioms until they are proved upon our pulses: We read fine – things but never feel them to thee [sic] full until we have gone the same steps as the Author. – I know this is not plain; you will know exactly my meaning when I say, that now I shall relish Hamlet more than I ever have done...[2]

This is not quite the same as Coleridge's saying that he finds something of Hamlet in himself, or Hazlitt's 'It is *we* who are Hamlet',[3] since both imply that Shakespeare has drawn the character in our own likenesses, or that we project our own preoccupations on to Hamlet. Instead, Keats says that Hamlet is a product of Shakespeare's own mind and experiences, and that it is only by going through similar experiences that we can fully understand or appreciate the creation. Keats maintains a fine but clear distinction between the artist's creation and our own lives. He wrote this in a period of mental pain. Subsequent comments amplify the idea of the connection between a poet's life and his works:

> A Man's life of any worth is a continual allegory – and very few eyes can see the Mystery of his life – ... Shakspeare led a life of Allegory; his works are the comments on it –[4]

Elsewhere, Keats makes another general comment that draws together Shakespeare's life and his creation:

> One of the great reasons that the english have produced the finest writers in the world; is, that the English world has ill-treated them during their lives and foster'd them after their deaths ... The middle age of Shakspeare was all c[l]ouded over; his days were not more happy than Hamlet's who is perhaps more like Shakspeare himself in his common every day Life than any other of his Characters.[5]

Keats draws a contrast between the Italian Boyardo, 'a noble Poet of Romance', and the English poet – no doubt with himself in mind as well as Shakespeare (and Milton) – as 'a miserable and mighty Poet of the human Heart'. We need not assume that Keats would agree with T.S. Eliot in saying that Shakespeare's identification with Hamlet interferes with his artistic objectification of certain impulses. Keats is not evaluating that play, but seeking to understand the mysterious connection between the artist and his work, and he maintains a distinction between the two. He is also working on the idea of creativity as an internalized reaction to events in everyday life. These may be unpleasant, but the result is the artist's speculation upon momentous issues of human existence, such as the nature of suffering and unhappiness, and out of speculation comes creation. Another reflection springs from the same train of thought:

> – Or, better – You are sensible no man can set down Venery as a bestial or joyless thing until he is sick of it and therefore all philosophizing on it would be mere wording. Until we are sick, we understand not; – in fine, as Byron says, 'Knowledge is Sorrow'; and I go on to say that 'Sorrow is Wisdom' ...[6]

In speaking of jaded worldliness, Byron is at the front of his mind, but the association of ideas may have come from reference to *Hamlet*. Among that character's preoccupations during the play is a morbid dwelling upon 'Venery', which explodes in his tirade to Ophelia upon female infidelity, and in his outburst of sexual disgust when he begs his mother not to go to her 'incestuous sheets', nor to lie in 'the rank sweat of an enseamed bed'. Hamlet is 'sick' in Keats's terms, and his philosophizing on sexuality as 'a bestial or joyless thing' comes from the state of Shakespeare's soul, according to Keats's reasoning. That Keats, in his phrase 'Knowledge is Sorrow' is picking up a reference from *Hamlet* is indicated when he quotes in the same letter to Reynolds:

> ... it is impossible to know how far knowle[d]ge will console us for the death of a friend and the ill 'that flesh is heir to' ...[7]

He is, of course, quoting from the 'To be, or not to be' speech:

> To die, to sleep –
> No more; and by a sleep to say we end
> The heart-ache, and the thousand natural shocks
> That flesh is heir to.
>
> (III. i.60–63)

Keats's allusion is apt to the moment in his own life, and to the context of the play. The 'friend' primarily in mind must be his brother Tom, since earlier in the letter he has spoken of Tom's feverish sleeplessness, and his own fit of gloom which has just lifted. There is some evidence that Keats at this time was thinking himself upon the subject of suicide. The problems of suffering, mortality and illness weigh so heavily upon him that he goes on to develop the allegory of the 'three chambers' of existence to explain his own awakened recognition of the primacy of suffering in a world 'full of Misery and Heartbreak, Pain, Sickness and oppression'.[8] He finds Hamlet apparently at the same point of discovery, although haunted not by physical suffering but by his father's death. Keats's statement, 'We are in a Mist',[9] can stand as a critical insight into the mental condition of Hamlet, so saturated is the passage in Hamlet's words. Both Hamlet and Keats are driven to nervous speculation about the future, wondering whether the knowledge which is dawning on them will prove a consolation, or an intensification of immediate suffering. The tangle of thoughts about dreams, sleeping and human misery, will eventually find poetic expression in Keats's own voice in the two versions of *Hyperion*. In the letter, his flippant dismissal of the problems, at least for the moment, in the phrase 'Wisdom is folly', as well as glancing at Lear's fool, may be Keats's own explanation of Hamlet's 'antic disposition', and marks his own adoption of the role.

Keats does not mark in his edition the 'To be, or not to be' speech, but it is a crucial reference point for him, and he quotes from it several times, in ways that can obliquely illuminate the passage for us. The first reference is perhaps not all that telling, though it proves the speech was important to him from an early time. He writes to Hunt in May 1817, alluding to Hamlet's 'bare bodkin' in saying that the amount he has written is merely a pin point compared with the whole which he envisages:

> When I consider that so many of these Pin points go to form a Bodkin point (God send I end not my Life with a bare Bodkin, in its modern sense) and that it requires a thousand bodkins to make a Spear bright enough to throw any light to posterity – I see that nothing but continual uphill Journeying?[10]

The allusion is little more than a joke, stimulated by a metaphor, although even here we detect Keats's and Hamlet's uncertainty about the future, the similarity between the concepts of posterity and an after-life, and correspondences between the notions of writing and living as a laborious process of bearing fardels, of grunting and sweating under a weary life.

Later in the same year, Keats relates Hamlet's speech more seriously to the suffering involved in life itself:

Such is this World – and we live – you have surely [been] in a continual struggle against the suffocation of accidents – we must bear (and my Spleen is mad at the thought thereof) the Proud Mans Contumely –[11]

At this moment, he is making a point about political oppression, after hearing with sympathetic anger of the way his friend Bailey was refused a curacy by a Bishop. Keats has glanced at Hamlet's lines:

For who would bear the whips and scorns of time,
Th' oppressor's wrong, the proud man's contumely,
...
The insolence of office...

(III. i. 70–3)

before going on to express his outrage at what appears to be an absence of worldly ways to find consolation for such problems. He continues:

O for a recourse somewhat human independant of the great Consolations of Religion and undepraved Sensations. of the Beautiful. the poetical in all things – O for a Remedy against such wrongs within the pale of the World!'[12]

The statement is part of a continuing attempt by Keats to discover or develop a humanitarian explanation for problems of suffering which religion and poetry, in their own ways and with their own limitations, seek to answer. Appalled at this moment by the church's tyrannical hierarchy, and temporarily feeling the inadequacy of his own poetry to help the world, Keats is frustrated and angry at the impersonality of the forces bearing man down: 'The thought that we are mortal makes us groan I will speak of something else or my Spleen will get higher and higher...'[13] As one of the rare occasions on which Keats is angry (and at times of righteousness, 'anger hath a privilege'), his tone is considerably different from Hamlet's quizzical, patient voice, but again Keats's reference takes us back to the ambitiousness of the 'knowledge' which both seek. Not only are they wrestling with problems of man's inhumanity, they are seeking an answer to mortality itself.

A few months later, Keats returns to the speech, in developing another of his major ideas. Attacking Wordsworth's poetry, Keats writes:

It may be said that we ought to read our Contemporaries. that Wordsworth &c should have their due from us. but for the sake of a few fine imaginative or domestic passages, are we to be bullied into a certain Philosophy engendered in the whims of an Egotist – Every man has his speculations, but every man does not brood and peacock over them till he makes a false coinage and deceives himself – Many a man can travel to the very bourne of Heaven, and yet want confidence to put down his halfseeing. Sancho will invent a Journey heavenward as well as any body.[14]

One interesting aspect of this comment is that it indirectly explains why Keats in his earlier comments saw Hamlet as referring to a 'continual uphill Journeying'. He sees the metaphor buried in the lines :

> Who would these fardels bear,
> To grunt and sweat under a weary life,
> But that the dread of something after death –
> The undiscover'd country, from whose bourn
> No traveller returns – puzzles the will.
>
> (III. i. 76–80)

In a way not specified by Shakespeare, Keats has concretized the pictures of earth below and heaven above, the two connected by an uphill journey. The interpretation of the images may actually be explained by the fact that, at least in another context, Keats does not seem to understand the word 'bourne'. In his lines in *Endymion*,

> A thousand powers keep religious state,
> In water, fiery realm, and airy bourne;
>
> (III. 31)

he is seeing the bourne not as a boundary but as a plateau upon a hill, a meaning which is sanctified by the *OED* as a Keatsian coinage.[15] It is also quite likely that Keats is remembering Ophelia's line, which he underlines, 'Show me the steep and thorny way to heaven' (I.iii.48) in coming to the visual image. More important, however, the comment about Wordsworth which alludes to *Hamlet*, opens up a question about Keats's current attitude to the character. Is Hamlet's speech one of the 'great and unobtrusive' things that poetry should be, or is Hamlet brooding and peacocking over his own speculations, ending up by deceiving himself? Is he, indeed, an image of Coleridge, 'incapable of remaining content with half knowledge', or the man who is giving expression to the necessity to remain in ignorance before the 'penetralium of mystery'? In his new spirit of impatience with thinkers, Keats may by now have retreated somewhat from his strong personal identification with Hamlet's speculations in his brooding speech about mortality. His comment is too cryptic for us to answer these questions, but the quotation in this passage points to the fact that Hamlet's speech still lies behind his thinking on important issues, even if his particular attitude may change. Hamlet's 'To be, or not to be' speech is one of the Shakespearean passages which Keats echoes occasionally in his poetry[16] as well as in the Letters. It is clear that in the issues it raises and in its train of imagery, the speech was of considerable significance to him.

Another episode in *Hamlet* from which Keats draws in his Letters, is the grave-diggers' scene, although again he has not marked it in his edition. Just as this scene deals with serious problems in a comic way, so Keats's references occur in contexts where he is disguising problems under a flippant tone. For example, after asking Haydon to repay a loan which Keats badly needed, he writes to his brother and sister-in-law thus:

> I applied to him for payment – he could not – that was no wonder. but goodman Delver, where was the wonder then, why marry, in this, he did not seem to care much about it – and let me go without my money with almost non-chalance when he aught to have sold his drawings to supply me.[17]

Keats is annoyed and somewhat hurt, but the blithely comic use of the Grave-digger's, 'Nay, but hear you, Goodman Delver' (V. i. 14), not only points up the casualness of Haydon's 'non-chalance', but also serves to dress Keats's feelings in a light-hearted tone. In the play, the Grave-diggers are speaking in a legalistic, detached way about an event of human distress, Ophelia's death, just as Haydon's response to Keats's desperate need for money seems to have been uncharitably distant. Keats invokes the passage again in the same dire financial straits. He writes to Dilke in false gaiety, using circumlocution and legal jargon, to say how worried he is, and stating his intention to live by writing reviews in periodicals: 'Now an act has three parts – to act, to do, and to perform – I mean I should *do* something for my immediate welfare.'[18] The decision to write ephemera for money was an extremely distasteful one for a poet so intent on fame, and Keats could contemplate it only by being hard on himself, holding the fact at arm's length by adopting an uncaring, laconic façade. He felt it a prostitution of his poetic talents, but he also realized that he had procrastinated too long, and must now 'act'. In *Hamlet*, the words come just before 'Goodman Delver':

> CLOWN. ... For here lies the point: if I drown myself wittingly, it argues an act; and an act hath three branches – it is to act, to do, to perform; argal, she drown'd herself wittingly.   (V. i. 11–13)

Keats's use of the quotation is apt on several levels. He feels that his decision, although necessary in a blunt world, is a self-destructive act which must be passed through with a grim joke. In addition, the speech comes in the play at the precise point where Hamlet must stop prevaricating and 'act', or else, as he knows, his inaction will 'wittingly' lead to his death by assassination. Whichever way he turns, Hamlet sees self-destruction looming, and Keats, regarding poetry as his life, also finds the possibility of destruction in one way or another. The Grave-diggers' scene occurs to Keats in situations where he faces grim legal and commercial threats, and it obviously helps him to distance the distress through nervous humour.

In using another reference to *Hamlet*, Keats is in bitter earnest. In his last letter to Fanny Brawne, he writes:

> If my health would bear it, I could write a Poem which I have in my head, which would be a consolation for people in such a situation as mine. I would show some one in Love as I am, with a person living in such Liberty as you do. Shakspeare always sums up matters in the most sovereign manner. Hamlet's heart was full of such Misery as mine is when he said to Ophelia 'Go to a Nunnery, go, go!' Indeed I should like to give up the matter at once – I should like to die. I am sickened at the brute world which you are smiling with. I hate men and women more.[19]

This is one of the most distressing and unpalatable statements in all of Keats's writings, but it has its interest for the Shakespearean scholar. From hints in this and other letters, we find that Keats was darkly suspicious that Fanny was flirting with his friend Brown. Judging from the scrupulous kindness of Brown towards him, the idea seems to have been a fiction of Keats's bedridden solitude. Like Hamlet's outburst, the passage is a morbid and unjust accusation of infidelity from one whose sensitivity has become hidden behind a wall of callous disregard. The substantial point of interest is that Keats understands the line to mean that Hamlet wishes to put an end to his suspicions by having Ophelia more or less institutionalized in a place where chastity will be enforced upon her. The suspicious accusation cannot really be sus-

tained against Ophelia, but many commentators on the play have puz-
zled over Hamlet's 'nunnery' line, and have interpreted it in different
ways.

Hamlet, then, had great personal importance for Keats, and he
knew certain episodes so well that he could allude to them easily,
almost without realizing the indebtedness. Essentially, the impor-
tance lies in the fact that the play presents problems within art which
are also compellingly real to Keats in his own personal life. In the case
of this play, it is not just the fine phrases of the 'Shakespearean hierog-
lyphics' which enter Keats's consciousness, but the content of ideas
rooted in particular dramatic situations. Keats's reception of the play
is something of a tribute to Shakespeare's most 'intellectual' hero.

After the frequency of quotation in the Letters, the markings on
Keats's edition of *Hamlet* are not numerous. My guess is that he
marked the text when he knew the play well, and he is interested in
particular details on this occasion. He does not mark, for example, the
two episodes which have proved so important in his Letters, and Act
III is not marked at all. For the very reason of their relative scarcity,
the markings are of special interest since they lead us to parts of the
play, lines and scenes, which are not generally celebrated, and which
further demonstrate Keats's poetic tastes.

In I.i. Keats first underlines Francisco's two comments that create
what Coleridge describes as 'the shivery feeling' of the night:

> 'Tis bitter cold,
> And I am sick at heart.
> ...
> Not a mouse stirring.
>   (I. i. 8–11)

Then he notices Bernardo's specification of the time, reinforcing the
feeling that it is deep night, and creating ominous suspense which cul-
minates in the mysterious appearance of the Ghost:

> Last night of all,
> When yond same star that's westward from the pole
> Had made his course t'illume that part of heaven
> Where now it burns, Marcellus and myself,
> The bell then beating one –
>
>   ENTER GHOST
>   (I.i.35–40)

After the Ghost leaves, Shakespeare again pinpoints the time of dawn before the sun rises (although Keats is interested in just one striking word): 'MAR. It faded on the crowing of the cock' (I. i. 157). Then the sun begins to glimmer:

> HOR. ....the morn, in russet mantle clad,
> Walks o'er the dew of yon high eastward hill. (I. i. 166–7)

Whether Keats's interest lies in the beauty of the words, or in the content, his markings are pointing us towards Shakespeare's craftsman-like way of creating atmosphere by being precise about the time of day. In dwelling upon details of atmospherics in *Hamlet*, it is appropriate to glance briefly at the uses Keats makes of what he finds in the play. It is particularly noticeable in *The Eve of St Agnes* that some of the mood can be traced to *Hamlet*, as well as to *Measure for Measure*. The poem moves from the 'bitter chill' of evening to the 'honey'd middle of the night' and then to the cold morning when the lovers must awake and flee. One particular passage in *Hamlet* is used to evoke the sense of the party going on in the hall:

> The King doth wake to-night and takes his rouse,
> Keeps wassail, and the swagg'ring up-spring reels,
> And, as he drains his draughts of Rhenish down,
> The kettle-drum and trumpet thus bray out
> The triumph of his pledge.
>
> (I. iv. 8–12)

Although Keats does not mark the passage in his text, it is certain, as Allott points out, that he is echoing it in two places in his poem:

> The boisterous, midnight, festive clarion,
> The kettle-drum, and far-heard clarionet,
> Affray his ears...
>
> (258–60)

and

> Arise – arise! the morning is at hand; –
> The bloated wassailers will never heed: –
> Let us away, my love, with happy speed;
> There are no ears to hear, or eyes to see, –
> Drown'd all in Rhenish and the sleepy mead.
>
> (354–9)

Keats's echo is impressively accurate to the context in the play. He has not just chosen images which are suitable for his own poem, but he writes a passage which conjures up a beautifully apt memory of the opening of *Hamlet*, with its circumstantial atmosphere of rheumy cold outside, drunken wassailing within, and nervous portentousness. By noticing the allusion, we add a dimension to the *Eve* and sharpen our understanding of *Hamlet*. On such occasions, the mutually enhancing quality of the link between Keats and Shakespeare is made wonderfully clear.

The court at Elsinore is full of omens and portents, of which the appearance of the Ghost is one. The others are connected with the strange military preparations which are being made, described in a passage which Keats evidently finds interesting both in general and for one striking phrase:

> Good now, sit down, and tell me, he that knows,
> Why this same strict and most observant watch
> So nightly toils the subject of the land;
> And why such daily cast of brazen cannon,
> And foreign mart for implements of war;
> Why such impress of shipwrights, whose sore task
> Does not divide the Sunday from the week;
> What might be toward, that this sweaty haste
> Doth make the night joint-labourer with the day?
> (I.i.70–77)

Horatio explains that 'this post-haste and romage in the land' (I.i.107) is in anticipation of an attack by Fortinbras and his men. There is some superstitious talk of omens, led by Horatio:

> In the most high and palmy state of Rome,
> A little ere the mightiest Julius fell,
> The graves stood tenantless, and the sheeted dead
> Did squeak and gibber in the Roman streets;
> As stars with trains of fire, and dews of blood,
> Disasters in the sun; and the moist star
> Upon whose influence Neptune's empire stands
> Was sick almost to doomsday with eclipse.
> (I.i.113–20)

Keats is drawing attention to the air of mystery and nervous anticipation Shakespeare is carefully building up in this scene. By way of contrast, when the cock crows to herald the dawn, Marcellus recalls what he has heard about good omens, such as the cock crowing all night at Christmas, in celebration of Christ's birth:

> This bird of dawning singeth all night long;
> And then, they say, no spirit dare stir abroad,
> The nights are wholesome, then no planets strike,
> No fairy takes, nor witch hath power to charm,
> So hallowed and so gracious is that time.
>
> (I.i.160–4)

On this, and on the other occasion in the first Act when the Ghost appears, Keats traces the characters' curiosity about what it looks like. It is undoubtedly the old King, dressed in the very armour that he wore,

> When he the ambitious Norway combated;
> So frown'd he once when, in an angry parle,
> He smote the sledded Polacks on the ice.
> 'Tis strange.
>
> (I.i.61–5)

His 'martial stalk' still commands respect, and Marcellus rather amusingly shows himself as obedient to royalty dead as alive: 'We do it wrong, being so majestical, To offer it the show of violence.'

(I.i.143–4)

In the next scene, as Horatio relates to Hamlet what happened 'in the dead waste and middle of the night' (I. ii. 198), he is careful to recall the details:

> thrice he walk'd
> By their oppress'd and fear-surprised eyes,
> Within his truncheon's length.
>
> (I.ii.202–4)
>
> ...
>
> yet once methought,
> It lifted up its head and did address
> Itself to motion, like as it would
> speak.
>
> (I.ii.215–7)

Hamlet plies him with eager questions:

> HAM.   What, look'd he frowningly?
> HOR.   A countenance more in sorrow than in anger.

HAM.   <u>Pale, or red?</u>
HOR.   <u>Nay, very pale.</u>

(I.ii.230–3)

It is probable that Keats was interested in such details, because he was himself to draw a ghost, a 'pale shadow', who appears at 'The dull of midnight' to Isabella. Keats's ghost, like Shakespeare's, is in purgatory, chanting alone the holy mass. Its final word is also the old Hamlet's:

The Spirit mourn'd "Adieu!" – dissolv'd, and left
The atom darkness in a slow turmoil.

Keats's interest in the Ghost extends to the precise descriptions of its appearance by the witnesses:

HAM.   Stay'd it long?
HOR.   While one with moderate haste might tell a hundred.
MAR., BER.   <u>Longer, longer.</u>
HOR.   <u>Not when I saw't.</u>
HAM.   <u>His beard was grizzl'd?</u> <u>no?</u>
HOR.   <u>It was, as I have seen it in his life,</u>
<u>A sable silver'd.</u>

(I.ii.236–41)

The paradoxical colour reference 'sable silver'd is, ironically, exactly the kind of compound adjective condemned in Keats by contemporary critics.

The rest of the underlinings in Act I reveal different aspects of Hamlet's character, and more pertinently a kind of language and poetic construction typical of the meditative passages in the play:

QUEEN.   Do not, <u>for ever with thy vailed lids</u>
<u>Seek for thy noble father in the dust.</u>
...
HAM.   <u>'Tis not alone my inky cloak, good mother,</u>
<u>Nor customary suits of solemn black,</u>
<u>Nor windy suspiration of forc'd breath,</u>
<u>No, nor the fruitful river in the eye,</u>
<u>Nor the dejected 'haviour of the visage,</u>
<u>Together with all forms, moods, shapes of grief,</u>
<u>That can denote me truly.</u>

(I. ii. 70–83)

It might be argued that the passage illustrates a characteristic of Shakespeare's style in this play, which Keats in his markings of individual phrases elsewhere makes clear: the preponderance of expressive adjectives, such as 'vailed', 'inky', 'solemn', 'windy', and 'fruitful' in particular. By choosing such words, Shakespeare allows himself to use metaphors with a glancing quickness and economy, without drawing attention to particular metaphors by expanding them. It is one of the secrets of Shakespeare's code or 'hieroglyphics' in this play, whether or not Keats saw it as such.

Keats goes on to mark a few phrases in the bluff, patronizing speech by the King, as he encourages his stepson to 'be a man':

> 'tis unmanly grief;
> It shows a will most <u>incorrect to heaven.</u>
> (I.ii.94–5)

Here is one of the several snippets marked by Keats which establish that Denmark is a Christian society. The fact raises many interesting problems concerning the moral status of actions in the play, but it is quite possible that Keats was primarily interested in such information because of his running debate with friends about Shakespeare's religious inclinations, a question on which Keats seems to have chosen to remain neutral.[20] The other phrases by Claudius are noteworthy for his own characteristically ceremonious rhetoric:

> And with no less <u>nobility of love,</u>
> ...
> <u>Here in the cheer and comfort of our eye</u>
> ...
> No jocund health that Denmark drinks today
> But <u>the great cannon to the clouds shall tell.</u>
> (I.ii.110–26)

Keats's strong interest is next engaged by Hamlet's first soliloquy, and the manner of the marking indicates that it is partly the rhythm to which he is pointing:

> O, that this too too solid <u>flesh would melt,</u>
> <u>Thaw, and resolve itself into a dew!</u>
> Or that the Everlasting had not fix'd
> His canon 'gainst self-slaughter! O God! O God!
> How <u>weary</u>, stale, <u>flat</u>, and <u>unprofitable</u>,
> Seem to me all the uses of this world!

> Fie on't! Ah, fie! 'tis an unweeded garden,
> That grows to seed; things rank and gross in nature
> Possess it merely. That it should come to this!
> But two months dead! Nay, not so much, not two.
> So excellent a king that was to this
> Hyperion to a satyr; so loving to my mother,
> That he might not beteem the winds of heaven
> Visit her face too roughly. Heaven and earth!
> Must I remember? Why, she would hang on him,
> As if increase of appetite had grown
> By what it fed on; And yet, within a month –
> Let me not think on't. Frailty, thy name is woman! –
> A little month, or ere those shoes were old
> With which she followed my poor father's body,
> Like Niobe, all tears – why she, even she –
> O God! a beast that wants discourse of reason
> Would have mourn'd longer – married with my uncle,
> My father's brother; but no more like my father
> Than I to Hercules. Within a month,
> Ere yet the salt of most unrighteous tears
> Had left the flushing in her galled eyes,
> She married.

(I.ii.129–56)

By breaking his underlining within lines, or sustaining it from line to line, Keats is effectively pacing out the rhythm, as it fluctuates between chopped, 'weary' snatches, angry bursts, and flows of emotion as he remembers his dead father. The rhythm follows Hamlet's moods, through reverie, bitterness and ennui. Of course, there is much more of interest in this passage, as there is in any of Hamlet's soliloquies; the reference again to Christianity, the brief and direct revelation of Hamlet's respective attitudes towards his mother, father and stepfather; his incipient suspiciousness of women. Perhaps most important of all, the passage conveys Hamlet's mood of weary distaste for the world which confronts him; the mood described by Keats in his letter when he concludes, 'Until we are sick, we understand not.'

After the first two scenes, Keats turns his attention almost completely to Ophelia, although he does not mark the 'nunnery' scene nor the scene of her madness. He begins by heavily marking the double-barrelled harangue she receives from her brother and her father. He notes her docility in 'I do not know, my lord, what I should think'

(I.iii.104), as well as more obviously striking lines such as 'A violet in the youth of primy nature' (I.iii.7), 'Unsifted in such perilous circumstance' (I.iii.102), 'the steep and thorny way to heaven' and 'the primrose path of dalliance' (I.iii.46–52); all underlined, amongst longer passages. In the light of the subject-matter of young love in *The Eve of St Agnes* and *Isabella* it is not surprising that Keats marks the image of innocence destroyed:

> That canker galls the infants of the spring
> Too oft before their buttons be disclos'd;
> And in the morn and liquid dew of youth
> Contagious blastments are most imminent.
>
> (I. iii. 39–42)

He underscores some of Polonius' sententious phrases as well as his later 'This is the very ecstasy of love' (II.i.102; also side-marked), and Ophelia's striking description of Hamlet entering her room in disarray, 'Pale as his shirt' (II.i.76–101). II.ii is lightly marked. Later in the play, Keats marks the wonderful set-piece spoken by Gertrude on the death of Ophelia, delivered as if she were transfixed before the scene (or by her imaginative re-creation of it), unable to help but reaching out with a heart full of suffering sympathy. Keats underlines the whole passage (IV.vii.167–84), except the two lines on the 'dead men's fingers', an image which is strangely incongruous with the rest. (It has been rather prosaically suggested that Keats did not mark the lines because 'perhaps he felt the hint of coarseness was inappropriate to the rest of the scene'.[21]) The poet would, of course, have been attracted by the sheer beauty of this serene but dismaying passage. With her own kindness and restraint, Gertrude is able to make something beautiful out of an event which could have appeared ugly and shocking. Later, she shows the same restrained gentleness in speaking of the way Hamlet's madness usually turns to quietness:

> Anon, as patient as the female dove
> When that her golden couplets are disclos'd,
> His silence will sit drooping.
>
> (V.i.280–82)

Keats regularly uses the dove as an image of pathos, most often in *Endymion* and most memorably in *The Eve of St Agnes*: 'A dove forlorn and lost with sick unpruned wing' (line 333), a fact which is not explained by its occurrence in *Hamlet* but which indicates that he was especially predisposed to notice Shakespeare's image here.

More intriguing is Keats's heavy marking of one scene in isolation, IV.vii, in which Claudius skilfully goads Laertes into murderous intent towards Hamlet. Apart from the occasional striking image such as 'like a spendthrift's sigh, That hurts by easing' and

> There lives within the very flame of love
> A kind of wick, or snuff, that will abate it;
> (IV.vii.107–23 *passim*; most sidemarked)

the scene is not distinguished for its poetically arresting quality, and in many productions nowadays it is reduced in length. The main point that emerges is the King's adroit political manipulation, and as we shall see in examining *Antony and Cleopatra* Keats was not beyond admiring such effects of character-depiction. His interest in the scene, as judged from his markings, really remains a mystery, but to put the matter in a different way, Keats's implicit appreciation of the scene as a whole can lead us to examine the subtle effects of a neglected aspect of a play so well-known that its familiar passages can dull us to other sections.

In Act V, Keats marks very little. No doubt with his own poetic preferences in mind, he underlines Laertes' Spenserian hyperbole:

> Now pile your dust upon the quick and dead,
> Till of this flat a mountain you have made
> T' o'er-top old Pelion or the skyish head
> Of blue Olympus.
> (V.i.245–8)

But if Keats finds such archaism attractive, he can also appreciate its parody from Hamlet's mouth:

> And, if thou prate of mountains, let them throw
> Millions of acres on us, till our ground,
> Singeing his pate against the burning zone,
> Make Ossa like a wart! Nay, an thou'lt mouth,
> I'll rant as well as thou.
> (V.i.274–8)

Reading back with this exchange in mind, we might feel that Hamlet's first words in the long-awaited meeting between himself and Laertes are just as burlesquing, sarcastically and contemptuously mocking inflated rhetoric:

What is he whose grief
Bears such an emphasis, whose phrase of sorrow
Conjures the wand'ring stars...

(V.i.248–50)

These exchanges may have interested Keats because they raise questions about appropriate poetic diction for the writer who is seeking to express emotion, a problem confronting Hamlet himself when he hears the actor counterfeiting grief for Hecuba. His final marking is Hamlet's declaration to Horatio of a new, fatalistic philosophy which will allow him to act uninhibitedly:

Rashly,
And prais'd be rashness for it – let us know,
Our indiscretion sometime serves us well,
When our deep plots do pall; And that should learn us
There's a divinity that shapes our ends,
Rough-hew them how we will.

(V.ii.7–11)

The statement is important, for it explains the new, ruthlessly spontaneous and laconic Hamlet who has returned from England, and who helps to precipitate the ending of the play. However, it may have been the idea which attracted Keats's attention.

There is little that is truly consistent in Keats's markings of *Hamlet*, although he does show interest in certain threads and scenes. However, his markings can show us many unexplored corners of the play, particularly in the fields of character presentation and Shakespeare's use of different kinds of poetry and speech-gestures. Taken together with the evidence in the Letters and poems, the markings of this particular reading establish that Keats knew the play so intimately that he could find interest in points of detail which are often overlooked, rather than concentrate merely upon the set-pieces which are well known. We find also that his interest is distributed equally between fine, sententious phrases, poetic language, and exchanges which hold little interest outside their immediate dramatic contexts. I hope that such a detailed listing of the portions marked by Keats has proved profitable, at least insofar as it indicates a diverse and eclectic appreciation on his part of the the play as a whole. He clearly held no exclusive interest in the play to the neglect of other concerns, and the marking reveals a side of his 'negative capability' exercised in the act of reading.

Much the same conclusion could be drawn from the markings on the Johnson-Steevens edition of *Macbeth*, although in this case it must be said that Keats was equally interested in *all* facets of the play. The evidence points to a single reading which was carried out with careful concentration upon every detail. Keats has marked every scene in some way, except two short ones (V.iv and V.vi), and some are almost totally marked by underlining and side-marks. In the circumstances, it would be misleading to attempt a description, since inevitably the impression would be that Keats's markings were more systematic and more selective than in fact they are. Instead, we should take for granted that he appreciated virtually every line as poetically intense, and turn instead to the more general question of what sort of associations the play had for him, and what kind of influence it had on his own poetry.

Macbeth inspired the first recorded comment made by Keats about Shakespeare's works. When he was thirteen or fourteen, he is said to have expressed the opinion that no one would dare to read the play alone in a house at two o'clock in the morning.[22] He was, then, reading Shakespeare at this youthful age, and already exercising the personal involvement which is characteristic of his later, well-documented readings. Throughout his writing life, in fact, if we may judge from the number of identified sources from *Macbeth* found in his later poetry, the play influenced him deeply, particularly in the poems after *The Eve of St Agnes*. After *King Lear* and on a par with *The Tempest*, *Macbeth* is the play which Keats knew best, and the one which comprehensively claimed his imagination. As a rough and ready generalization, it can be said that his mind discovers memories of the play when he is in an anxious or despairing mood or he is thinking about human evils in the context not of an indifferent universe as in *Lear*, but of a vision of predatory nature involved in a battle for survival.

It is the sustained vividness of the poetry in *Macbeth* which fires the mind of Keats, as it does most modern readers. Hazlitt asserts that this play is pre-eminent amongst the tragedies 'for the wildness of the imagination',[23] and the utterances of Macbeth himself are instrumental in creating this impression. 'Rapt' in the fertility of images that come teeming into his mind, Macbeth is often in danger of entering a mental world that is out of touch with practical realities around him. It is this aspect of Macbeth's character which Keats alludes to when he suggests in a letter that an imaginative, self-absorbed man is immune to physical dangers:

An idle man; a man who is not sensitively alive to self interest in a city cannot continue long in good Health – This is easily explained. If you were to walk liesurely through an unwholesome path in the fens, with a little horror of them you would be sure to have your ague. But let macbeth cross the same path, with the dagger in the air leading him on, and he would never have an ague or anything like it.... I am convinced there is as harmful Air to be breath'd in the country as in Town.[24]

Keats is saying that it is not a physical environment primarily that causes illness, but the person's mental attitude. The idle man who has nothing to worry about except his health will be susceptible, whereas the man preoccupied with an obsessive project is immune to his surroundings. Macbeth feels safe from all dangers, until he meets Macduff in combat, and Keats has vividly captured his desperate, death-defying attitude. Hazlitt sums up the distracted, obsessive quality of Macbeth's mind more directly still:

In thought he is absent and perplexed, sudden and desperate in act, from a distrust of his own resolution. His energy springs from the anxiety and agitation of his mind. His blindly rushing forward on the objects of his ambition and revenge, or his recoiling from them, equally betrays the harassed state of his feelings.[25]

Hazlitt, not content with simply describing the character, also offers a subtle explanation in suggesting that Macbeth distrusts his own resolution.

One passage spoken by Macbeth particularly haunts Keats's memory, and again, for some reason, its recall is triggered by the thought of another's health. He quotes it three times in his Letters. When Macbeth hears that, although Banquo is dead, Fleance is still alive he cries:

> Then comes my fit again. I had else been perfect,
> Whole as the marble, founded on the rock,
> As broad and general as the casing air,
> But now I am cabin'd, cribb'd, confin'd, bound in
> To saucy doubts and fears.

(III.iv.21–5)

Keats quotes the passage each time that he feels anxiety about the state of somebody else who is close to his concerns or about his own welfare:

Every one enquires after you – and every one desires their remembrances to you You must get well Tom and then I shall feel 'Whole and general as the casing Air.'[26]

My dear Reynolds.

I am anxious you should find this Preface tolerable. if there is an affectation in it, 'tis natural to me. – Do let the Printer's Devil cook it – and 'let me be as the casing air'.[27]

(To his brother George, and his sister-in-law, Georgina) I wish I could hear from you to make me 'whole and general as the casing air'... [28]

It seems the phrase itself, out of context, appealed to Keats, although there is a pertinence in that on each occasion he feels 'anxious', because of a lack of some information that would give him peace of mind. In the second reference, the printers, whom Keats was fighting over *Endymion*, are amusingly put into the position of the witches, as agents of evil, although in this case the technical term 'Printer's Devil' is the main prompt. As anger evokes *Hamlet* in Keats's memory, anxiety leads him to recall *Macbeth*. As a suggestion it might be tempting to find in Macbeth's 'fit' the clue to Keats's interest in health in the first and third references, and a glance at the next page shows the character saluting his guests with

Now good digestion wait on appetite
And health on both!

(III.iv.37–8)

It is a whimsical connection, but not impossible.

A much more direct, and consciously critical comment on Macbeth's state of mind comes briefly when Keats admires Kean for representing Macbeth when 'his eye lays siege to scorn',[29] a striking description of Macbeth's feelings towards the end of the play, as he fluctuates between desperate bravado, his moral sense blunted, and moments of resigned life-weariness. Keats is, in fact, slightly adapting Macbeth's own phrase:

... Our castle's strength
Will laugh a siege to scorn.
(V.v.2–3; not marked)

In a very strange sonnet, 'Why did I laugh tonight? No voice will tell', Keats, speaking in the first person, seems to swing between the same emotions. The poem questions some moment of wild exuberance that seems to have no justification, and no voice from heaven or hell will answer. From the anguish of incomprehension ('O darkness! darkness!'), the poet turns to a weary death-wish:

> Yet could I on this very midnight cease,
>   And the world's gaudy ensigns see in shreds.

The poem ends on a note which might be despair or a new form of ecstasy: 'death is life's high meed'. The connection with *Macbeth* comes first in the borrowing of a metaphor. The lines

> Why did I laugh? I know this being's lease –
>   My fancy to its utmost blisses spreads:

comes from Macbeth's moment of triumphant hope, after he has seen the witches for the last time:

> Sweet bodements, good!
> Rebellion's head rise never till the wood
> Of Birnam rise, and our high-plac'd Macbeth
> Shall live the lease of nature, pay his breath
> To time and mortal custom.
>   (IV.i.96–9 not marked)

Macbeth's cry of joy is soon to be drowned out by his despairing desire that 'the estate o'the world were now undone' (V.v.50; not marked) – to continue the metaphor of the 'lease' – and he sees that death will come prematurely. More generally, and apart from the use of a common metaphor, the poem, and the play in its concluding stages, both seem to tap a shared emotion of near suicidal self-hatred. In a way that cannot quite be specified, the sinister and frightening poem seems to be close in tone to *Macbeth*. Keats's own comments on the poem give a little more insight into his mood at the time of composition. In a letter to the George Keatses, after describing himself as a 'speculative mind',[30] he introduces the poem with these words:

> I am ever affraid that your anxiety for me will lead you to fear for the violence of my temperament continually smothered down: for that reason I did not intend to have sent you the following sonnet – but look over the two last pages and ask yourselves whether I have not that in me which will well bear the buffets of the world. It will be the best comment on my sonnet; it will show you that it was written with no Agony but that of ignorance....[31]

It cannot be wholly accidental that there are several verbal reminiscences here of *Macbeth*, and the passages from which they come shed more light on Keats's state of mind. The phrase 'buffets of the world' is spoken by the Second Murderer:

> I am one, my liege,
> Whom the vile blows and buffets of the world
> Hath so incens'd that I am reckless what
> I do to spite the world.
>
> (III.i.107–10)

The words 'surmise' and 'smothered' are used by Macbeth together, as he contemplates for the first time the murder of Duncan:

> Present fears
> Are less than horrible imaginings.
> My thought, whose murder yet is but fantastical,
> Shakes so my single state of man
> That function is smother'd in surmise,
> And nothing is but what is not.
>
> (I.iii.136–41)

If the recipients of his letter recognized the allusions and knew the contexts, they may have worried all the more about Keats's mood.

The detailed annotations to Keats's poetry in Miriam Allott's edition reveal many lines which are verbally indebted to *Macbeth*, and there are enough of these to prove that the play was a major influence upon the young poet. What is of more general interest is that on some occasions he shows himself impressionable to ways in which scenes are organized by Shakespeare, and we see Keats following structural precedents from *Macbeth*. One example is the opening to *King Stephen*, Keats's fragmentary attempt at writing a play in the Elizabethan vein. The organization of I.ii follows the same pattern as I.ii in *Macbeth*. Both plays begin at the height of a battle (an opening paralleled in Shakespeare in only *III Henry VI*), and in both a superior figure is brought news of the action. Just as Duncan hears report of the prowess of Macbeth at the front, so is Gloucester brought word of Stephen's military might. Although specific verbal echo is limited (the 'villainies of nature' that 'swarm' upon MacDonwald become 'our swarming arms' which threaten Stephen), there is a clear similarity between the effect which Keats wishes to build up of breathlessly reported action, and the impression of the Sergeant's speeches in *Macbeth*. The poetic techniques used by both writers to create this effect bear comparison, since we notice that both use the device of sharing one line between two speakers to give pace to the dialogue, and both use verbal coinages such as 'unseam'd' in Shakespeare and 'havock'd' in Keats. Since Keats in *Otho the Great* uses more echoes from *Macbeth* than from any other work, it would appear that he found this play a model for the language of dramatic speech, as well as a structural parallel for opening *King Stephen*. The other work in which he bases a scene upon Shakespeare's practice in *Macbeth* occurs in the more often read narrative poem, *Lamia*. The banquet scene in which Lamia is exposed by Apollonius bears resemblance to III.iv in *Macbeth*, in which Macbeth sees the ghost of Banquo at the feast. Although there is a difference in the various roles played, responses from characters are similar. Lady Macbeth's 'Why do you make such faces' (III.iv.67) leads to Lycius's 'Wherefore dost thou start?' (II,4), and Macbeth's 'Avaunt, and quit my sight' (III.iv.93) is equivalent to Lycius's 'Begone, foul dream!' (II,271). Just as Macbeth 'spoils the pleasure of the time' (III.iv.97) by interrupting the feast, so does Apollonius, and in both an 'aching ghost' (II,294) causes the reactions. The whole organization of the banquet scenes in both works is comparable, although Keats provides more circumstantial detail:

> The many heard, and the loud revelry
> Grew hush; the stately music no more breathes;
> The myrtle sickened in a thousand wreaths.
> By faint degrees, voice, lute and pleasure ceased;
> A deadly silence step by step increased,
> Until it seemed a horrid presence there,
> And not a man but felt the terror in his hair.
>
> (II.262–8)

Macbeth 'spoils the pleasure of the time' (III.iv.98) when he sees the 'horrible shadow' (III.iv.106) just as spectacularly as Lycius when he recognizes the serpent in Lamia. Macbeth's lines, marked by Keats,

> Thou hast no speculation in those eyes
> Which thou dost glare with!
>
> (III.iv.95–6)

prefigure the empty coldness Apollonius finds in Lamia's eyes: 'There was no recognition in those orbs' (II,260). Finally, the image used by Lady Macbeth in her advice to her husband, 'look like th'innocent flower, But be the serpent under't' (I.v.62–3) is displayed literally in the figure of Lamia. When she is with Apollonius her sobs are 'self-folding like a flower That faints into itself at evening hour' (I,138–9) and her eyelids open like the blooming of 'new flowers at morning song of bees' (I,142). Afterwards, however, 'Left to herself, the serpent now began To change' (I,146–7) and adopt the reptilian shape. Although the moral problems are rather different in each work, *Macbeth* is unique in Shakespeare's *oeuvre* as *Lamia* is in Keats's in showing the terrors of evil and the difficulties in recognizing its presence when a plausible surface is maintained. A particularly acute set of moral problems pervades both works, and we can see imaginative reasons why Keats's memory of *Macbeth* should inform his poem.

No matter how important *Macbeth* was to Keats, it would be dangerous to try to be more specific about the nature of his interest. The evidence is not so full as in the case of *King Lear*, where the poet has left us several significant comments about the play as a whole. His interest in *Macbeth* appears generally to centre upon the language of poetic utterance, and more particularly upon the way the play explores the existence of active evil which may not be immediately obvious. However, with some qualifications it can be concluded that, no matter how deeply the play haunted his imagination and influenced the poetry, it seems to have provided less for Keats's conceptualizing intellect to develop into his own philosophies and ideas than, for example, *Lear* and *Hamlet*.

VI Tragedies of love

There is some point in grouping together the 'tragedies of love', since Keats does appear to have recognized in his writing on love in *Isabella*, *The Eve of St Agnes* and *Lamia* that there is a language and a range of feelings which are particularly apt in the context of sexual passion. In the final chapter we shall examine the distinction in more detail. On the other hand, the grouping of these three plays in particular, *Antony and Cleopatra*, *Troilus and Cressida* and *Romeo and Juliet*, does admittedly have an arbitrary element. Some of Shakespeare's comedies have just as much influence upon Keats's own treatment of love as any of these, and in addition even in his readings of these three plays, his interest was not solely confined to the treatment of love. In *Antony and Cleopatra*, he certainly pays attention to the language of lovers, and to the remarkable heroine as lover, but we also find amongst Keats's interests the wider issue of dramatic revelation of character. In reading and quoting from *Troilus and Cressida* Keats shows interest in the lover Troilus, but the markings on his text have an unusually textual emphasis. *Romeo and Juliet*, as well as providing the poet with considerable creative stimulus and sense of atmosphere when he comes to write his own narratives of love, also gives Keats evidence to reinforce his more general concern with contrast in drama and poetry. In discussing these plays, then, we should attempt fairly to represent the diversity of Keats's interests, rather than artificially concentrate upon the subject of love alone. *Othello* is not discussed, because we do not have enough evidence to generalize about Keats's interest in the play. Although he obviously knew it well, quoting in several letters (usually when he is revealing or discussing jealousy), and echoing in poems, he has not left on the text any explicit comments nor any markings through which we could have entered upon systematic discussion.

Antony and Cleopatra

Antony and Cleopatra has the highest actual number of markings in the Johnson-Steevens edition, and once again it is clear that Keats has read the play attentively. The comments he makes in his letters are of interest because they exhibit his ideas on how Shakespeare reveals character through significant gesture and through language. Cleopatra is the character he speaks about most fully and eloquently, and his comments illustrate his strengths as a non-discursive interpreter of Shakespeare.

Caroline Spurgeon describes the circumstances of a reading which may have been the occasion of the markings on the text:

> Writing to Haydon from Margate on Sunday, May the 11th, 1817, in the letter which is full of Shakespeare and of Shakespeare quotations and echoes from start to finish, he says, 'It was very gratifying to meet your remarks on the manuscript'. This refers to a letter by Haydon contributed to the *Examiner* for May the 4th, 1817, on the subject of a book much under discussion at the time, *Manuscrit Venu de St Hélène*. Keats goes on, 'I was reading Anthony and Cleopatra when I got the Paper'. Allowing, therefore, two or three days for the *Examiner* to reach Keats at Margate, he was reading and marking this play between the 6th and 11th of May in the great Shakespearian year 1817. Haydon himself links the topic to Shakespearian psychology; he gives a series of acute reasons for his belief that this life of Napoleon was dictated by himself and no other, and adds, 'all these and many more are touches of nature so true, of natural self delusion so intense, and of Satanic defiance so deeply characteristic, as could only have come from the heart that gave birth to them, or have been laid open by Shakespeare; and Shakespeare is no longer alive'. ...[1]

Keats is interested enough in the generalization about the revelation of character to test out Haydon's aside, in the context of the play he is reading at the time – a particularly apt one in its political content:

> I was reading Anthony and Cleopatr[a] when I got the Paper and there are several Passages applicable to the events you commentate. You say that he arrived by degrees [speaking of Napoleon], and not by any single Struggle to the height of his ambitions – and that his Life had been as common in particulars as other Mens – Shakspeare makes Enobarb say – Where's Antony Eros – He's

walking in the garden – thus: and spurns the rush that lies before him, cries fool, Lepidus! In the same scene we find: "let determined things to destiny hold unbewailed their way". Dolabella says of Ant(h)ony's Messenger

> "An argument that he is pluck'd when hither
> He sends so poor a pinion of his wing" – Then again,
> Eno – "I see Men's Judgments are
> A parcel of their fortunes; and things outward
> Do draw the inward quality after them,
> To suffer all alike" – The following applies well to Bertram
> "Yet he that can endure
> To follow with allegiance a fallen Lord,
> Does conquer him that did his Master conquer,
> And earns a place i' the story"

But how differently does Buonap bear his fate from Antony![2]

Keats is quoting respectively III.v.15–17, III.vi.84–5, III.xiii.31–4, all of which are observations by other characters on Antony; and III.xiii. 43–6, where Enobarbus's faith bears comparison to that of Napoleon's friend and confidant, General Bertrand. (All underlined in Keats's edition.) The last three quotations are similar insofar as they show us that the political downfall of Antony has important consequences for many other people, and in this sense they provide us with an insight into the play. In addition, the passage is important in signifying the spirit in which Keats marks. In many plays, his markings indicate moments when a personage inadvertently displays his own character, and often the revelation is that the man's life is 'as common in particulars as other Mens'. The first quotation is a good example of what Keats sees as a Shakespearean strategy, for it is a glimpse of Antony's impetuous temper, as he kicks the rushes in his frustrated anger at the weakness of Lepidus. We can find many other occasions on which the grand, heroic character betrays a petty humanity. The complexity of Cleopatra is largely defined in terms of her combination of regally elevated poetry and more self-interested, jealous statements, often noted by Keats: 'Bring me word how tall she is' (II.v.118). We find many such examples amongst his marked passages. Keats does not simply look for fine phrases and inspiring poetry. It might also be suggested that in his final comment on the difference between Napoleon and Antony, Keats is referring to the fact that Napoleon even in defeat was decisive, vigorous and ruthlessly political, whereas Antony's tactical judgment and singlemindedness become questionable after setbacks. His comments in this letter show, then, that Keats is interested in the political issues of the plays, and particularly in the presentation of characters who are important for their position in the state. This is not, however, to suggest that he does not have sympathy for Antony's commitment to love. On the contrary, he is profoundly interested in the love-plot, although we can assert that he does not allow this part of the play to blind him to the political sphere, nor to the general issue of character-revelation.

Keats marks much of Cleopatra's part in the play, and there is evidence in the Letters that he was powerfully attracted to the character. He delights in the realization that although she may have greatness and dignity as a queen, yet 'Cleopatra was a Gipsey',[3] a wily and volatile woman. He is interested in the contradictions in the woman, which are amply illustrated in the passages he comes to mark in his edition. He is specific and revealing in suggesting some criteria for judging such a woman, when he compares a person he has met with Charmian, whom he appears to regard as a character who shares, in a lesser degree, many of Cleopatra's attributes, although he also indicates appreciation of Charmian as an individual character:

> ...from what I hear she is not without faults – of a real kind: but she has othe[r]s which are more apt to make women of inferior charms hate her. She is not a Cleopatra; but she is at least a Charmian. She has a rich eastern look; she has fine eyes and fine manners. When she comes into a room she makes an impression the same as the Beauty of a Leopardess. She is too fine and too con[s]cious of her Self to repulse any Man who may address her – from habit she thinks that nothing particular. I always find myself more at ease with such a woman; the picture before me always gives me a life and animation which I cannot possibly feel with any thing inferiour – I am at such times too much occupied in admiring to be awkward or on a tremble. I forget myself entirely because I live in her.[4]

This is such a full and compressed description of Keats's conception of a 'Cleopatra type', from her appearance to the life and animation of a leopardess, that commentary would diminish its effectiveness. (I am assuming that Keats sees Charmian as inferior to Cleopatra only in the degree of her charm, not the Egyptian kind.) In a few words, Keats had caught the doubleness of response drawn out by the dramatic character, in the way she instinctively demands attention, stirring some to envious or moralistic dismissal, and others to spellbound admiration which can forestall the critical reason. The main words are 'Life and animation', and Keats goes on to amplify. In speaking of the petty women who hate and criticize such a person, he says:

> They call her a flirt to me – What a want of knowledge? she walks across a room in such a manner that a Man is drawn towards her with a magnetic Power. This they call flirting! they do not know things. They do not know what a Woman is. I believe tho' she has faults – the same as Charmian and Cleopatra might have had – Yet she is a fine thing speaking in a worldly way: for there are two distinct tempers of mind in which we judge of things – the worldly, theatrical and pantomimical; and the unearthly, spiritual and etherial – in the former Buonaparte, Lord Byron and this Charmian hold the first place in our Minds... As a Man in the world I love the rich talk of a Charmian; as an eternal Being I love the thought of you. I should like her to ruin me, and I should like you to save me.[5]

(He is addressing his sister-in-law.) The tone implies that Keats is including Charmian amongst the 'worldly', which may include or grade into the theatrical and pantomimical in her effect on others. He is not, in other words, creating three exclusive categories. He is contrasting the worldly, in its various manifestations, and the ethereal. The value of the statement is that it shows Keats denying first that narrow moral values, or secondly, spiritual criteria, are in any way appropriate when judging Charmian and Cleopatra. To those legions of critics who insist on carping at Cleopatra's 'faults' in isolation, rather than recognizing that they are part and parcel of an overriding fineness when judged in the 'worldly' terms of the effect on spectators, we can retort with Keats's strong statement. 'Flirting' is altogether too demeaning a word to describe the magnificently self-centred yet largely unconscious power that the woman breathes. Inevitably, critics feel compelled to 'place' Cleopatra in a way that diminishes the wholeness of her presence, seeing her, for example, as a regal queen, *or* an actress, *or* a courtesan of genius. Keats shows us that in his eyes she overrides categories, being 'a fine thing speaking in a worldly way', yet having 'faults' when judged on more specific terms. Her faults are those attending upon her greatest qualities, as she may show her theatrical or pantomimical sides. Keats's view, and even his language, may be coloured by Hazlitt, who says of Cleopatra that 'She had great and unpardonable faults, but the grandeur of her death almost redeems them.'[6] In Hazlitt's concentration upon her death, and the word 'almost', however, we detect a difference between the two readers, but even in drawing his distinction between two categories of people, Keats may be at least half-remembering Hazlitt, who writes:

> The character of Cleopatra is a master-piece. What an extreme contrast it affords to Imogen! One would think it almost impossible for the same person to have drawn both. She is voluptuous, ostentatious, conscious, boastful of her charms, haughty, tyrannical, fickle. The luxurious pomp and gorgeous extravagance of the Egyptian queen are displayed in all their force and lustre...[7]

Again, although the basic distinction between Cleopatra and Imogen is relevant to the distinction drawn by Keats, there is a difference in sympathy between the two readers. Hazlitt, while recognizing the same qualities in Cleopatra as Keats, is less able to allow his feelings to sway his judgment. We should, however, remind ourselves that Hazlitt is writing in the context of public criticism, rather than in a familiar letter to a friend, a fact which helps to define the contrasting strengths and weaknesses of the two men as readers of Shakespeare.

Early in *Antony and Cleopatra*, Keats, as already mentioned, makes one of his rare annotations on the text. He asterisks Antony's phrase, 'Fie, wrangling queen!' as Cleopatra taunts, and scribbles:

> How much more Shakespeare delights in dwelling upon the romantic and wildly natural than upon the monumental. see Winter's Tale, 'When you do dance, &c.'

Having an eye to the context and the comparison with Florizel's words, it would appear that Keats means by 'the romantic and wildly natural' simply the language of lovers as they speak to each other in moments of intense personal involvement. The 'monumental' might conceivably be some form of public rhetoric, addressed to the world at large. One could debate the general truth of the statement, but its application shows the spirit in which Keats read this particular play and it is an interesting perception. From the outset, he himself takes 'delight' in the love interest. He locates the real energy of the play not in its political content, although he is aware of this dimension, but in its exploration of the nature of passion. 'The wildly natural' is an apt phrase to describe the uncontrollable turbulence of the emotions of the lovers as they reach expression, spontaneously 'wrangling', provoking, insulting, abusing, as well as extolling and loving.

The markings on the text of *Antony and Cleopatra* give us a good example of Keats 'orchestrating' a play, recording with his pen his fluctuations of interest, in such a way that we can trace his sense of the peaks and troughs of poetic expressiveness and dramatic power. He pays attention to Philo's words, unsympathetic to the lovers and 'Roman' in attitude, which begin the play. In all his markings upon the plays, Keats shows himself willing to pay attention to many conflicting points of view, rather than concentrating simply upon one strand. Surprisingly, in the opening dialogue between Antony and Cleopatra, apart from the note already examined, he marks only a couple of lines, both by Cleopatra:

> | If it be love indeed, tell me how much.
>
> (I.i.14)

And

> | As I am Egypt's queen,
> | Thou blushest, Antony, and that blood of thine
> | Is Caesar's homager: else so thy cheek pays shame
> | When shrill-tongu'd Fulvia scolds.
>
> (I.i.29–32)

We have already had occasion to notice several blushes in Shakespeare which Keats has marked, and it is one of the noticeable facial gestures which clearly interested him. Keats leaves thinly marked the next couple of scenes, and returns with closer attention when Antony and Cleopatra quarrel over Antony's decision to go back to Rome after hearing of Fulvia's death. This is the first lengthy 'wrangle' between the lovers in the play, although it does not discharge all the energy felt on both sides, since Antony is cautious and determined at this stage. In I. iv, Keats shows interest in Caesar's attitude to Antony, which is not at this stage wholly dismissive, for Caesar voices a strong note of regret that Antony has fallen from his former greatness. Cleopatra's grief in the absence of Antony, and Charmian's mocking banter, are noted. In II.i, Keats is interested in Pompey's ambitious design to strike while Antony is in Egypt and the triumvirate is in disarray. Keats throughout does not allow the love interest to overwhelm his response to other issues in the play. However, the scene in which Antony and Cleopatra make their peace with each other and agree upon the arranged marriage with Octavia is hardly marked at all. These dealings are perhaps too muted and diplomatic, 'political' in a narrower sense, to be especially striking to Keats. Not surprisingly, though, Keats's interest returns fully at the end of the scene when Enobarbus launches into his glowing picture of Cleopatra on the barge. The section is almost entirely underlined, with some side-marking as well. Antony's little conversation with the soothsayer is the next part marked. By telling him how his 'spirit' is in the power of Caesar's, the soothsayer forebodingly accentuates in a private exchange the change in Antony's public fortunes. Some, but not a lot, of Cleopatra's lines are marked in the scene in which she receives news of Antony's marriage. Up to the end of Act II, in fact, Keats does not find the presence of Cleopatra overwhelming, and one could at least argue that the relatively unsustained poetic quality of her lines, is a part of Shakespeare's design at this stage of the play. The political negotiations with Pompey are touched by Keats only occasionally, but on the other hand, there is a denser marking of the drunken scene on board Pompey's barge. Here, however, Keats does not seem so interested in the plot to kill Antony and Caesar suggested by Menas to Pompey, as in the effects of the drinking on each character. He under-lines the comments by the two servants about Lepidus as an insignific-ant man in 'great man's fellowship', and the relative effects of alcohol, on the relaxed, expansive Antony:

> Come let's all take hands,
> Till that the conquering wine hath steep'd our sense
> In soft and delicate Lethe
>
> (II.vii.104–6)

and the stiffer self-consciousness of Caesar:

> and mine own tongue
> Splits what it speaks. The wild disguise hath almost
> Antick'd us all.
>
> (II.vii.121–3)

The ear does not have to strain too hard to hear in Antony's invitation to soft and delicate Lethe the hope expressed in 'Ode to a Nightingale' that wine will allow one to 'fade far away, dissolve...'[8] and to detect Caesar's words behind the 'wild ecstasy' of the figures on Keats's Gre-cian Urn.

Perhaps unexpectedly, Keats shows interest in the first scene of Act III, a short interchange between Ventidius and Silius, as they discuss the way they have, on behalf of Antony, defeated 'darting Parthia'. Ventidius gives a short lecture on the necessity for restraint in an underling, saying that although he could go on to conquer more, yet it would be dangerous to make himself through his efficiency his 'cap-tain's captain'. The scene does show the competence of Antony's army in his absence, perhaps as a way of emphasizing later the way it will be his own bad generalship that will lose the subsequent battles. The marking is not so surprising when we remember the constant undercurrent of Keats's interest, at least in the first half of the play, in the political and military issues insofar as they bear on character. In the rest of the Act, however, Keats concentrates upon those scenes in which emotions are more directly engaged, and the central issue is the mutual influence of the lovers upon one another: Cleopatra's jealousy when she asks about Octavia's physique (III.iii), Scarus's contemptuous report of Antony's ignominious retreat from the naval battle when 'Yon ribaudred nag of Egypt' flees (III.x.10), Antony's anger (III.xi), and the long, culminating encounter between Antony and Cleopatra, beginning with his jealousy and ending with reconciliation (III.xiii). In this Act, Keats seems unstirred by the presence of the quiet Octavia, although her inauspicious entrance described by Caesar after she has been deserted by Antony is marked down the side, as if the note of pathos has been observed. Caesar's curtly expressed contempt for Antony is underlined:

> No, my most wronged sister; Cleopatra
> Hath nodded him to her.
> (III.vi.66)

The compression of 'nodded', implying a contemptuous tone, is no doubt what attracted Keats. Keats also seems to admire, in the spirit of a fellow craftsman, Caesar's, or rather Shakespeare's, virtuosity in miraculously cramming into iambic pentameters a list of otherwise dull, polysyllabic, and apparently poetically unmanageable names:

> He hath assembled
> Bocchus, the king of Libya; Archelaus
> Of Cappadocia; Philadelphos, king
> Of Paphlagonia; the Thracian king, Adallas;
> King Manchus of Arabia; King of Pont;
> Herod of Jewry; Mithridates, king
> Of Comagene; Polemon and Amyntas,
> The kings of Mede and Lycaonia, with a
> More larger list of sceptres.
> (III.vi.68–76)

I cannot help feeling that in versifying here, Shakespeare is showing off, and he has impressed at least one admirer with his expertise. The young poet is not above flexing his own muscles in a similar way, for example, at various points of 'The Cap and Bells'. One could make a more serious point, in both examples, by gesturing towards the impressive evocativeness of such an array of names.

Act IV is likewise fragmented into many short scenes, and Keats is interested in the moments when strong and various feelings are brought into the high light of 'intoning'. Caesar has his moment of anger, ruthless and cold, when, having been called 'boy', he mockingly spurns the challenge from 'the old ruffian' to single combat (IV.i). When Antony quietly and melancholically draws out the grief of his followers, Keats side-marks (IV.ii), as he does also when Cleopatra fussily tries to help Antony with his armour (IV.iv). These three scenes remind us of the wide range of feelings presented in the play, even in very short scenes. A rich spectrum of emotions lies between anger and joyousness in the play. IV.viii shows Antony's jubilation and renewed vitality after the successful first day's battle, and Keats marks some, but not all the striking passages. In IV.xii, Keats marks only Scarus's commentary on the ill-omen of swallows building their nests in the ships' sails, and on Antony's 'fretted fortunes' and equally fretted moods. In IV.xiv, Antony's uncertainty about identity, gropingly expressed in the image of shifting clouds, attracts underlining, as does his premonition of the 'shame' of being 'window'd in great Rome' should he be taken alive (IV.xiv.71–5). In the final, longer scene of the Act (IV.xv), as the wounded Antony addresses Cleopatra from the base of her monument, the register of the poetry shifts into the high mode which will dominate the ending:

> CLEOPATRA.   O sun,
> Burn the great sphere thou mov'st in! Darkling stand
> The varying shore o'th'world...
>
> > (IV.xv. 9–11)
>
> ANTONY. I am dying, Egypt, dying.   (IV.xv. 18 repeated at 41)
>
> ... Then is it sin
> To rush into the secret house of death
> Ere death comes to us?
>
> > (IV.xv.80-3)
>
> Let's do it after the high Roman fashion,
> And make death proud to take us.
>
> > (IV.xv.87–8)

Act V opens with the eulogies spoken by Caesar and Dercetas on the death of Antony, both of which Keats side-marks. The rest of the Act belongs to Cleopatra, and Keats's markings emphasize Shakespeare's skill in manipulating our responses. He leaves unnoticed the periods of build-up, and concentrates upon the climaxes in which the poetry takes fire. After a lot of unnoticed hedging between Proculeius and Cleopatra, Keats's pen returns to the page when her passion rises, first to disgust at the possibility that she will be paraded in Rome, and then to her extraordinary, mythopoeic vision of Antony's magnanimity. There is another lowering of tone, in lines left largely unmarked, when Caesar gently reminds her that she has withheld many riches from her inventory of what she possesses, but again the marking is heavy when she becomes comically enraged with her servant. After Caesar leaves, Cleopatra prepares for her death-scene, and from here until she dies, Keats marks the lot, Clown and all. He stops when the Guard and Dolabella enter, but resumes for some twenty lines when they discuss with Caesar the scene before their eyes. The final tableau of Cleopatra in Caesar's words is marked:

> but she looks like sleep,
> As she would catch another Antony
> In her strong toil of grace...
> (V.ii.343–5)

and so is the Guard's knowledgeable description which adds a touch of verisimilitude:

> This is an aspic's trail; and these fig-leaves
> Have slime upon them, such as th'aspic leaves
> Upon the caves of Nile.
>
> CAESAR.   Most probable
> That so she died; for her physician tells me
> She hath pursu'd conclusions infinite
> Of easy ways to die. Take up her bed,
> And bear her women from the monument.
> (V.ii.348–54)

In the last Act, like a concert conductor, Keats is signalling by silence the premonitions to passion, and focussing upon each crescendo of poetry and passion in turn.

In very general terms Keats, although alert to many of the political issues in the play and to the presentation of character, is most interested in the 'wildly natural' speeches between the lovers, and the high style of the last Act. This is not altogether surprising from a romantic poet, and the fact allows us safely to say that on the major critical issue, Keats would endorse the view that the world is well lost for passion, and that the emotional vitality of Egypt surpasses the Roman ethos in attractiveness.

Some of the less conspicuous personages do not escape Keats's notice. He shows consistent interest in Enobarbus's wry observations on Antony (III.xiii.31–4; III.xiii.93–4; III.xiii.199–200; all marked), his bluff *bonhomie* in addressing Menas (II.vi.75–8; side-marked), and of course his sensuous and admiring description of Cleopatra ('The barge she sat in...'). Keats does not mark Enobarbus's desertion nor his death, but he does side-mark Antony's generosity in sending his treasure after him (IV.v.12ff). We recall that Hazlitt, Keats's teacher in many aspects of character appreciation, sees Enobarbus's repentance as 'the most affecting part of the play'.[9] Other minor characters whose moments of self-revelation are recognized by Keats are the pathetic schoolmaster, sent as an embassy by the broken Antony, and the brave, pragmatic Scarus.

In his markings of particular words and phrases, Keats concentrates, as in other plays, upon the loaded compression of Shakespeare's 'hieroglyphic' language. As a fellow-practitioner, intent in his own poetry upon giving every word maximum work to do, he homes in on phrases which are so concise and full in evocation that they can barely be paraphrased: 'scrupulous faction', 'Broad-fronted Caesar', 'My salad days', 'courtiers of bounteous freedom', 'darting Parthia', 'queasy with his influence', 'for I have savage cause', and 'were it carbuncled like holy Phoebus car'. There is one thing that strikingly connects these and other constructions marked by Keats in isolation in this play, and it is different from the aspect that links his markings of words and phrases in *The Tempest* or *Lear*. All the energy here springs not from verbs but from adjectives (including adjacent participles). In some metaphorical way, this characteristic of the expressive part in the syntax imitates a conspicuous trait of the two major characters. They are both infinitely bountiful and generous, and yet every component of their speech and action is packed with a spontaneous economy that is breathtaking. Defined by their magnanimity they have so much breath to give, yet defined by their age and maturity they have none to waste, and the unit of grammar they find to express both aspects is the adjective. To illustrate from a longer passage the suggestion that this is a characteristic of the language of the play, notice the weight that each adjective and participle, effortlessly chosen not only for precision but for resonance, carries in the following:

> ANT.   Eros,
> <u>Wouldst thou be window'd in great Rome, and see</u>
> <u>Thy master thus with pleach'd arms, bending down</u>
> <u>His corrigible neck, his face subdu'd</u>
> <u>To penetrative shame,</u>
>
> (IV.xiv. 71–5)

Take out the adjectives here and there is virtually nothing left, if we include past participles as adjectival in function. Keats feeds back into his own poetry some of what he has learned from the language of the play. It is unlikely that, without the existence of *Antony and Cleopatra*, we should have at least the following unique phrases from Keats:

> amorous-aching earth (*Otho*, IV.ii.27)

> High-fronted honour (*Endymion*, I.759)

> Aye, so delicious is the unsating food
> (*Endymion*, I.816)

> 'Cleopatra regal-dressed
> With the aspic at her breast'
> ('Welcome joy and welcome sorrow', l.16)

> A very gypsy is she, Nilus-born
> ('Fame, like a wayward girl...')

These phrases are chosen conservatively, because they are connected with the play's subject-matter, but it is likely that Keats's frequent use of adjectives and participles in strong positions would bear comparison with Shakespeare's *Antony and Cleopatra*.

For more general reasons *Antony and Cleopatra*, paticularly its final movement, must have impressed and influenced Keats's own poetic vision, giving him precedent for believing in the truth of imagination. Throughout the play, Antony and Cleopatra do not allow literal reality to dislodge their imaginative conceptions of each other:

> CLEOPATRA. <u>His legs bestrid the ocean; his rear'd arm</u>
> <u>Crested the world. His voice was propertied</u>
> <u>As all the tuned spheres, and that to friends;</u>
> <u>But when he meant to quail and shake the orb,</u>
> <u>He was as rattling thunder. For his bounty,</u>

> There was no winter in't; an autumn 'twas
> That grew the more by reaping.

(V.ii.82 ff.)

Such a rhapsody cannot be dismissed as the romantic gush of a besotted lover, for it is expressed by a mature woman from the centre of her generous mode of perceiving the world. The transforming power of metaphor is at work in Antony's epithet 'Mine nightingale' (IV.viii.18), used in a passage where he suggests that they should defy the grey hairs of mortality, and also by the extraordinary word used by Cleopatra, 'darkling', as in a participle she turns even the darkness of death into the twinkling star of life. Both find their way into the 'Nightingale' Ode. The great and non-Christian consolation afforded by this play is that poetry and metaphor steeped in the activity of living can be as powerful as religion, in turning death from a defeat or a torment into a triumphant consummation. Keats's constant attempts to transcend suffering and death by using metaphors, visions which all decisively embrace the variety of life, lie in the same territory as the play, and it is no wonder that he lived through it with such complete absorption. In fact, on at least one occasion he is reported to have said that *Antony and Cleopatra* was his favourite play.[10]

Troilus and Cressida

The markings and comments made by Keats upon his Folio text of *Troilus and Cressida* attest to a very careful reading, in which he is comparing the original edition with the edited text of his own day. His interest reaches from the technicalities of textual criticism to the most wide-ranging admiration for Shakespeare's thought and linguistic craft. Two relatively detailed annotations illustrate general and specific interests shown by Keats.

One passage early in the play is underlined and commented upon. Agamemnon reflects sententiously upon the observation that men rarely achieve their stated aims, and that plans are modified, or go awry, in the course of action designed to bring about a certain end. He is attempting to reassure his Greek colleagues in their temporary setbacks during the war, and a section of his speech is relevant to Keats's appended comment:

> Princes,
> What grief hath set these jaundies o'er your cheeks?

> The ample proposition that hope makes
> In all designs begun on earth below
> Fails in the promis'd largeness; <u>checks and disasters</u>
> <u>Grow in the veins of actions highest rear'd,</u>
> <u>As knots, by the conflux of meeting sap,</u>
> <u>Infects the sound pine, and diverts his grain</u>
> <u>Tortive and errant from his course of growth.</u>
> Nor, princes, is it matter new to us
> That we come short of our suppose so far
> That after seven years' siege yet Troy walls stand;
> *Sith every action that hath gone before,
> <u>Whereof we have record, trial did draw</u>
> <u>Bias and thwart, not answering the aim,</u>
> <u>And that unbodied figure of the thought</u>
> <u>That gave't surmised shape.</u>
>
> (I.iii.1–17)

With a cross, Keats draws attention to his own observation upon the thought embodied in this statement, relating it to his feelings about Shakespeare:

> The Genius of Shakspeare was an in[n]ate universality – wherefore he had the utmost atchievement of human intellect prostrate beneath his indolent and kingly gaze. He could do easily Man's utmost. His plans of tasks to come were not of this world – if what he purposed to do here after would not in his own Idea 'answer the aim' how tremendous must have been his Conception of Ultimates.

The comment takes little or no account of the dramatic context, since Shakespeare does not allow us to have great sympathy for the Greeks or the Trojans in their practice of the war. Instead, Keats, as he often does, is using Shakespeare's words in application to the dramatist's art, lifting the passage out of context in order to make a different point. Since the tone and intention of the note amount to uncritical admiration for the dramatist's achievement and the apparently limit-less potential of his art, perhaps not much of substance can be gleaned from it. On the the other hand, by considering the words of the note and the passage, we might argue that what Keats is admiring are quite particular and identifiable qualities. Shakespeare's grasp over the whole spectrum of human thought, he is saying, is so large and com-prehensive that he may be credited with having intellectual aims – a 'Conception of Ultimates' – and his art is his method of working towards these. However, when he can be presumed not yet to have reached his aim, this need not be regarded as in any sense a failure. Instead, the deviations from some abstract purpose are wilful and yet considered decisions to represent the variety of life by introducing a 'bias or thwart' into his 'course of growth'. Keats is gesturing towards a combination of qualities in Shakespeare which have been found by many other writers: a scrupulous and profound intellectual control, yoked with an apparently casual digressiveness, a daring wildness in plucking imagery from the most diverse areas of experience.[11] We risk reading too much into Keats's idolatry by going so far, and yet his language, as usual, magically entices us into a pregnant and open speculativeness about what lies just beyond the reach of the simple statement.

The other comment made by Keats upon his text is much more hard-edged, and it should be enough to draw respect from even that most formidable and rigorous regiment of Shakespearean scholars, the textual critics. He exhibits impatience for the modern editors' cavalier and unsound treatment of textual minutiae:

> I have not read this copy much and yet have had time to find many faults – however 'tis certain that the Commentators have contrived to twist many beautiful passages into common places as they have done with respect to 'a scorn' which they have hocus pocus'd in[to] 'a storm' thereby destroying the depth of the simile – taking away all the sourrounding Atmosphere of Imagery and leaving a bare and unapt picture. Now however beautiful a comparison may be for a bare aptness – Shakspeare is seldom guilty of one – he could not be content to the 'sun lighting a storm', but he gives us Apollo in the act of drawing back his head and forcing a smile upon the world – 'the Sun doth light a-scorn'.

Keats is commenting upon Troilus's lines which appear in his old-spelling text thus:

> I haue (as when the Sunne doth light a-scorne)
> Buried this sigh, in wrinkle of a smile:
> $\overline{\text{(I.i.37–8)}}$

In speaking of 'the Commentators', Keats no doubt has in mind mainly the indomitably commonsensical Dr Johnson, who incorporates the emendation which Keats rejects. Some recent editors, like Keats himself, retain the Folio reading of 'a-scorn', perhaps with more cautious motives than Keats, applying the maxim that the more difficult reading is likely to be correct when compared with a phrase of 'bare aptness'. What is impressive about Keats's comment is not the particular words upon which he is commenting, but the principle which he enunciates. It amounts to an interesting rationale of the modern editor's rule of '*difficilior lectio*', as he says that there are aesthetic rather than prescriptive or conservative reasons for retaining an unusual reading before a literally 'correct' one. By choosing the more unexpected, Shakespeare himself is packing into his images a greater complexity of thought and feeling, enhancing the 'depth of the simile', creating the 'beautiful' instead of the merely 'apt'. To have the opinion of a great poet upon such a matter of editorial principle must be intrinsically of value to commentators, as well as illustrating on a delicate, linguistic level Keats's perception that Shakespeare often, with an inspired wilfulness, strays from his literal or formal 'aims'. The lesson for us is that even in such a quasi-scientific area as textual criticism, there is an important and rigorous role to be played by the exercise of imagination and poetic tact.

In his text of *Troilus and Cressida*, Keats provides us with other textual details of correction or suggested emendation. Some come, as he says, from checking against his edited text, but even so they are invariably intelligent and display a scholar's understanding. Accordingly, they require little comment, and may quickly be tabulated. The main value of such details, for our purpose, is as evidence that Keats's interest in the text was by no means vague, impressionistic, or narrowly poetic. The lines will be quoted in old spelling, as Keats found them in his text. (Some, it should be pointed out, are simple misprints, which are obviously corrected.)

I.i.47–9

TROY.   Oh Pandarus! I tell thee Pandarus;
       When I doe tell thee, <u>th̸ere my hopes lye drown'd</u>:
       <u>Reply not in how many Fadomes deepe</u>

Keats's emendation has grammatical justification, but has not been adopted by modern editors.

III.ii.22

TROY.   <u>Death I feare me</u>
   woon*
<u>S̶o̶u̶n̶ding distruction, or some ioy too fine,</u>

This emendation (sanctioned by the Quarto), has sometimes been accepted and sometimes not in modern editions. It has the merit of eloquence, but is not strictly necessary.

III.iii.162

> Or like a gallant Horse falne in first ranke,
> Lye there for pauement to the abiect, ~~neere~~   rear*
> Ore-run and trampled on:

As in the preceding case, this (Quarto) reading, eliminating the comma and substituting 'rear', is adopted in modern editions.

III.iii.177

> Though they are made and moulded of things past,
>   *iv
> And góe to dust, that is a little guilt,

Again, this is a Quarto reading, adopted in modern editions.

IV.iv.40,41

> With the rude breuitie and discharge of ~~our~~ ne*
> Iniurious time/* now with a robbers haste   ./
> (semi-colon deleted by Keats)

Again, Quarto readings, adopted in modern texts.

IV.v.57, 59

> Nay, her foot speakes, her wanton spirites looke out
> At euery ioynt, and motiŭe* of her body:
> Oh these encounterers so glib of tongue,
> That giue a coasting welcome ere it comes;

The change from 'motive' to 'motion' is apparently Keats's own, and may well not be an emendation but a note for his own benefit, to remind him of the meaning of 'motive' in this context as 'moving part'.

There are a couple of other short notes made by Keats, and in these cases the centre of attention is not textual but critical. The first shows his admiration of Shakespeare's choice of an allusion which has multiple shades of appropriateness. The passage is a bantering dialogue between Pandarus and Cressida, concerning Troilus:

PANDARUS. But to prove to you that Helen loves him, she came
  and puts me her white hand to his cloven chin –
CRESSIDA. Juno have mercy; how came it cloven?★

(I.ii.114–15)

Keats's note runs as follows: '★ A most delicate touch – Juno being the
Goddess of Childbirth.' By drawing attention to the allusion, Keats
allows us to regard Shakespeare's choice as deliberate rather than
arbitrary, thereby adding a little more bite to Cressida's joke, implying
that Juno did not have mercy if he was born with a cloven chin. The
other note is attached to a passage which Keats, judging from his
markings alone, seems to have especially liked. He was in fact to use
a part of the quotation in a significant note on *King Lear*, which has
already been examined.

ULYSSES. I have a young conception in my brain;
  Be you my time to bring it to some shape.
NESTOR. What is't?
ULYSSES. This 'tis:
  Blunt wedges rive hard knots. The seeded pride
  That hath to this maturity blown up★
  In rank Achilles must or now be cropped
  Or, shedding, breed a nursery of like evil
  To overbulk us all.

(I.iii.312–19)

Keats's note runs thus:

  ★ 'Blowne up' etc. One's very breath while leaning over these Pages
  is held for fear of blowing this line away – as easily as the gentlest
  breeze despoils [sic.] Robs dandelions of their fleecy Crowns.

We have here more evidence of Keats's creative and inward contact
with Shakespeare's words. His imaginative attentiveness has pictured
an image which could easily have been glanced over as a mere word-
play. He has indeed *created* the buried image, by specifically envisag-
ing a dandelion, its seeds ready to be scattered. The picture is beauti-
fully apt to the passage, and as Keats observes, so delicate that it could
easily be missed.

  When we examine the markings which are clearly of an appreciative
rather than of a textual nature, we find his usual eclectic interest in a
wide range of poetic utterance displayed throughout. He marks the
text continuously and fairly heavily, and it is clear that his attention

was alert throughout the reading. There are some personal touches. For example, in the dawn scene between the lovers, Keats picks out, amongst more lyrical snatches, the references to the chilly morning:

TROILUS. Dear, trouble not yourself; the morn is cold.
(IV.ii.1)

TROILUS. ...
You will catch cold and curse me.
(IV.ii.14)

Bearing in mind Keats's obsession with the weather, for example in his injunctions to his younger sister, Fanny, to wrap up well in cold weather, we may detect in his markings a personal preoccupation as well as a characteristic interest in touches of atmosphere and time-references. These markings also draw attention to a strain of domestic detail in the scene which is not often mentioned by commentators. Cressida's 'Hark! there's one up' (IV.ii.18) as she hears Pandarus bustling about has the same effect of establishing the time in concise, palpable fashion. It seems, in fact, that as in other plays, Keats is interested in tracing some time sequence, although the search is not particularly profitable here, since it throws up only the following, of which the third is the most poetically arresting:

ACHILLES. That Hector by the fifth hour of the sun
(II.i.118)

PARIS. It is great morning.
(IV.iii.1)

ACHILLES. Look, Hector,how the sun begins to set;
How ugly night comes breathing at his heels;
Even with the vail and dark'ning of the sun,
To close the day up, Hector's life is done.
(V.viii.5–8)

It is not wholly surprising, as Spurgeon points out, that Keats marks most of Troilus's protestations of love, for it is clear from a couple of statements in his Letters that in his relationship with Fanny Brawne he sometimes identifies with this character. He fears that Fanny is 'a little inclined to the Cresseid',[12] and on another occasion he amplifies in this way:

Let me be but certain that you are mine heart and soul, and I could

die more happily than I could otherwise live. If you think me cruel
– if you think I have sleighted you – do muse it over again and see
into my heart – My love to you is 'true as truth's simplicity and sim-
pler than the infancy of truth' as I think I once said before.[13]

Despite this comment, to be fair to Keats, he appears to have control-
led any personal tendency to despondent jealousy about women when
he came to write his own narrative poems of love. His heroines are
faithful and trustworthy, from the goddess and Peona in *Endymion* to
Isabella. Madeline, prepared to be frank and realistic, is completely
committed to Porphyro by the time they flee into the night. Even
Lamia, a character whom Keats could easily have represented as
treacherous, emerges from the first section of the poem as holding
firmly the feelings of a woman totally in love and made vulnerable by
her emotions, a treatment which adds considerable pathos to her
plight and moral ambiguity to the poem as a whole. In his poetry,
Keats preserves an impression of women as thoroughly faithful and
practical in their concerns.[14] His prototype is Imogen rather than
either Cleopatra or Cressida, despite his fascination and fear in reality
when confronted with types of the latter. In making this point we are
noticing a remarkable capacity on Keats's part in all his poetry to sub-
merge or sublimate many of his own personal attitudes. The relation-
ship between comments we find in his letters and the poetic treatment
of certain subjects is as fascinating for what the poems exclude from
their vision as for what they include.

On the other hand, one feels quite a lot of Troilus in Keats as a man,
and the words of this character influenced some of his poetry. Several
writers, including Middleton Murry and Spurgeon, have suggested
that Keats identified with the character of Troilus, and more recently
one critic has argued for a specific relationship of indebtedness bet-
ween the play and 'Ode to a Nightingale'.[15] In a letter, Keats refers to
a passage that particularly struck him:

> Or I throw my whole being into Triolus [sic] and repeating those
> lines, 'I wander, like a lost soul upon the stygian Banks staying for
> waftage,' I melt into the air with a voluptuousness so delicate that
> I am content to be alone –[16]

The whole passage, with the poet's markings, reads thus:

> I stalk about her door
> Like a strange soul upon the Stygian banks

Staying for waftage. O, be thou my Charon,
And give me swift transportance to these fields
Where I may wallow in the lily beds
Propos'd for the deserver! O gentle Pandar,
From Cupid's shoulder pluck his painted wings,
And fly with me to Cressid!
                    …
I am giddy; expectation whirls me round.
Th'imaginary relish is so sweet
That it enchants my sense; what will it be
When that the wat'ry palates tastes indeed
Love's thrice-repured nectar? Death, I fear me;
Swooning destruction; or some joy too fine,
Too subtle-potent, tun'd too sharp in sweetness,
For the capacity of my ruder powers.
I fear it much; and I do fear besides
That I shall lose distinction in my joys;
As doth a battle, when they charge on heaps
The enemy flying.

                                        (III.ii.7–28)

Although it is difficult to put one's finger on a clearly identifiable echo in the 'Ode', the whole movement and idea behind the two passages is analogous. The imagination 'enchants' the senses of the respective speakers, leading them towards a pleasurable death. Douglas Bush independently suggests a recollection of the Shakespearean passage in the last verse of the 'Ode on Melancholy',[17] and here the parallel is closer, since Keats is speaking of the melancholy induced by the presence of a beautiful woman, and like Troilus the poet, feels he will be among the spoils of battle, 'cloudy trophies', if he allows himself to succumb to the seductive influence. It is enough to say that Troilus's speech is an important reference point for Keats's poetic thought. Given the romantic lushness of the language, this is not surprising. One other marking may be less than wholeheartedly sympathetic. As Aeneas fetches Troilus in the morning, there seems to be an edge of emotional betrayal in Troilus's desire to cover up knowledge of his night of love with Cressida:

            And, my Lord Aeneas,
We met by chance; you did not find me here.

                                        (IV.ii.70–1)

There may be a sharp perception into Troilus's unromantic prag-
matism behind the underlining. On the other hand, in the famous bet-
rayal scene (V.ii), Keats tends to pick out only the bitter statements
about woman's infidelity, as if he is content to take Troilus's words and
conduct at face value. Cressida does not command the same sort of
interest for Keats, at least in terms of her poetic language, and he
marks her phrases only sporadically in comparison with the heavy
marking of Troilus's words.

Apart from the love-plot, Keats pays attention to the scenes in
which the Greeks parley with each other, particularly I.iii, which is
almost all marked, and III.iii. It may strike the modern reader that the
circumlocutions and calculated sententiousness of the Greeks' speech
are dangerously close to bombast, but Keats would certainly be by no
means the last to be taken in by the rhetoric of Ulysses. At least after
the work of E.M.W. Tillyard, many commentators by ignoring con-
text, have facilely thought that Ulysses is something like a spokesman
for Shakespeare's own beliefs on social order and political stability.
However, the main impulse behind Keats's interest must be at least in
large part stylistic, as we can see from the way he 'counts' the rhythm
and weights every word in his broken underlining in this, for example:

> The heavens themselves, the planets, and this centre,
> Observe degree, priority, and place,
> Insisture, course, proportion, season, form,
> Office, and custom, in all line of order;
> And therefore is the glorious planet Sol
> In noble eminence enthron'd and spher'd
> Amidst the other, whose med'cinable eye
> Corrects the ill aspects of planets evil,
> And posts, like the commandment of a king,
> Sans check, to good or bad.
> ...
> Divert and crack, rend and deracinate,
> The unity and married calm of states
> Quite from their fixture!

(I.iii.85–101)

This manner of marking may even be carried out as an aid to the mem-
ory, but it indicates also Ulysses's emphatic way of speaking, and
discriminates by double underlining striking images. Keats must have
admired his lofty tone, for he has marked many of Ulysses' lines, and
is said by Bailey[18] to have known off by heart the speech beginning:

Time hath, my lord, a wallet at his back, Wherein he puts alms for oblivion. (III.iii.145ff; almost all marked).

It would appear that Keats takes a practitioner's interest in the kind of language used by Ulysses. It is perhaps the most 'Miltonic' in Shakespeare, and in this sense comparable with the choice of style in *Hyperion. A Fragment*. There is even a reference to Hyperion made by Ulysses, noted by Keats:

> And add more coals to Cancer when he burns
> With entertaining great Hyperion.
> (II.iii.191–2)

It is possible that a more detailed study than can be undertaken here would reveal a stylistic relationship between the language of the gods in Keats's first *Hyperion* and that of Ulysses in *Troilus and Cressida*, as if Keats chose the Greek as a rhetorical model alongside Milton.

Pandarus and Thersites introduce a more colourful note in their language, and Keats enjoys phrases and snatches of their speech. Thersites' invective, in particular, is striking:

> The plague of Greece upon thee, thou mongrel beef-witted lord!
> (II.i.13)

> He would pun thee into shivers with his fist, as a sailor breaks a biscuit.
> (II.i.38)

> and Mercury, lose all the serpentine craft of thy caduceus...
> (II.iii.12)

> it will not in circumvention deliver a fly from a spider...
> (II.iii.17)

> The common curse of mankind, folly and ignorance, be thine in great revenue! Heaven bless thee from a tutor, and discipline come not near thee!
> (II.iii.25–6)

> but he has not so much brain as ear-wax
> (V.i.51)

> the parrot will not do more for an almond than he for a commodious drab.
> (V.ii.191)

Thersites' bitter and biting commentary on the main figures emerges constantly in such inventive metaphors and parody. Keats, in a racy, affectionate burst of fun in a letter to Reynolds, asks him to send 'a few finch eggs',[19] and since he is repeating one of Thersites' insulting diminutives, it is probable that he is asking his friend to send the kind of bad, self-parodying popular poetry which he has been speaking of satirically in his letter. Thersites' phrase in context is much more gratuitously splenetic and literally demeaning:

> PATROCLUS. Out, gall!
> THERSITES. <u>Finch egg!</u>
> (V.i.33–4)

The phrases of Pandarus picked out by Keats seem to be notable for their homely ordinariness, which adds a special tone to the generally rhetorical language of the play: 'I'll be sworn 'tis true; <u>he will weep you, an 'twere a man born in April.</u>' (I.ii.167–8) Cressida here mocks his platitudinousness: <u>'And I'll spring up in his tears, an 'twere a nettle against May.'</u> (I.ii.167–70) Equally conventionally, Pandarus speaks of <u>'the spice and salt that season a man'</u> (I.ii.247), and Keats notes the following courteous but meaningless phrases:

> <u>Fair be to you, my lord,</u> and to all this fair company! Fair desires, in all fair measure, fairly guide them – especially to you, fair Queen! <u>Fair thoughts be your fair pillow.</u>

This time it is Helen who parodies his sycophancy: 'Dear lord, you are full of fair words.' (III.i.41–4) Keats's markings pick out the unconscious humour of this Polonius-like character. The interest may lie in the more poetic imagery (and again the blush) in such breathless rushes of verbiage as this:

> <u>She's making her ready, she'll come straight; you must be witty now. She does so blush, and fetches her wind so short, as if she were fray'd with a sprite. I'll fetch her. It is the prettiest villain; she fetches her breath as short as a new-ta'en sparrow.</u>
> (III.ii.28–33)

Keats also marks down the side a similar passage at III.ii.56–9. Although he is one of the '<u>Brethren and sisters of the hold-door trade</u>' (V.x.50) and a fussy voyeur, Pandarus, through the language which Keats notes, conveys the sense of an artless, homely man.

It seems that Keats's interest in *Troilus and Cressida* lies mainly in the language, its many figurative and rhetorical usages and its very variety and flexibility. At this level, little of value escapes his attention, even the words of an insignificant Servant, who produces the striking phrase, 'the heart-blood of beauty, love's invisible soul' (III.i.32). Keats is struck by the lover's casual familiarity of address, when Paris refers to the immortal Helen as '<u>Nell</u>' (III.i.129), and he is also arrested by the formally courteous description of the old man:

> Here's Nestor
> Instructed by the Antiquary times:
> (II.iii.244–5)

Keats picks up unusual words, such as 'unplausive' and 'derision med'cinable' (III.iii.43, 44); 'tetchy' (I.i.95) and 'observant toil' (I.iii.203), and many others. He notices unusual syntactical constructions:

> Do a fair message   (I.iii.218)
>
> your full consent Gave wings to my propension   (II.ii.132–3)
>
> who, like an arch, reverb'rate The voice again   (III.iii.120–1)
>
> he professes not answering   (III.iii.266)

We have seen illustrated time and again Keats's capacity to recognize and draw out Shakespeare's way of embedding pictorial images in his language in such a glancing way that they can be easily overlooked:

> Thou great commander, nerve and bone of Greece   (I.iii.55)
>
> A slave, whose gall coins slanders like a mint   (I.iii.193)
>
> were his brain as barren As banks of Libya   (I.iii.328–9)
>
> You fur your gloves with reason   (II.ii.38)
>
> To angle for your thoughts   (III.ii.151)

Such examples, culled more or less at random, further illustrate Keats's own claim that he looked upon fine phrases like a lover and they also prove his deep interest in the textual, stylistic and metaphoric aspects of this play. We may not be able to tell whether he had an overall impression or attitude, but that is in the nature of the 'philosophy of particularity' which he partly acquired from Hazlitt. There is certainly ample evidence of the kinds of detail which attracted him, as an attentive and subtle reader of *Troilus and Cressida*.

Romeo and Juliet

Keats marked lines and passages up to the end of III.i. from *Romeo and Juliet* in his Folio copy of Shakespeare. This is clearly not his only reading of the play, for elsewhere he shows a thorough knowledge of its poetry. *The Eve of St Agnes*, for example, is shot through with verbal reminiscence, and there are atmospheric touches that conjure up the spirit of the play. From one comment in a letter to Fanny Brawne, Keats indicates in an amusing but touching fashion that he at least knows the ending of the play:

> I fear I am too prudent for a dying kind of Lover. Yet, there is a great difference between going off in warm blood like Romeo, and making one's exit like a frog in a frost.[20]

One of his interests is the character of Juliet, whom he regards as a particular kind of ideal. We have already noticed that he compares Imogen and Juliet, not as fictional characters but as women,[21] confessing that although Imogen is the 'finest Creature', yet he feels such a 'yearning' towards Juliet that he 'would rather follow her into Pandemonium than Imogen into Paradize', and he heartily wishes himself a Romeo 'to be worthy of her and to he[a]r the Devils quote the old Proverb – "Birds of a feather flock together" – Amen'. On another occasion, Keats uses similar language of attraction when speaking of Juliet. As he wishes well to his friend Reynolds in his impending marriage, Keats mentions his own feelings:

> My sensations are sometimes deadened for weeks together – but believe me I have more than once yearne'd for the time of your happiness to come, as much as I could for myself after the lips of Juliet.[22]

It is not possible to identify exactly the qualities that Keats has in mind, but once he has drawn our attention to the differences between the two women, we may recognize the impulsive passion and lyrical nature of Juliet, the commonsense and practical outlook of Imogen. Hazlitt has some penetrating comments on the character of Juliet, and they help to clarify the nature of Keats's interest:

> The character is indeed one of perfect truth and sweetness. It has nothing forward, nothing coy, nothing affected or coquettish about it; – it is a pure effusion of nature. It is as frank as it is modest, for it has no thought that it wishes to conceal. It reposes in conscious innocence on the strength of its affections. Its delicacy does not consist in coldness and reserve, but in combining warmth of imagination and tenderness of heart with the most voluptuous sensibility.[23]

Undoubtedly Keats idealized women but at least he discriminated between different stereotypes of female attractiveness. His imagination seized upon three Shakespearean characters as his paragons: Cleopatra, the 'worldly' woman, mature and magnetic; Imogen, the patient, practical woman who has an 'ethereal' attractiveness because of her moral goodness; and Juliet, who embodies youthful vitality and spontaneity, a 'conscious innocence' that combines modesty and frankness in a spontaneous way. The contrast drawn with Imogen is partly explained by Hazlitt, who casually demonstrates a rather contemptous attitude towards the 'hero' of *Cymbeline*:

> We have almost as great an affection for Imogen as she had for Post-humus; and she deserves it better. Of all Shakespear's women she is perhaps the most tender and the most artless.[24]

Juliet is less safe, but more exciting; she is more impetuous, spirited, and romantically absorbed: more 'young'. She shares one characteristic at least with several other Shakespearean heroines, and Keats, as is his custom, picks out her blush for special attention. The same passage points towards Madeline's 'soft and chilly nest' (*The Eve of St Agnes*, line 235):

> NURSE. Then hie you hence to Friar Lawrence' cell;
> There stays a husband to make you a wife.
> Now comes the wanton blood up in your cheeks;
> They'll be in scarlet straight at any news.
> Hie you to church; I must another way,
> To fetch a ladder, by the which your love
> Must climb a bird's nest soon when it is dark.
> I am the drudge, and toil in your delight.
> (II.v.68–75)

It is evident, as we shall see in more detail, that *The Eve of St Agnes* is Keats's attempt to capture certain qualities of young love which he found in *Romeo and Juliet*, and the presentation of Madeline is perhaps his most detailed commentary on Juliet. There are only two women whom Shakespeare shows us in happy bedroom scenes at dawn, and the case of Juliet portrays the awakening of young sexuality which Keats dwells upon in *The Eve*.

Romeo and Juliet is full of 'anthologizable' poetic statements, and in the portion of the play that he marks, Keats indicates admiration for the famous passages and scenes. He sidemarks the Nurse's long and amusing speech to Lady Capulet; he underlines some fifteen lines of Mercutio's strange rhapsody on Queen Mab (I.iv.59–70 and 100–

103); he underlines the operatic dialogue when Romeo and Juliet shyly touch hands at the ball (I.v.93–104), and he pays concentrated attention to the language of the 'balcony' scene (II.ii), underlining and sidemarking so many lines here that it is clear he knew and appreciated the scene as a whole. Some shorter, equally quotable portions, attract Keats's attention, and it is no surprise that he picks out the images in Montague's regret at Romeo's reticence:

> As is the bud bit with an envious worm,
> Ere he can spread his sweet leaves to the air,
> Or dedicate his beauty to the sun.
> (I.i.149–51)

Like this quotation, the other short passages marked by Keats emphasize, perhaps inadvertently, that much of the imagery draws the lives of the characters in the play close to the natural world. Capulet, speaking of his daughter, Juliet, as 'the hopeful lady of my earth' (sidemarked), goes on to predict the merriment of the feast to be held at his house in terms of spring following winter:

> Such comfort as do lusty young men feel
> When well-apparell'd April on the heel
> Of limping winter treads, even such delight
> Among fresh female buds shall you this night
> Inherit at my house.
> (I.ii.26–30)

Much of the pathos at the end of the play derives from the delicate portentousness of such passages, as we anticipate that precious youth will be blighted. Juliet later speaks of

> the sun's beams
> Driving back shadows over louring hills.
> (II.v.5–6)

She continues, describing the tardiness of the Nurse in bringing news. Perhaps the marking is another example of Keats's interest in tracing the movement of time in Shakespeare's plays:

> Now is the sun upon the highmost hill
> Of this day's journey; and from nine till twelve
> Is three long hours, yet she is not come.
> Had she affections and warm youthful blood,
> She would be as swift in motion as a ball;

My words would bandy her to my sweet love,
And his to me.
But old folks – many feign as they were dead;
Unwieldy, slow, heavy and pale as lead.

(II.v.9–17)

Contrast, a central interest of Keats and Hazlitt in Shakespeare, is vital to such a passage, and other passages mark it as a principle particularly present in this play. Friar Lawrence's speech as he gathers weeds in his garden at dawn is side-marked (including the four lines describing the sunrise, now usually ascribed to Romeo) (II.ii.188–91 and II.iii.1–18), and his moralistic aside about this exercise is underlined:

And vice sometime's by action dignified.
Within the infant rind of this weak flower
Poison hath residence, and medicine power.

(II.iii.22–4)

Keats then shows interest in the Friar's greeting of Romeo:

What early tongue so sweet saluteth me?
Young son, it argues a distempered head
So soon to bid good morrow to thy bed.
Care keeps his watch in every old man's eye,
And where care lodges sleep will never lie;
But where unbruised youth with unstuff'd brain
Doth couch his limbs, there golden sleep doth reign.
Therefore thy earliness doth me assure
Thou art uprous'd with some distemp'rature.

(II.iii.32–40)

Again, the simultaneous awareness of youth and infirmity is important to the design and is one of the colourful and vital contrasts in the play.

One underlining by Keats may denote a central aspect of *Romeo and Juliet*, the depiction in its action and imagery of extreme states of feeling, 'intensity' described and conveyed:

But passion lends them power, time means, to meet,
Temp'ring extremities with extreme sweet.

(II. Prologue. 13–4)

Contrast is apparent in the images which Romeo chooses to use when his sight is first struck by the beauty of Juliet:

> ROMEO. What lady's that which doth enrich the hand of yonder
>   knight?
> SERVINGMAN. I know not, sir.
> ROMEO. O, she doth teach the torches to burn bright!
>   It seems she hangs upon the cheek of night
>   As a rich jewel in an Ethiop's ear –

(I.v.39–44)

And another speech, heavily marked by Keats, amplifies the idea of
extreme emotional states:

> Amen, amen! But come what sorrow can,
> It cannot countervail the exchange of joy
> That one short minute gives me in her sight.
> Do thou but close our hands with holy words,
> Then love-devouring death do what he dare;
> It is enough I may but call her mine.

(II.vi.3–8)

We are reminded of Keats's own injunction that 'the knowledge of con-
trast, the feeling for light and shade' is essential to the poet. Many of
the lines marked by Keats in the play exemplify this kind of 'know-
ledge' in Shakespeare himself. As the scene continues, the extremity
of joy in the young lovers is emphasized. First, the Friar describes it
from the outside, his rhythms holding a fragile weightlessness, as do
the images:

> O, so light a foot
> Will ne'er wear out the everlasting flint.
> A lover may bestride the gossamer
> That idles in the wanton summer air
> And yet not fall, so light is vanity.

(II.vi.16–20)

Next, Romeo describes the joy from the inside:

> Ah, Juliet, if the measure of thy joy
> Be heap'd like mine, and that thy skill be more
> To blazon it, then sweeten with thy breath
> This neighbour air, and let rich music's tongue
> Unfold the imagin'd happiness that both
> Receive in either by this dear encounter.

(II.vi.24–9)

With his markings on two separate parts of the text, Keats draws attention to the striking difference between the character of Tybalt and that of Romeo, and the quotations show that the contrast is built into the play. Keats marks with dashes down the side the first description of the 'fiery' Tybalt swinging his sword around his head (I.i.108–12), and with a combination of underlining and side-marking he picks out the juxtaposed picture painted by Benvolio of the love-sick pacifism of Romeo, stealing away from attending eyes by the sycamore grove at dawn (I.i.118–30). The last passage marked in this text draws the same contrast, with the dire consequences:

> PRINCE. Benvolio, who began this bloody fray?
> BENVOLIO. Tybalt, here slain, whom Romeo's hand did slay;
>   Romeo that spoke him fair, bid him bethink
>   How nice the quarrel was, and urg'd withal
>   Your high displeasure. All this, uttered
>   With gentle breath, calm look, knees humbly bow'd,
>   Could not take truce with the unruly spleen
>   Of Tybalt, deaf to peace, but that he tilts
>   With piercing steel at bold Mercutio's breast;
>   Who, all as hot, turns deadly point to point,
>   And, with a martial scorn, with one hand beats
>   Cold death aside and with the other sends
>   It back to Tybalt, whose dexterity
>   Retorts it. Romeo he cries aloud
>   'Hold, friends! friends, part!' and, swifter than his tongue,
>   His agile arm beats down their fatal points,
>   And 'twixt them rushes; underneath whose arm
>   An envious thrust from Tybalt hit the life
>   Of stout Mercutio; and then Tybalt fled;
>   But by and by comes back to Romeo,
>   Who had but newly entertain'd revenge,
>   And to't they go like lightning; for ere I
>   Could draw to part them was stout Tybalt slain;
>   And as he fell did Romeo turn and fly.

(III.i.147–71)

Keats, we remember, was to write, 'Though a quarrel in the streets is a thing to be hated, the energies displayed in it are fine; the commonest Man shows a grace in his quarrel',[25] and perhaps the 'quarrel' between Tybalt and Romeo was one of the literary examples he had in mind. The content of the description is violent and dismaying, but the speech is expressive in its energy and controlled rapidity. The sentence underlined is a poetically striking tableau of Mercutio's death.

When Keats marks single lines or words, he appears to be noticing Shakespeare's fertility of language and metaphor:

When the devout religion of mine eye   (I.ii.88)

That in gold clasps locks in the golden story   (I.iii.93)

But no more deep will endart mine eye   (I.iii.99)

Tickle the senseless rushes with their heels   (I.iv.36)

What man art thou, that, thus bescreen'd in night,
So stumblest on my counsel?   (II.ii.53)

Which to the high top-gallant of my joy   (II.iv.184)

Finally, there remains a slight puzzle in one other marking. When Mercutio is mocking 'fashion-mongers', Keats marks his final contemptuous phrase thus: 'O, their bonés, their bonés!' (II.iv.35) The explanation for the phrase is, as modern editors tell us in notes, that Mercutio is partly quibbling on the French 'bon', aping the dandyish affectations of the people he is condemning. The open question is whether Keats found this explanation in some editor's work, or thought of it himself. If the latter, which is quite possible since he obviously worked hard in order to find a meaning in difficult phrases, then he is showing again the acuteness of an editorial mind.

On this play in particular, we can imagine Keats being especially impressed by Hazlitt's commentary, for here the critic raises himself to a height of poetic rhapsody in defence of romantic love. His opening comments form an interesting link between the play and Keats's own poetry. First, in quoting Schlegel, Hazlitt gives us a description which could well be attached to the 'Nightingale' Ode:

It has been said of ROMEO AND JULIET by a great critic, that 'whatever is most intoxicating in the odour of a southern spring, languishing in the song of the nightingale, or voluptuous in the first opening of the rose, is to be found in this poem.' The description is true; and yet it does not answer to our idea of the play. For if it has the sweetness of the rose, it has its freshness too; if it has the languour of the nightingale's song, it has also its giddy transport; if it has the softness of a southern spring, it is as glowing and as bright.[26]

Such a statement, in its language and spirit, its references to the night-ingale, 'giddy transport' and 'a southern spring', would be irresistible to the writer of the 'Nightingale' Ode. (Perhaps in the phrase 'It has its freshness too' we find also an anticipation of Keats's 'To Autumn'.) Secondly, Hazlitt's analysis of the love between Romeo and Juliet may well have provided Keats with a set of aims which he was to realize in *The Eve of St Agnes*. Hazlitt is anxious to dispel the notion that there is anything 'sickly and sentimental' in the play (an important priority for Keats also in the *Eve*), and he uses his perception of the play to make a general philosophical point about the difference between inno-cence and experience:

> [Shakespear] has founded the passion of the two lovers not on the pleasures they had experienced, but on all the pleasures they had *not* experienced.[27]

This is the prelude to an attack upon 'the modern philosophy' (Wordsworth's in particular) 'which reduces the whole theory of the mind to habitual impressions, and leaves the natural impulses of pas-sion and imagination out of the action'. Quoting Wordsworth's 'Im-mortality' Ode, Hazlitt calls its backward-looking philosophy 'idle', and asserts,

> It is not from the knowledge of the past that the first impressions of things derive their gloss and splendour, but from our ignorance of the future, which fills the void to come with the warmth of our desires, with our gayest hopes, and brightest fancies... Desire and imagination are inmates of the human breast.[28]

A glance at the notes in Miriam Allott's edition of Keats's poetry reve-als the extent of verbal indebtedness in *The Eve of St Agnes* to *Romeo and Juliet*, and the overall atmosphere of the poem is suffused with the spirit of the play.[29] In addition, Hazlitt's comment allows us to iden-tify another point of contact. Keats has done his best to eliminate any-thing 'sickly and sentimental'[30] in his treatment of young love (some-thing which he felt he had not achieved in *Isabella*), and one might trace the final effect partly to the breathless speed of action, which the poem shares with *Romeo and Juliet* and partly to the absence of any nostalgia or hindsight knowledge in the narratorial voice. There are no *ex post facto* observations or philosophical reflections on the nature of love which could imply a Wordsworthian recollection. Instead, the tenses are often present or future, as a result of taking us into the con-sciousness of a character. Even in the first stanza, the mood shifts from the storyteller's preterite to the present of the beadsman 'while his prayer he saith'. Especially when we turn to Madeline, all is expectancy, apprehension and the 'visions of delight' that may occur in the evening, 'And all the bliss to be before tomorrow morn' (VIII). Hope and desire for impending, unknown pleasure mark the feelings of Madeline and Porphyro alike, just as Hazlitt says that 'passion, the love and expectation of pleasure' explains the intensity of feelings in *Romeo and Juliet*. The consummation of love in the *Eve* could equally well be described in the terms Hazlitt uses of *Romeo and Juliet*:

> The sense of pleasure precedes the love of pleasure, but with the sense of pleasure, as soon as it is felt, come thronging infinite desires and hopes of pleasure, and love is mature as soon as born.[31]

The remarkable quality in Keats's treatment of young love is its elimination of a range of tones such as regret or disappointment, or any point of view based on recollection which would detach the reader through jaded experience, wary cautiousness or self-indulgence from the full anticipation and robust genuineness of the lovers' feelings. These qualities he could have found in *Romeo and Juliet*, at least as interpreted by Hazlitt: 'The feelings of youth and of the spring are here blended together like the breath of opening flowers.'[32] The comment could apply as well to *The Eve of St Agnes* as to Shakespeare's play, and we recall the climactic lines of the poem:

> Into her dream he melted, as the rose
> Blendeth its odour with the violet, –
> Solution sweet.
>
> (XXXVI)

The great differences between the play and the poem, of course, lie in their respective endings. By choosing not to kill tragically his young lovers, Keats is perhaps being more consistent than Shakespeare to the inner vision as distinct from the generic convention. If the newly-awakened passion lies all in the future, as spring is the prelude to the rest of the year, then it is apt to send the lovers out into a harsh but challenging world of new experience, instead of celebrating any static quality in their feelings by seeing them die. If it is Juliet whom Keats would happily follow into Pandemonium, the ending of *The Eve of St Agnes* allows the reader similar scope for the imagination. Their initiation into love effected, Porphyro and Madeline face an unknown future together. Shakespeare may have been more faithful to the literary notion of *Liebestod* but paradoxically less realistic.

VII King Lear

We have already traced one of Keats's enthusiastic readings of *King Lear*, and it is no exaggeration to say that this play represented for him a momentous experience each time he read or thought about it. Its influence lies behind many of his meditations on poetic creativity and upon human suffering. The text in his Folio contains more markings of this play than any other, as well as several annotations (and a little picture-doodle!), and in addition Keats has marked and commented on Hazlitt's account of the play. Since we have at our disposal so much information about what Keats found significant in *King Lear*, it is a central example in our exploration of what interested him in Shakespearean drama in general. The markings on Keats's Folio copy of the play illustrate the kind of poetic 'intensity' so much admired by him, and give evidence for more detailed examination of one aspect of language in *King Lear* which the markings enable us to identify. Of fundamental interest is the way in which the play worked upon Keats's own creative mind, spurring him towards writing and thinking about poetry, and also enabling him to develop personal ideas on the nature of and justification for suffering in the mortal world.

Keats's markings of King Lear

In analysing Keats's markings on his text of *King Lear*, it is proper to make a couple of preliminary points. First, the Folio text does not represent the complete text of the play as we know it today in edited form, since it does not contain some one hundred lines which are found in the Quarto.[1] (In some other ways, the Folio is superior.) Keats would, however, have found the extra lines in his 'pocket' edition, and although this copy is unmarked, it is, as Caroline Spurgeon, says, well-thumbed.[2] Secondly, there is no reason or need to suppose that his markings of the Folio are the record of a single reading. For example, his dating of the words 'Poor Tom' (Oct. 4, 1818) is more than likely an isolated comment appended after the preliminary markings which may have been made in January 1818, when Keats wrote his Sonnet preparatory to a reading. When the Fool says, 'Shalt see thy other daughter will use thee kindly; for though she's as like this as a crab's like an apple, yet I can tell what I can tell' (I.v.13–15; Keats's underlinings). Keats, noticing that what the Fool is saying is that there is actually no moral difference between Goneril and Regan, ironically appends a phrase that comes from later in the play. He notes in the margin, 'Thy fifty yet doth double five and twenty' which comes at II.iv.258. (The two words underlined point to the pun on 'crab' and 'crabapple'.) Keats had either read the play before, or when he came to the second phrase he felt compelled to go back and compare it with the first. The problems raised by not knowing exactly when the markings were made need not, however, stand in the way of a critical evaluation. We may surmise that, whatever their provenance in time, they are in some sense a mature reflection of what Keats found interesting in the play.

Since the markings are more comprehensive than for many other plays, there is not much point in trying to be thorough in analysing them, nor in making speculations about why Keats marked any particular passage. On the other hand, a general description is revealing. For example, it can be said that although the markings are generally dense, yet they are also discriminating and show a selective mind. The first Act is some thousand lines long, yet Keats has marked fewer than four hundred, sometimes drawing attention to just a word or a phrase rather than a whole passage. The last Act is over four hundred lines, yet Keats has marked only seventy odd, of which thirty-five come in the last sixty lines. On the assumption that Keats is, generally speaking, drawn to the most poetically 'intense' portions, his ratio of markings in the last Act might be interpreted as confirmation of the judgment of some recent critics that the poetry just before the climax is relatively mediocre.[3] We might also conclude, on the basis of the evidence, that the most powerful and concentrated language in Keats's view comes on the heath before and after the storm in Acts III and IV, since here the markings are at their most frequent. Such a conclusion would probably accord with the general impression of most readers and audiences, and in this case we are enabled, as it were, to 'count' the quality.

With these qualifications, we can pick out some centres of interest dwelt upon by Keats. We shall, for the time being, leave aside the markings of individual words and phrases, to return to them later. In

Act I he has underlined the respective speeches made by Lear in savage indictment of two of his three daughters, as calls curses upon each. He shows early and continuing interest in the anger that erupts between Kent and the King and their reconciliation when Kent is in disguise, a strain which comes to a head as Kent sits in the stocks. Other markings in this Act are mainly of words and lines rather than passages, although Keats shows an interest in most of Edmund's speech on nature, side-marks Gloucester on astrology, and (as elsewhere) marks down the side most of the exchanges between Lear and the Fool. At this stage we can make a generalization which holds true throughout the play, that Keats's eye is constantly upon the language of King Lear himself. Act II builds up gradually in dramatic intensity, and Keats's markings reflect this judgment. The first three scenes are not much marked except for isolated words and phrases, and only three longer paragraphs are noticed. Kent's blunt attack on Cornwall is underlined (II.ii.69–74), and so is Cornwall's description of 'These kind of knaves' spoken in piqued response (II.ii.90–99). Edgar's decision to disguise himself as a Bedlam beggar is selectively marked, at the line 'The winds and persecutions of the sky' and then,

> Strike in their numb'd and mortified bare arms
> Pins, wooden pricks, nails, sprigs of rosemary;
> And with this horrible object, from low farms,
> Poor pelting villages, sheep-cotes, and mills,
> Sometimes with lunatic bans, sometime with prayers,
> Enforce their charity.
>
> (II.iii.15–20)

In happier tone, Kent's apostrophe to the sun which is about to rise attracts a mark:

> Approach, thou beacon to this under globe,
> That by thy comfortable beams I may
> Peruse this letter.   (II.ii.158–60)

After Lear's discovery of Kent in the stocks at the beginning of Scene iv, the pressure builds up in his arguments with his two daughters, and Keats underlines most of the scene until the storm breaks:

> STORM AND TEMPEST
> I have full cause of weeping; but this heart
> Shall break into a hundred thousand flaws
> Or ere I'll weep. O fool, I shall go mad!
>
> (II.iv.282–5)

There is a slight dramatic pause, as first Gloucester and then Kent and the Gentleman describe the stormy night and the King's high mood, and Keats marks just a few lines at a time.

From the opening of III.ii, with the entrance of the impassioned Lear defying the elements, Keats's markings are heavy and consistent, as if for him this is the most concentrated and powerful section of the play. He marks most of III.ii and all of III.iv. He does not mark Scenes iii and v, short interludes between Gloucester and Edmund back at the castle, and until the last episode of Act III just a few snatches are picked out for attention (although it should be pointed out that III.vi.17–55 are not in the Folio):

> LEAR. A king, a king!
> (III.vi.11)

> LEAR. To have a thousand with red burning spits
>   Come hissing in upon 'em –
> (III.vi.15–16)

> LEAR. The little dogs and all,
>   Tray, Blanch, and Sweetheart, see, they bark at me.
> (III.vi.61–2)

> LEAR. Then let them anatomize Regan; see what breeds about her heart. Is there any cause in nature that make these hard hearts? [To Edgar] You, sir, I entertain for one of my hundred; only I do not like the fashion of your garments. You will say they are Persian, but let them be chang'd.
> (III.vi.75–80)

In III.vii there are at first just two markings, both surprising insofar as they are side-issues to the main business of the scene, which is the blinding of Gloucester. The first is a vignette of the King:

> Some five or six and thirty of his knights,
> Hot questrists after him, met him at gate;
> Who...
> (III.vii.15–17)

Perhaps the marking indicates that Keats's attention is still upon the progress of Lear. The next phrase is Gloucester's graphic cry to Regan as she plucks his beard: 'You should not ruffle thus' (III.vii.40), and one presumes it is the vivid word which attracts his attention. It is surprising that Keats does not mark some striking phrases in this scene, such as 'corky arms', but his interest is firmly fixed upon the fortunes of Lear:

> REGAN. Wherefore to Dover?
> GLOUCESTER. Because I would not see thy cruel nails
> Pluck out his poor old eyes; nor thy fierce sister
> In his anointed flesh rash boarish fangs.
> The sea, with such a storm as his bare head
> In hell-black night endur'd, would have buoy'd up
> And quench'd the stelled fires.
> Yet, poor old heart, he holp the heavens to rain.
> If wolves had at thy gate howl'd that dern time,
> Thou shouldst have said 'Good porter, turn the key'.
> All cruels else subscribe, but I shall see
> The winged vengeance overtake such children.
>
> (III.vii.55–65)

The heavily marked phrase 'Yet, poor old heart' emphasizes the pathos of Lear's condition. Keats's only markings which relate to Gloucester's own predicament come at the end of the scene, when he underlines Gloucester's cry for help, side-marks the fatal intervention of the First Servant, and picks out the dismal cry, 'All dark and comfortless! Where's my son Edmund?' (III.vii.81–6). With his keen eye for poetry of the physical senses, Keats ends his marking of the Act with Regan's sneer:

> Go thrust him out at gates and let him smell
> His way to Dover.
>
> (III.vii.92–3)

It might be added here that there is more evidence later for Keats's interest in the Servant who sprang to Gloucester's aid, 'thrill'd with remorse', since he side-marks the account given by the Messenger to Albany of the incident at IV.ii.73–8.

The first five scenes of Act IV (Scene iii is not included in the Folio) attract Keats's pen only occasionally. He marks some of Edgar's and Gloucester's sententious observations (IV.i.1–9; 20–23; 47), and he pays exclamatory attention to one of these, as though Keats could himself feel a personal relevance in its sentiment:[4]

> As flies to wanton boys are we to th'gods –
> They kill us for their sport.
>
> (IV.i.37–8)

He underlines also Gloucester's brief description of Dover cliff (IV.i.74–7). There are two or three places where Keats shows a rare interest in the language of the 'evil' characters:

> GONERIL. ...
> <u>this kiss, if it durst speak,</u>
> <u>Would stretch thy spirits up into the air.</u>
> <u>Conceive, and fare thee well.</u>
> EDMUND. <u>Yours in the ranks of death.</u>
>   (IV.ii.22–5)

> GONERIL. <u>Milk-liver'd man!</u>
> That bear'st a cheek for blows, a head for wrongs.
>   (IV.ii.50–1)

In Scene iv Keats's hand returns heavily as Cordelia and the Doctor discuss the wild appearance and the condition of Lear (IV.iv.1–19), marked with a combination of underlining and side-marking). Scene vi presents a lengthy action in which the first two incidents, the 'suicide-attempt' by Gloucester on Dover Cliff, and the apparently incoherent speeches of Lear garlanded with flowers are very heavily marked. As we shall come to see, the former was very important to Keats. After Lear's exit, the text is left unmarked except for Gloucester's line, 'The bounty and the benison of heaven' (IV.vi.227), until Gloucester's grief-stricken outburst at the end of this scene:

> <u>The King is mad; how stiff is my vile sense,</u>
> <u>That I stand up, and have ingenious feeling</u>
> <u>Of my huge sorrows! Better I were distract;</u>
> <u>So should my thoughts be sever'd from my griefs,</u>
> <u>And woes by wrong imagination lose</u>
> <u>The knowledge of themselves.</u>
>   (IV.vi.279–84)

The final scene in Act IV is the moving reconciliation between Cordelia and Lear. Keats's interest quickens, as he underlines Cordelia's speeches at IV.vii.14–17; 27–9; 39–40, and he finishes the scene by marking virtually every line (45–85; the remaining twelve lines are not in his Folio).

The markings of Act V follow the pattern we have observed in the earlier sequences: a few sporadic and unsustained snatches, until the last hundred or so lines, beginning when Lear enters with his daughter in his arms (very heavily marked). The only passages of more than two lines marked by Keats in the section before this climax are Lear's speech beginning 'No, no, no, no! Come, let's away to prison...', together with the five lines before and the five after, which are side-marked (V.iii.4–23); and then the description by Edgar of his father's death:

> O our lives' sweetness,
> That we the pain of death would hourly die
> Rather than die at once! – taught me to shift
> Into a madman's rags, t'assume a semblance
> That very dogs disdain'd; and in this habit
> Met I my father with his bleeding rings,
> Their precious stones new lost; became his guide,
> Led him, begg'd for him, sav'd him from despair;
> ...
>   But his flaw'd heart –
> Alack, too weak the conflict to support! –
> 'Twixt two extremes of passion, joy and grief,
> Burst smilingly.
>   (V.iii.184–99)

From Lear's 'Howl' (V.iii.259) to the end of the play, Keats marks virtually all of Lear's own words, even down to the cryptic responses to Kent's revelation of his identity, 'You are welcome hither' and 'Ay, so I think'. The other lines marked in this section may be seen as comments upon the King. The first gives him a brief moment of restoration to the throne:

> ALBANY. ...
> What comfort to this great decay may come
> Shall be applied. For us, we will resign
> During the life of this old Majesty,
> To him our absolute power.
>   (V.iii.297–300)

The second is a plea for cessation of his sufferings:

> KENT. Vex not his ghost. O, let him pass! He hates him
> That would upon the rack of this tough world
> Stretch him out longer.
>   (V.iii.313–15)

Without presuming narrow intentions behind Keats's markings of *King Lear*, we can summarize their significance. First, the greatest concentration is upon Lear himself, his poetry of defiance and his suffering. This is consistent with Keats's note on Lear's character which we have already examined. Next, he shows greatest interest in other characters who are 'good': Cordelia (although she says little, virtually everything is noticed), the Fool (again, Keats marks most of what he says, and what is said about him), and to a lesser extent, Gloucester, Edgar and Kent. He does not show a lot of interest in the 'evil' people, perhaps because their poetry is not often arresting and perhaps also because he pays more attention to passages which blame the gods or a malign universe for the existence of suffering, rather than the malevolence of people.[5] Certain situations seem to interest Keats because they exhibit 'intensity' of one kind or another, and this concept we shall shortly explore. Finally, there is abundant evidence of what kinds of poetic language are most admired by Keats.

'Intensity'

In broadening the discussion into more general concerns, it is useful to quote once again a passage in one of Keats's letters which we have already looked at. It was written to his brothers, George and Tom, and is dated December 1817:

> I spent Friday evening with Wells & went the next morning to see *Death on the Pale horse*. It is a wonderful picture, when West's age is considered; but there is nothing to be intense upon; no women one feels mad to kiss; no face swelling into reality. the excellence of every Art is its intensity, capable of making all disagreeables evaporate, from their being in close relationship with Beauty & Truth – Examine King Lear & you will find this examplified throughout; but in this picture we have unpleasantness without any momentous depth of speculation excited, in which to bury its repulsiveness.[6]

It is clear that the reason Keats chooses to compare the picture with *Lear* is because they have something in common in their subject-matter: 'unpleasant' or 'repulsive' content. But whereas the play transcends its superficially disturbing subject, the painting does not, and the crucial element that makes the difference is 'intensity'. Nobody would hope or wish to pin down too rigorously the meanings of Keats's words such as 'intensity', 'beauty' and 'truth', since their magic lies in their range of resonances and connotations rather than any particular denoted meanings. It is quite possible that we feel we 'know what he means' without being able to use analytical language to explain it. We shall look soon at an example from the text but a few things may be said by way of preliminaries. 'Intensity' seems to be the process by which the reader (or perceiver) is irresistibly drawn into the life of the work of art, the point at which *its* reality becomes our own, and we are participating in its action with fully awakened feelings. Such a process allows us little scope for coolly judging the work whilst we are sharing its feeling-states, and 'depth of speculation' is merely awakened rather than answered. 'Beauty' and 'truth' are the keys to the process. By the former, Keats seems to mean sensuousness, the kind of tactile vividness which makes us 'mad to kiss' the representation of a woman. 'Truth' may be something like the recognizability of an imitation as existing in the same dimension of reality as the reader leads his own life, the quality that Aristotle in more sober language calls 'that which is probable' though not necessarily 'possible'. When the work of art is 'true' in Keats's sense, it is expressive of something which is made to be *important* to the perceiver in his own existence. 'Intensity' brings these qualities together in immediate forcefulness, a concentratedness which is the product of the active relationship between the reader and the work releasing and making real a potential. When such intensity occurs there are two consequences. First, the subject-matter is subservient to the immediate feeling excited, so that even the most unpleasant or disagreeable images lose their superficial ugliness. When represented by a great artist, a brick floor becomes an object of beauty (as Hazlitt points out in 'On Imitation') without losing naturalistic qualities. Secondly, just as our awareness of the surface literalism is suspended, so our moral faculties and our need to make judgments, are either subverted or suspended. The result is the arousal of a 'momentous depth of speculation', a grasp of the wonder involved in the existence of the thing, and its primary importance to us in the context.

Can such an aesthetic theory be exemplified from the evidence about Keats's reading of *King Lear*? Let us take an example, Keats's markings of the passage when Lear finds Kent in the stocks:

> LEAR. What's he that hath so much thy place mistook
>   To set thee here?
> KENT. It is both he and she,
>   Your son and daughter.
> LEAR. No.

KENT. Yes.
LEAR. No, I say.
KENT. I say, yea.
LEAR. No, no; they would not.
KENT. Yes, they have.
LEAR. By Jupiter, I swear, no!
KENT. By Juno, I swear, ay!
LEAR. They durst not do't;
    They could not, would not do't; 'tis worse than murder
    To do upon respect such violent outrage.

(II.iv.11–23)

Again, we cannot say why Keats marked such a passage so heavily, but we ought to be able to describe what a reader *might* find when his attention is directed to it. It is a useful example, since the exchange between Lear and Kent scarcely seems to merit inclusion in anthologies of the conventional 'beauties of Shakespeare'. Its interest must lie partly in the context itself. The 'argument' creates an intensity of feeling between the characters which may transfer itself to the reader or audience, and the intensity itself obscures partly the banality and faint ridiculousness of the content and language to create a powerful sense of the expenditure of emotional energy in violent cross-fire. This is not to deny that a roughly comic aspect can be present as well to the perceiver, even in the anger of the speakers. The source of such intensity might be located in what we have learned of the characters, and particularly Lear's irascibility, his furious impotence in the face of adversity, and his impetuous willingness to deny the facts around him in order to sustain his own illusions. Lear's crescendo of rage in such circumstances can be cited as an example of what Keats found in the character himself, in whom negative attributes are often invested with an energy that makes them positive in their force: 'self-will and pride and wrath are taken at a rebound...and mounted to the clouds...'. On the general notion that our recognition of repulsive events may be suspended in a moment of intensity, we might remember the famous statement made by Keats on another occasion:

> Though a quarrel in the streets is a thing to be hated, the energies displayed in it are fine; the commonest Man shows a grace in his quarrel – By a superior being our reasoning[s] may take the same tone – though erroneous they may be fine – This is the very thing in which consists poetry ...[7]

No matter how 'hateful' an event, the energy or 'intensity' of engagement which is displayed may give a 'grace' to impulsive action. By employing a language which is in some appropriate way forceful and sensuous (beautiful) in a manner that makes it recognizably human or mimetic (true), the poet can tap an area of amoral enjoyment and make even 'erroneous' ideas convincing, a phenomenon which is precisely what worried Hazlitt in *Coriolanus*.

The example quoted may be a small one, but it is by no means isolated. When we hear Lear's terrible curses upon his daughters, when we watch the blinding of Gloucester, and when we hear the howls of Lear in the last scene, we are in each case witnessing an event of appalling repulsiveness in subject-matter, but because of the powerful mode of expression employed by the dramatist, we are not allowed simply to reject the horror of the content. We are transfixed, suspending certain intellectual faculties, directly in touch with an intensity of feeling which is expressed in language conveying, enhancing and stimulating emotion. Here we may even have a Keatsian version of 'catharsis', an explanation for the strange fact that, for all its brutality, the play is not completely depressing to Keats, but unnervingly exhilarating. Out of such an experience is aroused 'depth of speculation', since our thinking about the subject-matter and the moral issues must proceed from the participation in events which impress upon us a sense that they are immediately important to our personal understandings of the world. It is this general theory that allows Keats to go on in his letter to say, 'that with a great poet the sense of Beauty overcomes every other consideration, or rather obliterates all consideration'.[8] It allows him to say elsewhere of the poetic character that 'It has as much delight in conceiving an Iago as an Imogen. What shocks the virtuous philosopher, delights the camelion Poet'.[9] It explains why Keats as a reader marks with apparently equal attentiveness the beautiful words of reconciliation between Lear and Cordelia, full of understatement and tenderness, and also the defiantly unsociable prayer by Edmund to the laws of bastardy, and passages in the scene of Gloucester's blinding.

However, as I argued when speaking of Hazlitt's influence on Keats, 'intensity' does not always remain in the poet's mind as a purely aesthetic matter which excludes moral considerations from writing and reading. 'Speculation' came to take on greater importance for him. Five months after the letter mentioning West's painting, Keats reaches beyond the instantaneous intensity of poetry, to its usefulness and dangers. 'Knowledge' can inform and broaden the reader's response to poetry and at the same time the poetry itself can expand knowledge and understanding of painful experiences:

> An extensive knowlege is needful to thinking people – it takes away the heat and fever; and helps, by widening speculation, to ease the Burden of the Mystery: a thing I begin to understand a little ...[10]

The phrase 'the Burden of the Mystery' is taken from Wordsworth whom Keats has been reading, but behind both poets lie King Lear's words as he hopes with Cordelia to 'take upon's the mystery of things' (V.iii.16; Keats's underlining).[11] It is no coincidence that at the time Keats was working on *The Fall of Hyperion* in which the moral utility of poetry, and the responsibilities it confers on the creator, are presented as more important than intensity of effect. Moneta gives the poet a power 'of enormous ken, To see as a God sees'.[12] Keats is speaking of a desire to widen speculation rather than be arrested by the moment, and again *Lear* is a part of his thinking. Knowledge is seen as providing a set of checks and balances which hold the 'heat and fever' of intensity under control, and leads to an exercise of the thinking power over simple sensations. Keats makes clear that he is not contradicting his earlier statements but telling us how one can cope with the power of sensation and intensity as primary responses, without losing one's bearings:

> The difference of high Sensations with and without knowledge appears to me this – in the latter case we are falling continually ten thousand fathoms deep and being blown up again without wings and with all [the] horror of a bare shoulderd Creature – in the former case, our shoulders are fledge[d], and we go thro' the same air and space without fear.[13]

Informing Keats's 'bare shoulderd Creature' is Lear's 'Poor, bare forked animal', at the mercy of the elements, but with 'knowledge' to interpret the 'sensations' he may maintain control and balance.

Keats goes on characteristically to test the axioms of philosophy on the pulses of his feelings, this time by comparing Milton and Wordsworth, but again Shakespeare is not far behind. His axiom is that suffering and wisdom are intrinsically related:

> Until we are sick, we understand not; – in fine, as Byron says, 'Knowledge is Sorrow', and I go on to say that 'Sorrow is Wisdom' – and further for aught we can know for certainty! 'Wisdom is folly'...[14]

The phrase 'folly is wisdom', if not Keats's variation, is as old as Eras-
mus's *Praise of Fools* but the particular cluster of thoughts and lan-
guage (knowledge/sorrow/wisdom) which we have seen to be
associated with *King Lear* in Keats's mind, inevitably points to Lear's
'wise fool'. The playful, paradoxical tone of the letter disguises a seri-
ous association. It is clear from his markings of the play that Keats
pays consistent attention to the words of Shakespeare's Fool. He side-
marks almost all the character's lines, and underscores comments
about him:

> Since my young lady's going into France, sir, the Fool hath much
> pined away. (I.iv.72)

> KENT. But who is with him?
> GENTLEMAN. None but the fool; who labours to out-jest
>   His heart-struck injuries.
>
>   (III.i.14–16)

Keats shows his serious appraisal of the Fool's role by annotating
Hazlitt's superficial reference to the character's 'well-timed levity'.
Keats writes,

> This is almost the last observation from Mr. Hazlitt. And is it really
> thus? Or as it has appeared to me! Does not the Fool by his very lev-
> ity – nay it is not levity – give a finishing touch to the pathos;
> making what without him would be within our heart-reach nearly
> unfathomable. The Fool's words are merely the simplest transla-
> tion of Poetry as high as Lears.

> > 'Since my young Ladies going into France
> > Sir, the Fool hath pined away.'

The word which springs to mind, once again, is 'intensity'. Hazlitt
goes further in his paragraph, acknowledging that the Fool 'carries
pathos to the highest pitch of which it is capable', and Keats is forced
to retract some of his criticism: 'Aye, this is it – most likely H. is right
throughout. Yet is there not a little contradiction?' Keats had thought
deeply upon the Fool, he values him dearly, and he recognizes the
important function of the character. Given the association of ideas and
words which *King Lear* often provokes in his mind, it is quite likely
that the phrase 'wisdom is folly' is prompted by a memory of the Fool
in *Lear* (and as we have seen, *Hamlet*). If so, it provides us with a sur-
prisingly modern insight, for even Coleridge, although admiring the
'wonderful' creation of the 'inspired idiot', tends to emphasize the

contrast between the King and the Fool rather than their closeness.[15] It is clear at least that the role of the Fool manifests 'intensity' to Keats, in his private meaning of the word.

At one point, Keats comes close to making an explicit statement about the different kinds of intensity encountered in *King Lear*, by implicitly drawing a distinction between the 'high' poetry and more peripheral but still functional passages. He scribbles beside II.i.94–7 the following brief observation:

x This bye-writing is more marvellous than the whole ripped up contents of Pernambuca or any buca whatever – on the earth or in the waters under the earth –

This is not merely uncritical panegyric of Shakespeare's writing, for the notion of 'bye-writing' introduces an analytical note. The passage to which the note is attached is a 'by-the-way' discussion about Edgar:

x REGAN. Was he not companion with the riotous knights
     That tended upon my father?
GLOUCESTER. I know not, madam. 'Tis too bad, too bad.
EDMUND. Yes, madam, he was of that consort.
                              (II.i.94–7)

Why should such an insignificant snatch be so 'marvellous'? We can only guess, but perhaps the passage displays a different kind of 'intensity', showing the remarkable capacity of Shakespeare's imagination to work on several levels of interest simultaneously, as he weaves the fabric of a closely observed verisimilitude.[16] Each comment is exactly true of the typical tone of each character: Regan's dismissive petulance, Gloucester's distraction and confusion, Edmund's cryptic, political opportunism. It shows that Shakespeare has not forgotten his other 'bye-writing' when Lear invited Poor Tom to join his men, and the recollection adds to the sense that we are observing a closely-knit, self-sufficient world, created by attention to verisimilitude in points of detail. Although apparently gratuitous, the conversation 'fits' the overall world of the play, and demonstrates Shakespeare's control over the detail of his work. Keats continually points us towards darting details which give flesh to the bones in Shakespeare's writing, adding a dimension of life-likeness to the central plot. It is something that Keats himself strove to do in his poetry, and when he was to advise Shelley to 'load every rift with ore' we sense that he is speaking primarily of his own poetic priorities. He is as careful to give 'intensity' to the 'bye-writing' of his own poems, as Shakespeare is in his plays. Hazlitt sums up the matter:

> Shakespear's mastery over his subject, if it was not art, was owing
> to a knowledge of the connecting links of the passions, and their
> effect upon the mind, still more wonderful than any systematic
> adherence to rules …[17]

Another note which Keats writes beside a passage in Hazlitt's
Characters further explains the poet's understanding of intensity in
poetry, and tells us more of his conception of composition. Hazlitt
writes the following words and Keats signals his interest by placing
two crosses beside them, and underscoring:

> XX That the greatest strength of genius is shewn in describing
> the strongest passions: for the power of the imagination, in
> works of invention must be in proportion to the force of the
> natural impressions, which are the subject of them.[18]

This is one of the four things which 'struck' Hazlitt in reading *Lear*.
Keats's comment is not simply a paraphrase, for it adds something of
his own preoccupations, and is expressed in his own unique language:

> If we compare the Passions to different tons and hogsheads of wine
> in a vast cellar – thus it is – the poet by one cup should know the
> scope of any particular wine without getting intoxicated – this is the
> highest exertion of Power, and the next step is to paint from
> memory of gone self storm.

We have already heard Keats speaking of the 'burgundy mark' that
distinguishes each identity from others, and here he is applying the
same metaphor to the quality of individual, intense experiences. The
nature and power of a feeling can be 'tasted' in the same way as wine,
by experiencing a small quantity. The sip will be just as potent, but not
as intoxicating, as a larger amount. In this way the writer may under-
stand many states of feeling without losing his artistic control, and
then he may write from the knowledge of many intensities. Keats's
final phrase, 'the memory of gone self storm' is perhaps his own cryp-
tic version of Wordsworth's 'emotion recollected in tranquillity'. It
links up with many of his central priorities: the need to experience
things on the pulses with maximum intensity, the need to counteract
the powerful effect of such feelings with the exercise of 'disinterested-
ness', and the need to build up and apply a body of 'knowledge' in
order to find and write from a centre of stability which will control the
fluctuations of the emotions. As a whole, the passage illustrates

Keats's consistency of thought and his adeptness at using other ideas – in this case Hazlitt's and indirectly Shakespeare's – to develop his own. Once again, it is the particular 'intensity' of *King Lear* which generates the train of thought.

Language

It would be time-consuming and not especially profitable to examine the linguistic detail of longer passages marked by Keats in his copy of *King Lear*. However, a presentation of the isolated words and phrases singled out helps us to understand both Keats's taste in language and also something of the unique idiom of the play. For example, he locates compound epithets which occur with great frequency in *Lear*:

'ear-bussing arguments' (II.i.9)[19]

'threading dark-ey'd night' (II.i.119)

action-taking...one-trunk-inheriting slave (II.ii.13–15)

'Alack, bare-headed' (III.ii.60)

'Milk-liver'd man!' (IV.ii.50)

'...this child-changed father!' (IV.vii.17)

'A most toad-spotted traitor' (V.iii.138)

Keats himself was to invent such compound adjectives himself, and judging from the evidence amassed by A.D. Atkinson[20] this aspect of his poetry seems to be something of a distinguishing mark of the young poet. It would of course be dangerous to conclude that Keats found the device in *King Lear* since it is used (although less frequently) in other plays by Shakespeare, but it is certain that his ear was attuned to spotting its recurrence, and that his markings guide us to one element which contributes to the verbal inventiveness in the play.

The great advantage of the compound epithet is its capacity for energetic compression, cramming several words together to form a single, compound idea. The same tendency towards packed, cryptic compression marks other words noticed by Keats for their isolated uniqueness. These, for example, are technically nouns used in a verbal sense:

Hath rivall'd for our daughter (I.i.191)

... stranger'd with our oath (I.i.204)

That monsters it (I.i.220)

A little to disquantity your train (I.iv.248)

elf all my hairs in knots (II.ii.10)

His nighted life (IV.v.13)

Such usages enable Shakespeare to express in a concise, active voice what would otherwise have to be presented in a longer, passive construction. Again, the effect is one of dense compression, many jets of verbal energy which contribute to the 'intensity' of the play as a whole. The language of *Lear* has an idiosyncratic vitality, as meaning expressed forcefully breaks the rules of orthodox syntax. It is certainly an aspect which invites the craftsman's eye of Keats. Ironically, it is precisely this linguistic trick in Keats's own poetry which is singled out for a special ridicule and condemnation by an unsympathetic reviewer. Apparently unaware of the Shakespearean example (in fact, blaming Leigh Hunt's bad influence), John Croker in the *Quarterly* attacks Keats's habits of 'verbalizing' nouns, of inventing compound epithets and coining neologisms, all of which find ample precedent in *King Lear*.[21]

As an extension of such verbal effects, we find in *Lear* many sentences and phrases which manage somehow to live beyond their means, creating memorable richness and expressiveness by the most poverty-stricken methods out of monosyllabic plainness and thrift. Here are some picked out by Keats's pen:

The quality of nothing (I.ii.33)

Ho? I think the world's asleep (I.iv.47)

Are you our daughter? (I.iv.217)

I know his heart (I.iv.331)

O me, my heart, my rising heart! But, down. (II.iv.119)

Who put my man i'th'stocks? (II.iv.181)

Is this well spoken? (II.iv.235)

I gave you all. (II.iv.249)

Let me alone. (III.iv.3)

Wilt break my heart? (III.iv.4)

A king, a king! (III.vi.11)

It is partly the context and partly the economy of language which account for the power of such snatches, and again Keats's notion of intensity is relevant. More recent, analytical studies (and particularly deconstructionist readings) may explain what is happening linguistically, but Keats as a fellow poet has already noticed and intuitively understood the special verbal texture of *King Lear*. Of course, his alertness to certain kinds of linguistic inventiveness in the play tells us primarily about his own tastes and interests, and more detailed studies would certainly illuminate his own poetry. However, the evidence of his choices of 'fine phrases' can also sharpen our own perceptions into potential in the language of the play which we may not fully have noticed. Keats is the one who like Lear says 'Look there, look there!' and he acts as a discriminating but unassertive guide for us, for when we look we find many details that we had never bothered to focus upon. His eye roams from the blunt and pithy to the rhetorical flourishes from characters whose phrases often proclaim their falseness by their verbal conspicuousness. By following his guidance, we must share something of Keats's inwardness with the 'hieroglyphic visnomy' of the play's surface as well as finding new insights of our own. Broadly speaking, Keats leads us to recognize *King Lear* as a play marked by action, energy and spontaneous outbursts rather than introspection or sustained reflectiveness. In terms of its language, it is a verbal play in the active voice, a model of 'intensity'.

King Lear *and Keats's creativity*

Early in his poetic career, Keats has a premonition that Shakespeare will somehow be accompanying and helping him along the path to come. It is an understandable feeling, since during early 1817 he was voraciously reading the plays. In particular, the scene between Edgar and Gloucester on Dover Cliff haunts him. He begins a letter to Haydon on 10 May 1817 by quoting the first seven lines of *Love's Labour's Lost*, a clarion call to 'Fame' which he knew would appeal to his egotistical correspondent. He then goes on to speak of his own poetry, swinging from a feeling of inadequacy to one of renewed confidence:

> ... truth is I have been in such a state of Mind as to read over my Lines and hate them. I am "one that gathers Samphire dreadful trade" the Cliff of Poesy Towers above me – yet when, Tom who meets with some of Pope's Homer in Plutarch's Lives reads some of

those to me they seem like Mice to mine. I read and write about eight hours a day ... Thank God! I do begin arduously where I leave off, notwithstanding occasional depressions: and I hope for the support of a High Power while I clime this little eminence and especially in my Years of more momentous Labor. I remember your saying that you had notions of a good Genius presiding over you – I have of late had the same thought. for things which [I] do half at Random are afterwards confirmed by my judgment in a dozen features of Propriety – Is it too daring to Fancy Shakspeare this Presider?[22]

The allusions are to the following lines in IV.vi of *King Lear* (Keats marks the former but not the latter):

> Half-way down
> Hangs one that gathers samphire – dreadful trade!
> Methinks he seems no bigger than his head.
> The fishermen that walk upon the beach
> Appear like mice.
>
> (IV.vi.14–18)

GLOUCESTER. When shall I come to th'top of that same hill?
EDGAR. You do climb up it now. Look how we labour.

(IV.vi.1–2)

There are several things to remark upon in Keats's statement. First, in a cryptic way he locates perhaps the most mysterious aspect of imaginative creation: the poet writes 'half at Random' yet afterwards the details are seen to have 'a dozen features of Propriety' that can be recognized and analysed by the logical mind. Perhaps Keats had already read Hazlitt's remarks about Shakespeare's 'knowledge of the connecting links of the passions ... still more wonderful than any systematic adherence to rules', but it is equally the quality of Shakespeare praised by critics of all generations in their own languages. The neoclassical critics praised the dramatist's truth to 'nature' in which, as science has always confirmed, once we discover one pattern of order, many others follow as a consequence. Even twentieth-century analysis of items of language, style, imagery, plot and so on, is often engaged in confirming the unexpected 'propriety' of detail on several levels.

It is remarkable also that Keats's conception of composition, where imaginative links are formed between ideas in an almost instinctive way, can be applied even to the letter itself for it has its own imaginative propriety. Seeking to express his thoughts on the related subjects of poetry, Keats finds, apparently accidentally, the scene in Shakespeare which is perfectly inward with creativity itself. The scene on Dover Cliff, whatever else may be said about it, is a sublime example of the power of the poet's imagination to create a landscape full of palpably perceived detail, using nothing at all but words and sounds. Edgar's spellbinding descriptions, first from the top of the cliff and then from its base, belie the evidence of the senses left to Gloucester and allow the audience to transcend the ocular proof of a flat, bare stage. We are even tricked into wondering whether Edgar is really playing a trick on his father or not, so convincingly is the landscape conjured up. By utilizing the language of the senses and acting as the eyes for a blind man, Edgar teases us out of the literalism of the reasoning power. In a virtually literal sense beauty *is* truth, for there is nothing else. Such an example is profoundly important to Keats's poetic development. Each of his great Odes works its own spell in a similar way: by supplying light where there is no light but only sound, he creates the 'Nightingale' Ode; by supplying movement where there is stasis he creates the 'Grecian Urn'. Just as the function of Edgar's verbal trick is to restore Gloucester's faith in living on, so its wider function is to compel faith in the power of poetry to create something which is not physically before the eyes of the audience – a primary aim of much dramatic poetry. Keats's use of the allusion is beautifully apt. At this point, we unearth another 'propriety' in his choice. The poet is, metaphorically at least, leading a blind man up a hill, just as Shakespeare, again metaphorically, is leading the young, faltering poet up the little eminence of Poesy. Keats feels there is something as guided and involuntary about his own progress as about Gloucester's.

The other allusion made by Keats is to the 'one that gathers samphire, dreadful trade!' Even in its context this image has an oddly tantalizing quality. Its very irrevelance to the situation in which Gloucester wishes to commit suicide and his son prevents him, gives a strange conspicuousness to the figure halfway down the 'cliff' (it is, we must remember 'all in the mind'). Perhaps in the context he has a symbolic function, as one whose strength is to hang on between life and death, despair and hope. Perhaps also, the figure of the samphire-picker gives us an intimate, Breughelesque vignette of ordinary, diurnal existence as a poor man pursues diligently his hazardous and humble trade. If so, the moment is similar in quality of perception to the glimpse of servants applying flax and egg-whites to Gloucester's bleeding eyes, or the common humanity shown to Gloucester by the old man who is his tenant and wishes to help his blinded landlord – moments of warm, common decency against which is set the fierce dispute of royalty. Such a feeling is intensified by our knowledge that 'above' him (in many senses of the word) high-born characters are playing out a profound spiritual struggle. Whatever private significance a reader may find in the samphire-gatherer, Keats adds his own dimension of meaning. By likening the lonely figure to the poet, he is being at his most Romantic, finding an image for himself which is comparable to Wordsworth's leech-gatherer:

> He told, that to these waters he had come
> To gather leeches, being old and poor:
> Employment hazardous and wearisome![23]

In the introduction of the samphire-gatherer into Keats's train of thought, as in the introduction of the leech-gatherer into Wordsworth's poem, the figure enters the poet's landscape at a point of change from despair to hope, a moment of hanging on to the possibilities in life however modest, rather than submitting to despondence and gloom. It is the point which Gloucester has reached with Edgar's aid. Finally, in imagining himself to be the samphire-gatherer in his own poetic enterprise, Keats is commenting on the poet's position. He is adopting the climber's point of view, looking up to see the cliff of poesy towering above him, and looking down to see the mice which are Pope's poems. Poetry itself, Keats implies, is a dangerous, 'dreadful' trade, for the poet must cling to his own perceptions which may come as rarely and with as much preciousness as samphire or leeches (both associated with healing). Shakespeare's imagined gatherer is given no interior life, and he pursues his task oblivious of things around, but once we have seen him from Keats's perspective the idea of his life does not easily leave us.

Edgar's confidence in his word-power is a liberating influence upon Keats himself. A single, simple line from *Lear* acts as a stimulus, triggering his own creative freedom. He slightly misquotes Edgar's line, 'Hark, do you hear the sea?' to which Gloucester replies 'No, truly' (IV.vi.3–4), and turns it into a whimsical question to an absent correspondent:

> From want of regular rest, I have been rather *narvus* – and the passage in Lear – 'Do you not hear the Sea?' – has haunted me intensely.

On the Sea.

> It keeps eternal Whisperings around
> Desolate shores, and with its mighty swell
> Gluts twice ten thousand Caverns; till the spell
> Of Hecate leaves them their old shadowy sound.[24]

And the beautiful sonnet unfolds itself, according to its own internal, rhythmic laws, laced with delicate half-echoes, never fully present, from Shakespeare's own sea-music scattered through his plays and sonnets. Keats's poem weaves us into the 'spell' of the sea's presence, and like Edgar's descriptions it evokes an imaginary landscape, this time based on sound. Poetry creates a spell, 'Until ye start as if the Sea Nymphs quired –'. To be rather bluntly literal for a moment, it can be noticed that it is not only the memory of the Shakespearean line which is haunting Keats at this time. The memory also has a stimulus, the sea itself, for Keats is staying on the coast at the Isle of Wight:

> ... beautiful green Hedges along their steps down to the sands. –
> But the sea, Jack, the sea – the little waterfall – then the white cliff
> – ...

We need go no further than the white cliff to see where the association with *Lear* comes from. But for our purposes, and as far as Keats will divulge, it is Shakespeare's line which has inspired the later poet towards his own creativity, 'once again'.

King Lear *as consolation*

We may turn now to the general ideas which Keats appears to have associated with *King Lear* and from which he forged many of his own attitudes to life. These we may roughly call moral considerations[25] in order to distinguish them from the more aesthetic concerns which have so far occupied us. The outlines of the issues have already been sketched in the first chapter, but we may now say more.

Although Keats is so saturated in *King Lear* that the overt references to the play may be few, yet amongst unobtrusive echoes lies proof of its presence as part of the web of his own thinking. These echoes are invariably present when he is considering the great problem, 'Why suffering?' In a fairly late, and very long letter of February – April 1819 written to his brother and sister-in-law in America, Keats returns after many attempts to the problem and develops his ideas further. By this time of his life the allusions to Shakespeare are few and far between, and he seems to have outgrown his buoyant idolatry of 1817, when it had appeared that Shakespeare could always sum things up in more sovereign fashion than himself. For this reason, by 1819 even a single, isolated quotation carries great weight as the distilled residuum of what Keats's memory retains as important to his own experience. Now he is directly confronting the problem of suffering, without celebrating the palliative or cathartic effects of poetry and drama. He is no longer the 'dreamer' but a realist. He attempts to create a personal mythology which will develop and fortify his idea that during a lifetime a human being is travelling through a 'Vale of Soul-making'. He is returning again to Hamlet's question, how man is to cope with 'a sea of troubles', and this is a question which, for Keats, is implicitly raised by the whole action of *King Lear*. As on other occasions, his personal thoughts on suffering are closely identified with the play, and this time the specific prompt for his thoughts comes in the words of Lear in III.iv. on the heath, at a moment of moral lucidity:

> Is man no more than this? Consider him well. Thou ow'st the worm no silk, the beast no hide, the sheep no wool, the cat no perfume. Ha! here's three on's are sophisticated! Thou art the thing itself: unaccommodated man is no more but such a poor, bare, forked animal as thou art. (III.iv.102–6)

The implication which Keats works upon is that for people in general, as for Edgar stripped almost naked, suffering is unavoidable and an intrinsic part of his element, a proof of vulnerability.

Keats argues that the nature of the world, and the existence of mortality itself, will not admit 'perfectibility':

> the inhabitants of the world will correspond to itself – Let the fish philosophise the ice away from the Rivers in winter time and they shall be at continual play in the tepid delight of summer.[26]

Although a poem like 'To Autumn' attempts to do just this, to philosophize away the rigours of winter by using the image of the migrating swallows, yet even in the Ode there is a sense that it cannot rationally be done because the human observer remains with his wider perspective. It is as impossible for man to ignore discomforts when they come as for a fish to ignore the ice in winter. Keats speculates that one possible justification for adversity may be that it exists for the purpose of training the soul as it develops into an identity from the elements of the intelligence and the emotions. 'Negative capability' might develop from something self-delighting into a comprehensive and painful sympathy and understanding. Discomforts and suffering are imposed from outside the identity and they work upon it, moulding it and acting as agents for 'soul-making'. Keats is thinking for himself in this letter, and his tone is one of relentless sombreness, but as so often it is Shakespeare who opens the debate:

> The whole appears to resolve into this – that Man is originally 'a poor forked creature' subject to the same mischances as the beasts of the forest, destined to hardships and disquietude of some kind or other. If he improves by degrees his bodily accomodations and comforts – at each stage, at each accent [*for* ascent?] there are waiting for him a fresh set of annoyances – he is mortal and there is still a heaven with its Stars abov[e] his head.[27]

As we have seen, Keats is here conflating two Shakespearean passages, the one from *King Lear* and the other spoken by the Duke in *Measure for Measure*:

> ... Thou art not noble;
> For all th'accommodations that thou bear'st
> Are nurs'd by baseness. Thou'rt by no means valiant;
> For thou dost fear the soft and tender fork
> Of a poor worm.
> (*Measure for Measure*, III.i.13–17; Keats's markings)

The association between the two passages is partly verbal, picking up the words 'accommodations' and 'fork' used by Lear and by the Duke straight after the pertinent phrase 'Servile to all the skyey influences'. But the association lies also in the respective contents, since both passages stress man's helpless vulnerability and mortality. The more resonant connection is with *Lear*. Keats's development of thought, like the words of Lear, depict a recurrent pattern informing a play which systematically destroys every glimmer of hope. Every illusion or wish that happiness is just around the corner is dashed with a reminder that all is dark and comfortless. Words like 'affliction' occur again and again, as a mockery of the vanity of human wishes. As in Keats's passage so in *Lear* the very stars above seem to the characters to be malign, indifferent or simply another illusion to beckon towards hope. The 'gods' exist in the play only as yet another assertion of man's mortal confines. If the word Keats intended to use is indeed 'ascent', then we may have another association, this time with the despairing Gloucester toiling up what he is told as part of the illusion is a steep hill. In short, Keats through an allusion, as so often linking us imaginatively with more general patterns, guides us towards an interpretation of the play.

However, Keats turns despair itself into energy and hope, by finding some justification for the suffering in *Lear* and in life. Working from the ubiquitous presence of the play in his thinking, we might suggest that it is the experience of *King Lear* itself which may act for the receptive reader as a 'vale of soul-making', helping to shape identity into a new understanding. The play provides both the origin and proof of the general idea, in a way that life itself, lacking the structuring, concentration and repeatability of a work of art, can do only partially. Full of unmitigated suffering and submission to pain, *King Lear* schools the soul towards a modified, more integrated knowledge of human limitations and human potential. However, by now placing the emphasis upon the hardship rather than the fulfilment, Keats is perhaps recording a more bleak and embattled response to a play which, more than a year before, he had celebrated in verse for its capacity to provide 'new Phoenix wings' of hope. *King Lear* seems now to represent for him less an exhilarating challenge leading to renewed optimism, and more a hard-won, modest form of consolation for the existence of discomfort, suffering and death. We still learn from the play, it may still change us, but the lesson is more sobering. Keats has not changed his thoughts on the play, but developed them, as if he has passed as he hoped from the chamber of maiden-thought into the dark passages. In doing so he confirms the experience of every reader that a great and rich work of art may hold different but closely related significances at different times in a person's life. The point will be confirmed later when we come to examine *The Fall of Hyperion*. *King Lear*, freshly re-encountered by Keats during his life, has a potent influence upon his development as poet and thinker. Our analysis, which has been forced by Keats's modes of expression to blur distinctions between 'source' and 'influence', between art and life, and even between Keats's understanding of Shakespeare and what he helps the critic to discover independently, adds up to a confirmation of an interesting, general point made by Jack Stillinger:

Keats's notions about poetry got more complicated as he rapidly grew up in the course of a very short career; serious worries about human life began to intrude on and conflict with esthetic theory; and by the time he entered on his best period of creativity, beginning with 'The Eve of St Agnes' in January 1819, he was writing much more concentratedly about life than about poetry or art. Art of course still figures frequently in his major poems, but it is now most often art as a hypothetical alternative to life.[28]

It is impossible to make clearcut distinctions because Keats's commitment to 'life', his withdrawal from 'art', is itself a process partly built up by deepening reassessment of works of art themselves, and preeminently *King Lear*.

VIII Keats and tragedy

Keats's relationship with any literary text he happened to be reading was one based on qualities of receptivity and creativity. Attempting to co-operate with the spirit of the text, he would by temperament rather than by effort retain an openness of mind that borders on self-annihilation, a consequence of exercising 'negative capability'. He wished to experience the work intensely, without imposing his own demands or preconceptions. However, we have observed that even such a sensitively open reader as Keats did indeed have centres of interest which made him particularly susceptible to recognizing certain effects in Shakespeare's poetry. It is his acknowledgement of such tastes which allows him to build into his philosophy of reading and thinking a vital component of creativity, by which the act of reading gives him the material for individual composition and self-creation. He uses the twigs and branches of others' words and ideas as the points upon which he, like the spider, will weave his own unique web.[1] The relationship is in no way parasitic, but rather it involves a mutual exploration in which both reader and text contribute equally, the one actualizing a potential in the other, whilst keeping a tactful distance from each other. To some extent I have tried to maintain a similar relationship towards the material of this book, reconciling a discreet distance which will allow the subjects to speak through their own words, with a necessarily coercive, interpretative need to shape the ideas and draw a general significance from them. The intention has been to show some of the 'fine things' which Keats found, first through Hazlitt and then more directly in Shakespeare, while he remained impressionable. Inevitably, the opportunity has often been taken to glance at the possible uses Keats himself made of what he found, when he came to write his own poetry. At this point, it should be possible to switch our attention more centrally to Keats himself, and observe his own struggle towards poetic self-discovery. His thoughts on the nature of tragedy in poetry and in human existence were forged partly through the practice he found in Shakespeare's tragedies, but they also involve much that was special in his own feelings and experiences. To this extent Keats's views on tragedy will be different from Shakespeare's, although they are intimately related.

Even if we cannot say with certainty that Keats discovered an understanding of tragedy in its literary form through reading Shakespeare, at least he found confirmation in the dramatist's works of his own belief in certain essentials. Some of these have been amply illustrated in the course of this book: intensity of feeling expressed through language which is powerful in its context, selfless participation in the physical and mental sufferings of others, and above all a grasp of contrast between 'light and shade' and between different modes of feeling. Such contrast is equally observable in the comedies, where Keats discovers moments of melancholy, and it is clear from his comments and practice of marking that he would not see comedy and tragedy as exclusive categories. This complementarity of mood is just as important to the Odes in which dark touches tinge a golden world of the imagination, as in the whole enterprise of *Isabella*, in ways that we shall analyse. We shall examine Keats's own presentation of tragedy, first as an aesthetic principle in his tragedy of love, *Isabella*, then in his dramatic tragedy, *Otho the Great*, and finally in his most direct confrontation with the nature and purpose of tragedy as a mode of perceiving, in *The Fall of Hyperion*.

Isabella; or The Pot of Basil is a relentless attempt to raise in a narrative the Aristotelian tragic feelings of pity and fear, but in a context which draws upon romantic comedy as well as tragedy. Like *Romeo and Juliet*, the poem deals with the tragic waste of young love, threatened first by the murderous actions of a vindictive family and secondly by the heroine's self-destructive grief. I do not wish to judge the quality of the poem, but simply to understand it in its own terms, although I can say that I believe the poem to be better than most critics admit. The fact that Keats gave himself the worst possible press by seeing the work as too 'smokeable'[2] should not be used as an excuse for critics in self-congratulatory fashion to dismiss it as well, since Keats was almost certainly obeying the artist's inner law that he must put certain works behind him in order to write others. One point is important, and seldom made about the kind of poem *Isabella* is. Although there are many tragedies of love in English written in the form of drama and prose which are highly valued, one is hard-pressed to find such works successfully cast in the form of the narrative poem. (*Troilus and Crisede? The Rape of Lucrece?* A few Victorian poems which themselves are influenced by *Isabella*?) It may be possible that there is something in the nature of the poetic narrative which denies us entrance into full tragic feelings, and this, I suspect, is something to do with the fact that we are rarely able to enter the consciousness of the characters and share their feelings. The ballad is an instructive contrast, for here tragedy exists, but it is built up mainly by way of relating action through understatement about people's feelings and through a laconic use of simple description, but there is no attempt fully to take us into the feelings of the characters. Keats appears to have recognized the difficulties and technical problems involved in the poetic, narrative love tragedy, discovered how the effect can be dangerously close to melodrama, and never repeated the effort. Instead, he chose to make narrative romance the vehicle either for an optimistic, celebratory point of view (*The Eve of St Agnes*) or something like moral instruction (*Lamia*), two strong capabilities of poetic romance which had been tried and proven over centuries. Or he used the equally traditional form of the ballad, to produce a short, perfect work, 'La Belle Dame Sans Merci'.

Although Boccaccio provides the source for *Isabella*, we can find at least indirect influence from Shakespeare and Jacobean tragedy. *The Duchess of Malfi* in particular holds strong analogies in the plot and colouring. We have a high-born woman who falls in love with a man below her social status, to the active disgust of her two malevolent brothers who murder the man. The atmosphere of macabre and sinister cruelty comes from details of imagery that are Jacobean in quality. Three Shakespearean plays in particular contribute towards the composition. In the overall enterprise (as well as in the specific figure of the nurse who accompanies Isabella into the woods), we find echoes of *Romeo and Juliet*, and Keats could hardly have written a tragedy of young love without recalling that acknowledged masterpiece on the subject. The tragedy in *Isabella*, although not caused by a feud between families, is precipitated nevertheless by conflict within the family, and there is the same concentration upon a threat to affections, the waste of young lives, social violence, as well as the shy reverence involved in the inception of love itself. Furthermore, just as we noticed that one of Keats's centres of attention when he read the play was imagery linking the characters with nature, seasonal cycles and references to the blighting of young flowers, so it is noticeable that in *Isabella* the pictorial qualities of nature are so insistent and functional that they form virtually a principle of construction for the poem:

> Great bliss was with them, and great happiness
> Grew, like a lusty flower in June's caress.
>> (lines 71–2)

>> She withers, like a palm
> Cut by an Indian for its juicy balm.

>> 57

> O leave the palm to wither by itself;
>> Let not quick Winter chill its dying hour!–
>>> (lines 447–50)

Very often in the poem when Keats is narrating, the imagery wanders into the world of natural growth in a way that owes as much to Spenser as Shakespeare. The natural scenery is more memorable than the human travellers as the two brothers take Lorenzo into the forest, and the exact scene where the body is buried, as described by the ghost, is more dominant than the murdered man himself. The effect is all the more poignant, too, when Isabella keeps fresh her grief by lavishing it upon a plant which grows from her lover's head. By partly creating a thematic structure out of such close attention to imagery of nature, Keats may well risk the criticism of banality from literal-minded readers (as does Wordsworth occasionally), but he is attempting an effect which he had observed partially in *Romeo and Juliet*.

Hamlet and *Macbeth* are the other two tragedies that lie behind some moments in *Isabella*, bearing in mind that we are not seeking 'sources' but exploring Keats's general notion of tragedy as manifested in the poem. We have already seen that Keats studied the presentation of the Ghost in *Hamlet*, and we have observed the similarity to his own treatment. The stanza that dwells upon graveyards, although no doubt nodding towards eighteenth-century poems in the genre, includes the 'old mole' that can 'work i'th'earth so fast' when Hamlet speaks to the Ghost (I.v.162), and an evocation of Shakespeare's hero brooding upon skulls:

> Who hath not loiter'd in a green church-yard,
>> And let his spirit, like a demon-mole,
> Work through the clayey soil and gravel hard,
>> To see scull, coffin'd bones, and funeral stole;
> Pitying each form that hungry Death hath marr'd,
>> And filling it once more with human soul?
>>> (lines 353–8)

If there is a ghoulish element in *Isabella*, it is present also in *Hamlet*, down to the particulars of the death of the old king in the play, poisoned through the ears. *Macbeth*, a play which directly deals with problems of evil, is relevant insofar as *Isabella* is Keats's only poem which includes specifically human evil, in the form of the brothers. Macbeth's ambition for power reappears here in a form perhaps more dangerously comprehensible to the nineteenth and twentieth centuries, not as a desire to become king but as a desire for commercial profit. Keats vehemently questions the existence of evil as it is manifested by the avaricious, capitalist brothers, and he juxtaposes it with precious human values involving young love. When Lorenzo is murdered in the 'forest quiet for the slaughter' (line 216), the killing of Banquo springs to mind, and the murderers in the one work, 'break-covert blood-hounds of such sin' (line 221), bear resemblance to the bestial murderers in the other:

> MACBETH. Ay, in the catalogue ye go for men;
> As hounds, and greyhounds, mongrels, spaniels, curs,
> Shoughs, water-rugs, and demi-wolves, are clept
> All by the name of dogs.
>
> (III.i.91–4; Keats's markings)

The fact that these three tragedies are echoed in *Isabella* allows us to draw a distinction between types of tragedy which may be Keats's own. A week after his review of Kean's acting in *The Champion* there appeared another review. It used to be thought that Keats wrote this too, although more recently it has been strongly argued that Reynolds was the author.[3] The disputed authorship of the piece need not prevent us from using it, for we remember that it was precisely at this time that Keats and Reynolds were discussing their project to produce a series of versified adaptations of Boccaccio's tales, of which the product, less than two months later, was *Isabella*. It is inconceivable that the two men had not discussed the issue raised in the review:

> The poetry of 'Romeo and Juliet,' of 'Hamlet,' of 'Macbeth,' is the poetry of Shakespeare's soul – full of love and divine romance. It knows no stop in its delight, but 'goeth where it listeth' remaining, however, in all men's hearts a perpetual and golden dream. The poetry of 'Lear', 'Othello', 'Cymbeline', etc., is the poetry of human passions and affections, made almost ethereal by the power of the poet...[4]

If we examine the statement for its analytical content, we find ourselves slightly baffled by the groupings (and particularly by the inclusion of *Cymbeline* in the second batch), but as usual it is a passage reflecting an impression, rather than an attempt to present a conceptual argument. In the first three plays there is indeed a kind of free-flying, imaginatively heightened and often lyrical quality about the verse, and one might argue that each deals in a different way with the truth of the imagination as it confronts an unsympathetic reality. These three plays could be seen more easily as dramatic poems, held together by threads of imagery and by poetry for its own sake, than can *Lear* at least, where the language is generally bare, the poetry is rarely sustained in description or rhapsody (except in Edgar's speech on Dover Cliff), and speech is functionally designed to be expressive of momentary and conflicting feelings in the characters. If the distinction between the 'golden dream' and 'the poetry of human passions and affections' has any validity, however, it probably tells us more about Keats's practice of tragedy than Shakespeare's, for it can be applied to describe the differences between *Isabella* and the later *Hyperion*. The first deals with love, its imagery is from the world of nature, its poetry often takes off into conspicuously lyrical, romantic passages, and its language has a self-conscious lusciousness. *Hyperion* is altogether more 'in earnest', dealing with the mysteries of suffering, its voice that of the anguished poet speaking his feelings, with little attention paid to scenery or digressive incident. In such ways, the poetry reflects a deeper distinction between types of tragic awareness. *Isabella* is an observation from the outside of the fate of young lovers, and it attempts to catch such qualities as pathos, adolescent sentiment and Gothic horror, all described with the jewel-like clarity of a pre-Raphaelite painter's attention to exterior detail and significant gesture:

> Then 'gan she work again; nor stay'd her care,
> But to throw back at times her veiling hair.
>
> (lines 375–6)

Hyperion: A Fragment deals with the tragedy of the individual consciousness faced with ultimate issues of pain and suffering, seriously presented. *Isabella* is about grief, about love-relationships in a malign society, and about the turning inwards of feelings, all observed in a narrative story.

To be a little more precise about the tragic dimension in *Isabella*, we can say that the poem paradoxically presents as a total incident the kind of potential tragedy which Keats found existing within Shakespearean comedy, the veiled melancholy that dwells even in the very temple of delight. It gives the story of Julia in *The Two Gentlemen of Verona* or Viola in *Twelfth Night* played out to the bitter end, without the reprieve offered by the happy ending of the comic structure. *Twelfth Night*, perhaps the romantic comedy that takes us closest to tragic feelings in its presentation of frustrated love, is the more relevant comparison at this point. Keats's poem is in the spirit of the kind of song liked by the melancholy lover Orsino, a work that 'dallies with the innocence of love, Like the old age'. Its tone is that of the song which Feste sings for him:

> Come away, come away, death;
> And in sad cypress let me be laid;
> ...

(II.iv.46–65 *passim*; Keats's marking)

Although the one work is tragic and the other comic in form, they both deal centrally with 'concealment, like a worm i'th'bud' (II.iv.110) and they both provide a heroine who metaphorically sits 'like Patience on a monument, Smiling at grief' (II.iv.113–14). Both works present characters who are so wholeheartedly committed to romantic love that they invite ridicule for self-indulgence. It is interesting to speculate on whether Keats and his critics would have found the poem too 'smokeable' in its sentiment, if he had managed to build into the structure of the poem, as Shakespeare does in his play, the comic form and more overt awareness of the potential bathos; if the narrator had distanced himself more firmly from his characters. But such a possibility does not necessarily point towards a better poem, and it would certainly be a different one. We are on safer ground by merely pointing out the poetic and thematic similarities between the poem and the play, by comparing, for example, the description of the mourning Olivia:

> But like a cloistress she will veiled walk,
> And water once a day her chamber round
> With eye-offending brine; all this to season
> A brother's dead love, which she would keep fresh
> And lasting in her sad remembrance;

(I.i.28–32)

with the no less plaintive picture of Isabella feeding 'with thin tears' the pot of basil which holds a relic of her dead lover, and her memories. The first seven lines of *Twelfth Night*, Orsino's words on the dying fall in music, are invoked in a choric statement which mingles its words with those of Feste's song, and those of Viola smiling at grief:

> O Melancholy, linger here awhile!
> O Music, Music, breathe despondingly!
> O Echo, Echo, from some sombre isle,
>   Unknown, Lethean, sigh to us – O sigh!
> Spirits in grief, lift up your heads, and smile;
>   Lift up your heads, sweet Spirits, heavily,
> And make a pale light in your cypress glooms,
> Tinting with silver wan your marble tombs.
>
> (stanza 55)

It is in such comparisons that we find the nature of the tragic feelings which Keats is dealing with in this poem. Melancholy, the grief of lost love which can become all-consuming and self-destructive and the pity involved in observing the waste of precious youth, mark the kind of 'tragic order' of *Isabella*, and create the 'amusing sober-sadness' which its author picked out as the secret of its modest success.[5] The precarious achievement is at least in part attained by the inbuilt resistance to sentimentality represented by the close and conscious presence of comic memories. The narrator's stance is also at times the distanced one of the teller of romance stories:

> O for the gentleness of old Romance,
>   The simple plaining of a minstrel's song!
> Fair reader, at the old tale take a glance,
>   For here, in truth, it doth not well belong
> To speak: – O turn thee to the very tale,
>   And taste the music of that vision pale.
>
> (lines 387–92)

The technique is one encountered by Keats in Chaucer, but more pertinently in Shakespeare's romance, or tragi-comedy, *Pericles* in the use of Gower:

> It hath been sung at festivals,
> On ember-eves, and holy-ales;
> And lords and ladies of their lives
> Have read it for restoratives:
>
> …
>
> I life would wish, and that I might
> Waste it for you, like taper-light.
>
> (Prologue, 5–16 *passim*; Keats's markings)

Furthermore, there are some structural analogies where Shakespeare appears to be attempting similar kinds of effect, and where even his success is as problematical as Keats's. In *Measure for Measure* the existence of Mariana adds a risk of sentimentality to the play, and the dilemmas of Isabella – as unformed and immature as Keats's heroine of the same name – pose a genuine problem in assessing how far the dramatist is trying to distance us from her feelings. A similar problem comes in *Cymbeline* when Imogen weeps over the headless body of Cloten whom she thinks to be her lover. What links these examples with *Isabella* is the writer's choice to place a heroine in a situation which draws from her fully tragic feelings in a context which prevents the reader or audience from completely accepting, without irony or mature distancing, these almost hysterical and certainly self-obsessed emotions.[6] The instances cited are notorious 'problems' in Shakespearean drama, and the problem is always stated in terms of genre: to what extent are the plays intended as tragedies in comic contexts or comedies in potentially tragic contexts? The same questions hover over Keats's *Pot of Basil*, and the consistency with which Keats through verbal reminiscence gestures towards these and other Shakespearean comedies indicates that he is experimenting with effects of contrast which are very peculiar to Shakespeare. While such an approach to the poem may not vindicate it as a masterpiece, at least it provides symptoms of an artistic complexity that we find in the other poems Keats was writing at the time.

Although we have concentrated upon Keats as a reader of Shakespeare, we should not forget he was a keen theatre-goer, and his admiration for the acting of Kean, shared with Hazlitt and expressed effusively in his review for *The Champion*, shows that he had no closeted scorn for the stage. It is not necessary here to rehearse the evidence of his experience of the theatre, especially since the job has been conveniently done by Harry. R. Beaudry in *The English Theatre and John Keats*.[7] It is sufficient to say that one of Keats's greatest ambitions was to write a play for Kean to act in (which would certainly make it a tragedy), and that it is clear he knew from the outset what the play's essential nature would be:

> My having written that [Passage]...is my first Step towards the chief Attempt in the Drama – the playing of different Natures with Joy and Sorrow.[8]

Such an intention is quite consistent with all that Keats found in his reading of Shakespeare and Hazlitt, and in what he praises in Kean's acting. Eighteen months later, whilst engaged in writing *Otho the Great*, he writes to Bailey:

> One of my Ambitions is to make as great a revolution in modern dramatic writing as Kean has done in acting – another to upset the drawling of the blue stocking literary world.[9]

And again, a few months later, he tells his publisher, John Taylor:

> The little dramatic skill I may as yet have however badly it might show in a Drama would I think be sufficient for a Poem – I wish to diffuse the colouring of St. Agnes eve throughout a Poem in which Character and Sentiment would be the figures to such drapery – Two or three such Poems, if God should spare me, written in the course of the next six years, would be a famous gradus ad Parnassum altissimum – I mean they would nerve me up to the writing of a few fine Plays – my greatest ambition – when I do feel ambitious...[10]

God did not spare him, and he did not write his few fine plays. All he left in pursuing his goal were *Otho the Great* and four scenes of *King Stephen* (which we shall not look at here because it hardly gives evidence of Keats's concept of tragedy). No matter how modest and incomplete is such a corpus of tragic drama, however, it does show Keats putting into practice some of the lessons he has learned from his reading of Shakespeare.

If *Isabella* is a work manifesting Keats's understanding of the tragic emotions as they are latent in young love, *Otho the Great* is a more ambitious attempt to portray a comprehensive view of the circumstances and kinds of characters who make the tragic condition, 'the playing of different Natures with Joy and Sorrow'. It is, however, a rather intimidating task to attempt to make serious claims for *Otho the Great* when in the past it has been roundly condemned and dismissed by many distinguished critics.[11] Again, they use as evidence for their opinion some casual remarks by Keats himself, and once more it might be retorted that they are mistaking the devastating honesty of a remarkably self-critical poet for an example of Keats's own unerring taste in literary matters. The fact that Keats 'agreed to clothe with rhetoric the preposterous skeleton of Brown's *Otho the Great*' is complacently assumed to be the poet's a priori judgment on the whole enterprise.[12] On the other hand, Keats's enthusiasm for the project is also well-documented, whilst his disappointment when it became clear that Kean could not act in the play, and our knowledge of his own artistic integrity, attest to his own feeling that it was a first attempt at his highest ambition, the writing of tragic drama. As such, *Otho* is a crucial document for the purposes of the present work, and there is enough evidence to claim licence for treating it with respect, if not with quite the admiration reserved for Shelley's *The Cenci*. Verse written for the theatre must be different from that required in a concentrated, narrative poem or an ode, and for this reason too we should accept the intention behind *Otho the Great* as a valid one, different from that applying in Keats's other works. Great artists have rarely contented themselves with giving us what *we* want. They effect their aims, and solve their artistic problems, in the way they are capable of at the time of writing, and it is wise to pay attention to what Keats was trying to do.

It would not be particularly helpful to go through *Otho* tabulating verbal and situational debts to Shakespeare's plays, abundant as they are. Keats could hardly have written a complete, five-act tragedy without drawing somewhere upon his acknowledged mentor in the field. C.L. Finney, one critic who does give generous attention to the play as a competent dramatic composition, points to significant likenesses with *Much Ado About Nothing, Cymbeline,* and *Hamlet.*[13] Beaudry amplifies the range of reference to include *I Henry IV* and *Macbeth,* as well as indicating that the debt is more general. He also helpfully mentions several contemporary plays which Keats must have known.[14] In the example of this play, however, discovering sources and echoes for individual lines and dramatic situations does not really tell us a lot about Keats's notion of tragedy. Instead, we should look at the work as a whole, remembering that even if Brown gave him the plot it was Keats who supplied the poetry which conveys the vision, and it was Keats who apparently took over in shaping the dénouement according to his own artistic conscience.[15] If it is true, as Joan Grundy interestingly suggests, that Keats was always less effective at conveying character as temperament than working upon emotional situations and moods,[16] then we may be able to describe the kind of overall effect or 'colouring' which conveys his awareness of a tragic dimension to life at the end of *Otho the Great*. In doing so, we shall be finding a deeper level of indebtedness to Shakespearean tragedy than we could discover by merely finding verbal reminiscences. First, however, a word should be said about the limitations upon the Shakespearean model. Although I believe Keats is drawing important elements from his reading of Shakespeare's tragedies, he (or perhaps Brown) is basing the design upon different practice.

There is some justice in Harry R. Beaudry's contention that *Otho the Great* owes more to plays of Keats's own age than to the Elizabethans', and to this extent the work is against his own grain. On the other hand, it should be pointed out that many motifs remind us strongly of Beaumont and Fletcher, writers whom Keats read and admired. It is likely that he did have these twin dramatists sometimes close to his mind, since the enterprise of writing *Otho* was a collaboration in the same tradition. As Brown fed him the story and he supplied the poetry, Keats must have felt something like a Fletcher to his companion's Beaumont. We find similarities of construction. Beaumont and Fletcher concentrated on dramatic situation and scenic effectiveness rather than on depth of characterization, a mark of *Otho* which has been held up as a fault. They were also adept at constructing their plots around a series of relationships which are intense, intricate, and involving duplicity and a measure of sexual blackmail (as in *A King and No King* and *The Maid's Tragedy*), instead of employing the Shakespearean method of concentrating upon one tragic protagonist essentially. Again, then, it may be quite a conscious decision that 'there is no particularly outstanding character in the play as a whole', but that 'each major personage is able to hold the reader's interest' at some stage of the action.[17] Finally, there are two character types which are reminiscent of Beaumont and Fletcher: Ludolph is very like their rather passive heroes who are acted upon rather than asserting themselves (for example, Philaster); and Erminia, like Evadne, is the even more passive, suffering figure of virtue. If such important similarities be granted (and the case has never been put), then *Otho the Great* may yet be judged as an effective drama written in the vein of plays which had been enormously popular in the early seventeenth century, and which Keats admired.

This is not the place to advance the argument further, since it would be a digression, but one of the points mentioned is of central importance since it helps us to locate the conception of tragedy which Keats holds in the fifth Act when, according to Brown, he felt most liberated to supply his own vision through the poetry. We might speak of Conrad and Auranthe as effective embodiments of evil, but little sentiment can be spared over their deaths which are in accordance with the rules of poetic justice. (One suspects, moreover, that Keats was temperamentally incapable of understanding evil with any subtlety.) It is Ludolph, and to a lesser extent Albert and Erminia, who emerge as the ones involved in tragic predicaments. Ludolph goes mad as a consequence of the situation which has confronted him. All the time,

although he is introduced as a warrior and a man of pride and right-
eous anger, Ludolph is given very little choice over what happens to
him. He is reconciled with his father through the accident of Otho rec-
ognizing his son through the disguise of an Arab soldier, he is married
off to Auranthe (not against his wishes, certainly, but not of his own
volition), he is completely tricked by his wife and her evil brother, but
he clings to his trust in her honesty. Albert, the man of truth 'Whose
words once utter'd pass like current gold' (III.ii.210) is faced with a
conflict of loyalties, between supporting the truth which Erminia
speaks and telling a lie to protect Ludolph's marriage and his feelings.
The lie which he tells cannot go unchanged in such a pillar of truth-
telling, and in attempting to rectify it he loses his life. His death is re-
presented with tragic intensity (V.ii), for he dies full of grief and guilt
which have not yet been atoned for. His motives can ultimately be
traced back to a praiseworthy loyalty to Ludolph and to Otho. Finally,
although Erminia does not die, the eventual revelation of her honesty
and virtue after she has been publicly calumniated during the action
of the play, comes too late to help the situation or her immediate repu-
tation. She witnesses the events of the ending in possession of a total
understanding denied to anybody else, and she speaks words of pity
recalling Cordelia's: 'Alas! Alas!' (V.v.167). The figures whose fates
represent the tragic spirit in the play, then, are all people who suffer
for their sympathy or their honesty, and they are helplessly caught in
a web of circumstances which are none of their doing. Evil lies outside
them, in the characters of Conrad and Auranthe. They are, in fact,
people who live and die by their 'negative capability'.

There is a consistency here with what Keats was thinking about in
the two or three months before he began writing *Otho the Great*. The
long letter to his brother and sister-in-law of April 1819, in which he
sees life as 'the vale of soul-making'[18] emphasizes the helplessness of
the sensitive individual in controlling his circumstances. There is
more than a hint of tragic consciousness in the description of such a
fate:

> For instance suppose a rose to have sensation, it blooms on a beau-
> tiful morning it enjoys itself – but there comes a cold wind, a hot
> sun – it cannot escape it, it cannot destroy its annoyances – they are
> as native to the world as itself: no more can man be happy in spite,
> the world[l]y elements will prey upon his nature ...[19]

The parable Keats presents as an optimistic answer to the 'vale of
tears' emphasizes the creative, self-instructive potential in the act of

enduring, and the possibility of gaining ever more wisdom. We have seen that such a conception is intimately linked in Keats's mind with the experience of *King Lear*. A month later, he comes to the same point of recognizing the world's adversity, and again chooses optimism as his own personal answer: he chooses 'energy' over 'despair'. [20] In life as he lives it, Keats strives consciously to transcend his awareness of the tragedy of the helpless mortal, buffeted by circumstances. In art, however, he can legitimately play out the negative feelings in a tragic form which belongs to literature: the fates of Ludolph, Albert and Erminia represent the result. It is more than possible that Keats's ultimate intention in writing the final act of *Otho* was to raise in the spectator the feelings he had himself on reading *King Lear*: the bracing, invigorating effect of burning through a tragic recognition, to discover a newly awakened personal optimism that would enable the reader to choose energy rather than despair. Furthermore, if it be accepted that Keats may have been influenced by Beaumont and Fletcher, and if Philaster is partly a model for Ludolph, it is clear in turn that Philaster was modelled upon Hamlet, another character who is acted upon, tempted by despair and eventually chooses energy against a sea of troubles. Whether Keats succeeds or not in his attempt to emulate the effect of Shakespearean tragedy is, of course, open to question, but we can say at least that in *Otho the Great* Keats places the concept of tragedy in the fates of people who, unlike, say, Macbeth or Richard III, have little room for active decision-making, and to this extent they reflect many of his own feelings and ideas. He did not need to follow this particular notion of tragedy, since others were available even in Shakespeare. That he did so is an indication of his discovering in some plays by Shakespeare a pattern which he found congenial to his own ideas.

Keats's first version of *Hyperion*, the work known as *Hyperion: A Fragment*, is by his own description, an attempt to emulate Milton in the epic mode. [21] This fact governs the choice of language and versification, and it also determines the overall strategy of the poem as primarily narrative rather than dramatic, although dialogue is employed as in *Paradise Lost*. Consistent with the model of Milton's work, *Hyperion: A Fragment* uses the narrative as a vehicle for myth, in the sense of a thematic centre which presents an archetypal pattern. The myth chosen by Keats is not Christian, but the pagan story of the fall of the Titans who are overthrown by Apollo. This choice allows Keats the opportunity of dealing with many of his beliefs in a series of patterns overlapping the central theme. Predominant is the basic stress upon process and change which is observed and implicitly accepted by the narrator. Change is seen as necessary progress, and based on the 'eternal law' acknowledged even by the vanquished that 'first in beauty should be first in might'. The young and splendid Apollo must succeed Hyperion, just as Hyperion and the Titans had followed Saturn. Process itself becomes a paradigm for many aspects of evolution which Keats often affirmed: political change from an ancien regime to a new order,[22] the triumph of poetry, represented by Apollo, energetic change in the order of things which accompanies creativity of any sort, the overriding existence of memory (Mnemosyne) as a principle of stability and accumulated knowledge which survives change, and Keats's own personal myth of the kind of inner, psychological change from youthful, receptive enthusiasm to a darker, wiser knowledge of suffering and pain.

It is clear even from this bald description that the choice of myth held enormous promise for Keats, in its capacity to carry so many variations and dimensions based upon the inner dynamism of change. It is perhaps this kind of fertility Keats was discovering as he went along, that led to his perception that 'things which [I] do half at Random are afterwards confirmed by my judgment in a half dozen features of Propriety'.[23] That Keats left the epic unfinished has been explained in various ways, all of them holding a part of the truth. One possible reason lies in Keats's developing interest in tragedy, which he came to find was not fully accommodated in the work as he began it. After showing us the tragedy of the passive and sensitive in *Otho*, he was now determined to show a more active, self-determining character. In drawing a distinction between *Endymion* and his plan for *Hyperion*, Keats writes,

> that the Hero of the written tale being mortal is led on, like Buonaparte, by circumstance; whereas the Apollo in Hyperion being a fore-seeing God will shape his actions like one.[24]

But it is clear that at the time he was writing the poem, his feelings were not optimistic enough to sustain such a vision, and that his interests still really lay amongst the 'mortal' and in tragedy itself rather than progress. Apollo was far too ebullient, and his part was so shaped by the design that he could never become the symbol of knowledgeable sorrow that Keats wanted. The tragic situation of the Titans, again in conformity with the story, had more or less been exploited to the full in the first two books, and Keats was well aware that no matter how sympathetic he made them the real thrust of the book had to be towards the new, non-tragic order represented by Apollo. Somehow he found the pattern back-to-front, as if it moved from the 'vale of soul-making' backwards to the chamber of maiden-thought, instead of the other way around. To counter the danger, he begins to develop the goddess Mnemosyne as the carrier of tragic wisdom, but he realized again that if he should make this character too full and central, then Apollo's role would be diminished and the kind of progress represented by the new order would appear naive. No matter how potentially rich was the myth he had chosen, Keats found himself trapped between it and his own preoccupation. Simple change did not offer a true answer to the suffering of mortals which is the stuff of tragedy.

When Keats took up the work again for revision, he probably had no clear idea of how to solve these structural problems, since he appears to be sticking to the original shape of the story. Perhaps he wrote at this stage from a kind of instinct rather than from a plan, concentrating locally upon the texture of the poetry rather than the overall architecture. The poetry, as commentators have pointed out, is less Miltonic, owing more to Dante, and perhaps it is even more 'Shakespearean', richer and wider in its range of imagery. What he does have, however, is a surer knowledge of what really interests him at this stage, and he is prepared to spend more attention upon clarifying it. Process is no longer the central interest, for Keats has discovered that his real centre of gravity is suffering, as comprehended by the patient wisdom of Mnemosyne (or Moneta, as she becomes in the second version). His subject, in short, is the tragic condition itself, and everything in *The Fall of Hyperion: A Dream* illuminates Keats's current conception of this subject. Keats may well have known from the outset that he would again be forced to leave the poem incomplete for largely the same reasons, but at least now he strives to make the fragment as full and sustained a vehicle as possible for his central preoccupation, rather than compelling his interests to serve the overall myth. If *Hyperion: A Fragment* exists 'Upon the boundaries of day and night', drawing on 'grief and radiance faint' (lines 303–4), then *The Fall of Hyperion*, as its title suggests, turns its full gaze upon grief itself, unmitigated and pure. Here it is the loss involved in change, the 'Fall', which concerns the poet, rather than the potential for new growth. The new myth works not on change and progress but on the suffering of stasis.

Right from his decision to open the revised poem with a first person narration from the poet, probably following Dante, Keats strives to 'humanize' the action. The intention, however, is not merely to make comprehensible to mortal ears the feelings of the gods, 'Making comparisons of earthly things' (II, 1–6), but to concentrate wholly upon the mortal condition itself. The two goddesses are observing, and carrying much of the burden for, the suffering of ordinary people. Since they feel the pain as if they suffered it themselves, but yet do not die as mortals do, they are existing eternally at the quintessential point of tragedy itself which they cannot escape. Keats always seems to have felt that death is a cessation of pain, and that tragedy lies in the living awareness of suffering in oneself or more especially others. *The Fall of Hyperion* concerns human nature and human pain, observed from an all-seeing, all-suffering and never-ending perspective – in short, tragedy distilled to its greatest intensity. That the poem is centred so firmly upon the mortal condition is consistent with Keats's deepest convictions about the primal importance of simple existence proved upon the pulses of the senses. There are no 'havens' offered, and no form of religious consolation in the poem, for the living are placed at the centre, as they are at the centre of Keats's view of life: 'Wonders are no wonders to me. I am more at home amongst Men and women'.[25] The mortals in *Hyperion* who are held up as models are those who do not aspire to the godlike position of passively observing pain in their world but, accepting their mortality, attempt to 'Labour for mortal good' (I, 159): 'They seek no wonder but the human face' (I, 163). The poet himself is in an extremely ambiguous position, and Keats honestly represents the tension he finds in himself. The distinction made by Moneta is between the poet as 'dreamer' who 'vexes' the world by confusing pain and pleasure to such an extent that neither feeling can be felt purely any more – the person who writes and thinks self-indulgently, without concentrating upon the reality around him – and on the other hand the genuine poet who 'pours out a balm upon the world' by offering accurate observation of feelings and humanistic consolations for the real pain that he sees, helping his fellow beings to endure without despair. The fact that Keats places himself provisionally amongst the dreamers is surely not just a result of modesty, but displays consistency of thought in the poem. If the poet's words should survive his own death and continue to give 'balm' to the world then he will attain the status of immortality held by the goddesses, but it is not until after death that this can be judged. When he is living, the poet must place himself among the dreamers. Shakespeare, to take an example, would be one of the genuine philanthropists, one who helps mankind to endure and who also happened to be a writer. His works have continued after his death to pour balm upon the world of suffering, although Keats admits that some day a 'superior being' may relegate even Shakespeare to a lower level.[26]

Pain and suffering are represented in two episodes which make up the first Canto. After enjoying first the loveliness of complete acceptance of all the mortal senses, the narrator must die into knowledge through pain felt upon the senses. The ascent is described in poetically powerful lines which represent the most significant advance in this poem over the former fragment. As he laboriously struggles up the steps, feeling only physical sensation – chillness, numbness and sharp, piercing pain – he is initiated into the experience of dying, although he is not yet immortal. The other depiction of suffering is one of mental and spiritual pain, as we observe Saturn in his impotent misery. His suffering lies mainly in an incapacity to act or create. He has the vision of fruitful change:

> Let me hear other groans, and trumpets blown
> Of triumph calm, and hymns of festival
> From the gold peaks of heaven's high piled clouds;
> Voices of soft proclaim, and silver stir
> Of strings in hollow shells; and let there be
> Beautiful things made new for the surprize
> Of the sky children.

> > (I, 432–8)

But he feebly ceases to hope. Lacking the capacity to effect change by creativity, he must give way to a more potent regime, as the new order must eventually relinquish its sovereignty. The description of Hyperion in the fragment of Canto II is full of colour, vitality and life after the stasis of Saturn's misery. Saturn, left behind but still immortal, must endure the suffering forever.

The two goddesses who are in attendance upon Saturn stand at the very centre of the tragic vision informing the whole poem. Moneta is like Dante's Virgil, the prophetess guiding the poet's responses and perceptions, and in her role as Mnemosyne, 'shade of memory', she has omniscient knowledge of the past. Thea expresses compassion for Saturn and strengthens him in endurance. They are the ones who embody calm, feeling sympathy for the suffering. As such they are the immortal equivalent of those poets who pour balm upon the world with their eternally reassuring lines. The difference between the two appears to be that Moneta, the prophetess, is active in giving knowledge whilst Thea is passive in total fellow-feeling with the sufferer, 'softest-natur'd' of the brood of immortals. Together they show understanding, wisdom and spiritual support, and they provide between them the capacities of corporate, accumulated memory which exists in the world even though it may not reside in a single individual. They both share the quality that Keats had described as 'negative capability', which is now revealed as no pleasure but as an awesome responsibility, a 'curse' (I, 243), and a never-ending, vicarious suffering:

> 'None can usurp this height,' return'd that shade,
> 'But those to whom the miseries of the world
> Are misery, and will not let them rest.
> All else who find a haven in the world.
> Where they may thoughtless sleep away their days,
> If by a chance into this fane they come,
> Rot on the pavement where thou rotted'st half.' –
> (I, 147–53)

In presenting with poised maturity such an unflinching humanistic vision, Keats is working on a lonely height of his own. He appears to have left Shakespeare behind. However, I hope it is evident from the argument of this book that he could not have attained such a point without having absorbed, assimilated and transmuted much of what he found in Shakespeare. *The Fall of Hyperion* is a logical growth from the sonnet 'On Sitting Down to Read King Lear Once Again', and here Keats, firmly rejecting the golden tongue of romance, turns to the impassioned clay of mortal existence as his subject matter. That the poem is his own considered attempt to write 'tragedy' is clear from the significant use of the word itself, placing the concept at the centre of the poem but just beyond human comprehension:

> So at the view of sad Moneta's brow,
> I ached to see what things the hollow brain
> Behind enwombed: what high tragedy
> In the dark secret chambers of her skull
> Was acting, that could give so dread a stress
> To her cold lips, and fill with such a light
> Her planetary eyes; and touch her voice
> With such a sorrow.
> (I, 275–82)

One phrase from *King Lear* itself, a favourite with Keats, 'and take upon's the mystery of things' is echoed and amplified by the poet narrator:

> Whereon there grew
> A power within me of enormous ken,
> To see as a God sees, and take the depth
> Of things as nimbly as the outward eye
> Can size and shape pervade. The lofty theme
> At those few words hung vast before my mind,
> With half unravel'd web.
>
> (I, 302–8)

Keats's attentiveness to aspects of *King Lear* which emphasize the primacy of human suffering, the importance of endurance and sympathy and the courageous rejection of despair, blossoms at the very heart of *The Fall of Hyperion*.

Finally, Keats's two goddesses who preside reverently over human tragedy owe something to Cordelia as the scene is close to *Lear*. His admiration for this character and recognition of the symbolic value of her demeanour are shown as early as 'Sleep and Poetry', when Keats asks,

> What is more gentle than a wind in summer?
> ...
> More serene than Cordelia's countenance?
>
> (lines 1 and 9)

The main description of her face in *King Lear* comes in a scene which does not appear in Keats's marked Folio, although he would certainly have read it in his well-thumbed copy of *Lear* in the Johnson-Steevens edition:

> KENT. Did your letters pierce the Queen to any demonstration
> of grief?
> GENTLEMAN. Ay, sir; she took them, read them in my
> presence,
> And now and then an ample tear trill'd down
> Her delicate cheek. It seem'd she was a queen
> Over her passion, who, most rebel-like,
> Sought to be king o'er her.
> KENT.   O, then it mov'd her?
> GENTLEMAN. Not to a rage; patience and sorrow strove
> Who should express her goodliest. You have seen
> Sunshine and rain at once: her smiles and tears
> Were like a better way. Those happy smilets

That play'd on her ripe lip seem'd not to know
What guests were in her eyes, which parted thence
As pearls from diamonds dropp'd. In brief,
Sorrow would be a rarity most beloved
If all could so become it.

(IV.iii.10–24)

The same tender tears express her silent feelings in the beautiful, serenely moving reconciliation between Cordelia and Lear (IV.vii), a scene which is heavily marked in Keats's Folio. He picks out her gentle, healing words of blessing:

O my dear father! Restoration hang
Thy medicine on my lips, and let this kiss
Repair those violent harms that my two sisters
Have in thy reverence made.

(IV.vii.26–9)

He notes the passages which illustrate Cordelia's innate sympathy:

Mine enemy's dog,
Though he had bit me, should have stood that night
Against my fire; and wast thou fain, poor father,
To hovel thee with swine and rogues forlorn,
In short and musty straw? Alack, alack!

(IV.vii.36–40)

For thee, oppressed King, am I cast down;
Myself could else out-frown false Fortune's frown.

(V.iii.5–6)

One other quotation demonstrates Cordelia's faith not in gods nor in an afterlife, but in humanly accessible gifts of nature, sleep and 'simples operative':

All blest secrets,
All you unpublish'd virtues of the earth,
Spring with my tears; be aidant and remediate,
In the good man's distress.

(IV.iv.15–18)

Like the goddesses in *The Fall of Hyperion*, Cordelia presides over suffering mankind, full of sympathy, patience, tears and a sharing of suffering, and like them her attitude is fundamentally humanist in its outlook, offering no religious consolation but instead the balm of pity. In her father's eyes she eventually attains the superiority of perception linking her with Keats's pagan goddesses:

> Upon such sacrifices, my Cordelia,
> The gods themselves throw incense.
>
> (V.iii.19–20)

These two lines could be used as an epigraph to *The Fall of Hyperion*, and although Cordelia is no goddess herself her human qualities are those which eternally pour a balm upon a suffering world.

Keats lived with all these lines close to his consciousness for at least three years before he wrote the poem, and when their echoes come in his own lines they appear in no simple manner identifiable as a 'source' but in a pervading, visionary way. Moneta, 'Of accent feminine, so courteous' (I, 215), shedding 'long treasured tears' (I, 221) strews incense of cinnamon and spice-wood upon the sacrifice of Saturn. When she parts her veil, the poet sees 'a wan face',

> Not pin'd by human sorrows, but bright blanch'd
> By an immortal sickness which kills not;
> …
> But for her eyes I should have fled away.
> They held me back, with a benignant light,
> Soft mitigated by divinest lids
> Half closed …
>
> (I, 256–71 *passim*)

Thea is more 'human', less detached, 'in her sorrow nearer woman's tears', and her dramatic role is more closely akin to Cordelia's, as the 'poor lost King' (I, 354) is close to the 'poor perdu' (IV.vii.35) addressed by Cordelia:

> One hand she press'd upon that aching spot
> Where beats the human heart; as if just there,
> Though an immortal, she felt cruel pain;
> …
> the while in tears
> She press'd her fair large forehead to the earth.
>
> (I, 344–6 and 378–9)

The whole description as Thea watches and weeps over the sleeping Saturn has an inescapable similarity to the emblem of Cordelia by the awakening Lear, and her words to the 'hoary majesty' recall the situation in *King Lear* as civil war rages around the exhausted, sleeping king:[27]

> Thy thunder, captious at the new command,
> Rumbles reluctant o'er our fallen house;
> And thy sharp lightning in unpracticed hands
> Scorches and burns our once serene domain.
>
> (I, 362–5)

The last picture we see in the first Canto is of Thea leading Saturn, white in beard and hair, 'A midday fleece of clouds' (I, 454) like Lear's 'white flakes' (IV.vii.30), melting into the woods towards

> the families of grief,
> Where roof'd in my black rocks they waste in pain
> And darkness for no hope.
>
> (I, 460–3)

In the scene in *Hyperion* we find a tableau of Lear awakening beside his daughter:

> Until old Saturn rais'd his faded eyes,
> And look'd around, and saw his kingdom gone,
> And all the gloom and sorrow of the place,
> And that fair Goddess at his feet.
>
> (I, 400–3)

The feeble 'old man of the earth Bewailing earthly loss' (I, 440–1) is again distinctly reminiscent of Lear. Of course Keats's originality is too great for us to say he is 'copying' or that the literary memory is a conscious one, but the reader's recognition of the dimly observed source, one of the most moving scenes in Shakespeare, enriches the thematic concentration upon the bereft old king, the healing understanding of Moneta and the womanly sympathy of Thea, by reference to a dramatic moment which captures the same effects. Middleton Murry may be too melodramatic in saying that when Keats gave up the revised *Hyperion* 'Shakespeare had triumphed over Milton',[28] and the conclusion is also not accurate. Shakespeare had triumphed already in the rewriting. The effective changes made by Keats were, first, the shift away from Miltonic narrative towards first-person experience of the poet's persona – from the epic mode towards the dramatic mediated through Dante – and secondly, the deepening of the tragic stasis by the development of the specific analogue from *King Lear*. But these are artistic decisions rather than a matter of turning away from the influence of one writer and towards another. From his by now ample and mature repertoire of literary experience, Keats has detected that the Shakespearean model is more appropriate to his revised intentions – the raising of genuinely tragic *catharsis*, and the presentation of human sympathy as the most powerful antidote he can discover for the problem of human suffering. The 'Miltonic inversions', apt to the earlier intention of epic, are getting in the way of the dramatic effect.

Some commentators on *The Fall of Hyperion* take the Shakespearean analogy even further. Helen Vendler in *The Odes of John Keats*, arguing that the poem internalizes suffering in 'representational tragedy' by dwelling on Moneta's mind, emphatically declares:

> *The Fall* is finally not a Miltonic or a Dantesque poem so much as an homage to Shakespeare, not the Shakespeare of the plays as we have them, but the Shakespeare who preceded the plays, the Shakespearean mind-in-creation.[29]

This view is rather an interpretative approach to the poem than a statement about literary influence, but its significance here is that Vendler enables us to extend the analysis to show that the apparently passive sympathy of Moneta and Thea has in fact a creative function, far from the inertia of Saturn. By adopting the first-person narration, Keats shows us the poet learning and sharing the paradoxical qualities of creative sympathy. The pattern is not so distant from that of 'On Sitting Down to Read *King Lear* Again' – through self-annulment to creativity.

It seems that after a lifetime striving to understand and accept suffering, Keats has come full circle, to a knowledge that the only consolation one can accept is the existence in the real world of total, self-denying sympathy. Behind the mysterious brow of Moneta and the soft nature of Thea, just as behind the inscrutable but sorrowing tears of Cordelia, lie no ultimate answers to 'high tragedy'. 'It is, And my heart breaks at it.' (*King Lear*, IV.vi.141–2 spoken by Edgar). It seems a simple theme to find at the end of so long a struggle on Keats's part, but sometimes it takes more courage to 'rest in half knowledge' than to continue the pursuit. The courage with which Keats came to face his own death, learned through observing helplessly his dying brother and partly schooled by the emblem of Cordelia, finds a moving voice in this fundamental poem, 'a personal art brought to its moral limits'.[30]

We observed that Keats found *King Lear* more bracing than bleak, full of an energy which is stylistic and linguistic as well as spiritual, and in the play despair is encountered by Keats only to be transcended. This is all the more reason why we must do justice to Keats's own determination to ward off in the mortal condition the temptation to inaction and hopelessness which his vision sometimes invites. His own form of transcendence owes much to what he found throughout Shakespeare, a loving attentiveness to small detail, a treasuring of the inadvertently revealing gesture of a character caught off-guard, an intense celebration of 'the simple worship of a day'.[31] As Blake had said in more rebellious spirit, 'Everything that lives is holy, life delights in life'. In short, through dwelling upon the richness and diversity felt in the moment of living and apprehending with all the senses, Keats finds not only an antidote to despair but a potent challenge to the necessary condition of suffering, which in oneself must be met as an educative experience and when observed in others must be treated with humane and humanistic sympathy. We find such strength, accepting and holding onto real experience, learned on the pulses, in many a personal touch in Keats's letters, such as in one where both *Hyperion* and 'To Autumn' are quoted:

> I should like a bit of fire to night – one likes a bit of fire – How glorious the Blacksmiths' shops look now – I stood to night before one till I was verry near listing for one. Yes I should like a bit of fire – at a distance about 4 feet 'not quite hob nob' – as wordsworth says...[32]

Keats, standing watching and feeling the warmth of the fire, gives an image holding in itself the combination of stasis and movement, the barely-moving encountering the actively-living, which is one of his most characteristic poetic notes. We find it in the image of Saturn in *The Fall of Hyperion*, although the observer is here the active one, eventually led to exert his sympathies and feelings on behalf of the deadened Saturn:

> I set myself
> Upon an eagle's watch, that I might see,
> And seeing ne'er forget. No stir of life
> Was in this shrouded vale, not so much air
> As in the zoning of a summer's day
> Robs not one light seed from the feather'd grass,
> But where the dead leaf fell there did it rest.
>
> (I, 308–14)

The active determination of the narrator to set himself to 'see' as the describing poet dwells upon the minutiae of the scene down to the dead leaf, becomes something of a quiet but meaningful reproach to those who would sink into a static disregard for the human and unrepeatable gift of reflecting upon what is offered merely by the ability to see, and to hear, to smell, touch and taste. The image of Saturn being watched by the poet-narrator gives us a representation of the two sides of Keats himself, and it is the latter, by his decision to feel and to live, who establishes an active moral principle, characterized in Moneta and Thea.

Keats's determination to value concrete experience for its own sake found confirmation in his readings of Shakespeare who, as we have seen, is admired by the poet for his attention to detailed observation, sometimes to the neglect of more formal concerns such as plot, thematic unity and consistency of characterization. It is precisely the quality which A.C. Bradley associates with both Keats and Shakespeare:

> Now this spirit, it is obvious, tends in poetry, I do not say to a realistic, but to what may be called a concrete method of treatment; to the vivid presentment of scenes, individualities, actions, in preference to the expression of unembodied thoughts and feelings...Scott had it in splendid abundance and vigour; but he had too little of the idealism or the metaphysical imagination which was common to those [Romantic] poets, and which Shakespeare united with his universal comprehension; nor was he, like Shakespeare and like some of them, a master of magic in language. But Keats had that magic in fuller measure, perhaps, than any of our poets since Milton; and, sharing the idealism of Wordsworth and Shelley, he possessed also wider sympathies, and, if not a more plastic or pictorial imagination than the latter, at least a greater freedom from the attraction of theoretic ideas.[33]

In this judicious summation of Keats's empirical achievement, Bradley specifies those qualities which, as we have seen, the poet found most abundantly and learned from in Shakespeare: concreteness of perception and presentation, wide sympathies and 'magic' in language.

In Keats's thought, a part of the meaning of tragedy lies in the fact that he can glimpse a precious, post-tragic awareness, where one can write from a state of 'gone self-storm'. It is the loveliest of all the 'chambers':

Tom has spit a leetle blood this afternoon, and that is rather a damper – but I know – the truth is there is something real in the World Your third Chamber of Life shall be a lucky and a gentle one – stored with the wine of love – and the Bread of Friendship.[34]

Just as in *King Lear* after the 'violent harms' comes the kiss of Cordelia as medicine to repair the frame of the moral world with love, so Keats's knowledge of the worst gives him a firm point of sanity and rest, no less 'real' for its being against the grain of distressing experience: 'Ripeness is all'. Keats the artist is untouchable and inviolable from such a point of visionary refuge and inner peace, itself the product of powerful, humanistic and humane sympathy as reflected in *The Fall of Hyperion*. It is generally agreed that in 'To Autumn' he speaks from such a perspective where the certainties of death and pain, moved just out of focus, gather on the horizon. 'Gone self-storm' is perhaps an equivalent for Aristotelian catharsis, Miltonic 'all passion spent', or the Shakespearean 'full close' after the final words of a tragedy have been spoken, as distress is comprehended and encompassed within a wider understanding of life going on. In a mood of quiet compassion, the poet guides us away from glimpses of the soft-dying day, the mourning of the small gnats, back into a full apprehension of the ripe forces available in the experience of living. This in itself is a great gift to discover in the poetry of Keats and the drama of Shakespeare alike, and it is one that has more to do with experience on the pulses than with art, or rather the point at which the two meet. It is the sanctifying of common experience, and paradoxically the concrete embodiment of sacred mysteries, which we find demonstrated in the mature poetry of Shakespeare and of Keats.

Conclusion
Keats as a reader of Shakespeare

If we give equal weight to each word in the title of this book, we should
be able to answer with some confidence three questions:

What have we learned about Keats?

What have we learned about Shakespeare?

What have we learned about the nature of reading?

As a reader John Keats carried in his mind many ideas about Shake-
speare and literature which were current amongst critics of his time,
and particularly Hazlitt. This means that his primary interests lay in
'impressions' of the play, both momentary and overall, in the presenta-
tion of character, in the vividness of figurative language, in feeling
states aroused in the individual reader, and in the breadth of contrasts
presented in a play. He also adopted the central idea that poetry is
important to the reader in helping to formulate his own ideas and
philosophies about morals and experience. All of these concerns we
have seen illustrated many times by the evidence, and Keats's
approach was so uniquely individual that he discovered his own
answers. He was always drawn to admire 'fine phrases' and in his
markings on the texts and in his letters he shows that the unexpected-
ness and aptness of Shakespeare's images and turns of phrase lie at the
heart of his interests:

> One of the three Books I have with me is Shakespear's Poems: I
> neer found so many beauties in the sonnets – they seem to be full
> of fine things said unintentionally – in the intensity of working out
> conceits – Is this to be borne? Hark ye!

> When lofty trees I see barren of leaves
> Which [erst] from heat did canopy the he[a]rd,
> And Summer's green all girded up in sheaves,
> Borne on the bier with white and bristly beard.

He has left nothing to say about nothing or any thing: for look at

Snails, you know what he says about Snails, you know where he talks about "cockled snails" – well, in one of these sonnets, he says – the chap slips into – no! I lie! this is in the Venus and Adonis: the Simile brought it to my Mind.

Audi – As the snail, whose tender horns being hit,
Shrinks back[s] into his shelly cave with pain,
And there all smothered up in shade doth sit,
Long after fearing to put forth again:
So at his bloody view her eyes are fled,
Into the deep dark Cabins of her head.

He overwhelms a genuine Lover of Poesy with all manner of abuse, talking about –

"a poets rage
And stretched metre of an antique song" –

Which by the by will be a capital Motto for my Poem [*Endymion*] – wont it? – He speaks too of "Time's antique pen" – and "aprils first born flowers" – and "deaths eternal cold" – By the Whim King![1]

The very tone of delighted exhilaration tells us a lot about the kind of breathless joy in the phrases of Shakespeare which makes Keats reach for his text. The fact that he can move from the Sonnets to *Venus and Adonis* via a phrase recalled from *Love's Labour's Lost* shows that he sees the same kind of language manifested in all Shakespeare's texts, and that it can be pulled out of context and still be admired. He is most aware of the provocativeness of Shakespeare, in chastising poets 'with all manner of abuse' as well as in creating a line of thought apparently arbitrarily ('unintentionally') by following where the conceit leads him. Shakespeare is the 'Whim King' letting his thoughts follow where his language leads him. We see also that Keats finds a direct line between Shakespeare and his own poetry, the former lending inspiration, confidence in poetic language, and even a post-script or 'Motto' for his poem. At other points in the letters we see Keats building upon a phrase or an idea from Shakespeare to develop his own philosophies of life and literature, a habit most eloquently displayed through his readings and recollections of *King Lear*. At the same time, we are aware of what Keats is *not* attempting to do. He does not have a strict notion of exact context or the dramatic autonomy of any one work (although, as we have seen, his 'misrememberings' can be intuitively revealing about connections in Shakespeare's use of recurrent situations). He shows little interest in matters of structure (although, again, he can notice chronology observed in a play like *Measure for Measure*), nor in overall problems of plot or consistent moral stance. His approach has the great strengths of one who could read with 'negative capability', surrendering himself to the power of a moment, celebrating contrast and diversity rather than intellectual coherence of the whole or consistency of dramatic presentation. At the same time despite his enjoyment of the theatre he has all the 'weaknesses' of one who is a reader rather than a critic, a closeted bardolater rather than one who sees the end product of a play as the performance in the theatre.

Bardolatry, however, is not a solemn and humourless stance for Keats. Acknowledging the ability to sum things up in sovereign manner, he irreverently appropriates Shakespeare's words in his letters. He jokingly asks Reynolds in an early letter, 'lend me thy hand to laugh a little',[2] glancing towards Prince Hal's words to his own friend Poins, in the play he marks in the Folio, *I Henry IV* (II.iv.1–2). A few months later, we find an equally informal absorption into Keats's language and experience of Hal's next speech, as the young Prince boasts of picking up low-life slang in the tavern. Hal's words to Poins read in part:

> ... They call drinking deep, dyeing scarlet; and when you breathe in your watering, they cry 'hem!' and bid you play it off. To conclude, I am so good a proficient in one quarter of an hour that I can drink with any tinker in his own language during my life... (II.iv.20–4)

Keats writes to his brothers, George and Tom, in early January 1818:

> I have had a great deal of pleasant time with Rice lately, and am getting initiated into a little Cant – they call dr[i]nking deep dying scarlet, and when you breathe in your wartering you bid you cry hem and play it off – they call good Wine a pretty tipple, and call getting a Child knocking out an apple, stopping at a Tave[r]n they call hanging out – Where do you sup? is where do you hang out?[3]

The examples are lightly instructive, for time and again Keats asks Shakespeare to lend him his words to laugh a little, and expands not only his vocabulary but his range of tones and responses when maintaining his own unique version of *badinage* with correspondents by borrowing phrases, idioms and figures of speech.

We can never afford to forget that the interest in Keats as a reader follows from the fact that he was a very great poet in his own right. As such he was influenced by a host of poets, major and minor, ancient and modern, but his commitment to Shakespeare as the writer from whom he learned most was loyal and abiding. We have noticed many occasions on which Keats echoes Shakespearean language, never in so simple a way that it can be called copying, and more generally he discovered *methods* of coinage and effects. As a poet, Keats can show how much he has learned from Shakespeare in his own capacity to find fine phrases to express 'Beautiful things made new for the delight of the sky-children', the same unexpected aptness of image, the same utter devotion to the truth of a moment expressed through sensuous language, even at the risk of irrelevance to his narrative. There is, of course, a difference of temperament which can perhaps be hinted by the contrast between Shakespeare's 'quick forge and working-house of thought'[4] and Keats's 'wreath'd trellis of a working brain',[5] the one darting upon phrases with a sure aim before swiftly moving on to another image or thought, the other tenderly coaxing from his linguistic resources a patiently full scene of rich stasis. What Keats apparently did not learn from Shakespeare was the art of building a play or a poem with a fastidious concentration on the nuts and bolts of the artisan who sees his job as presenting a completed, seamlessly structured work. Only in *The Eve of St Agnes* does Keats manage this kind of overall control and completion in a longer poem, for here his imagination is fully engaged throughout.

About Shakespeare as poet and dramatist, I hope to have shown throughout this book Keats's ability suddenly to open up a seam of beauty or profundity that has not gained full attention from critics or anthologists of the dramatist's work. Because he became so deeply and imaginatively involved in Shakespeare's works, continually testing phrases and ideas upon the palate of his own taste, Keats exhibits few preconceptions about what he will find (although he does not escape a predisposition to notice some things more than others), but instead a constant sense of being freshly surprised. By looking at Shakespeare with a knowledge of what interested Keats, we too can be surprised even when approaching texts we thought we knew by heart. That this is so is first a measure of Keats's sensitive concentration but equally, extra proof of Shakespeare's large vision, encompassing the delicate and the immense at the same time. Our respect for Shakespeare cannot fail to be enhanced, our knowledge broadened, by newly perceiving what Keats has noticed, and also by what he has not – effects achieved not by 'whim' but by careful, concentrated labour.

The nature of reading is a very large subject, and only a few comments can be hazarded here in a spirit of suggestiveness rather than thoroughness. By respecting Keats's own habits and notions of reading we are oddly brought full circle to theories which are only recently being given acknowledgement by theorists and literary critics. The characteristic process adopted by Keats is to attempt first to forget his own limited 'identity' and reach out in sympathy and self-annihilation to a full recreation of the text in front of him. A simple part of the exercise is reading with pen in hand, ready to mark anything that attracts his attention. At a certain stage, however, (whether later in time or simultaneously-but-secondarily is a metaphysical question) he refers the verity of an idea, the aptness of a phrase, back to his own sense of self as a thinking person and a practising poet. Reading as a process then becomes an unbroken continuum between submergence in another's text and a creative effort on Keats's part, selecting and adapting to his own ends what remains of use to him. Broadly speaking, using his own analogy, the movement is from the function of the flower to the function of the bee, from passive receptivity to active self-assertion. The significant conclusion is that 'the text' does not exist as holding one definitive set of 'meanings' or even a body of structures which can be universally agreed upon. Whether the unit examined is the word, the phrase, the exchange between speakers, the scene, any number of other structural portions, the play as a whole or even genres or the canon as a whole, there is always the possibility of individual understandings and evaluations differing from reader to reader. The metaphor I have used elsewhere of a musician or conductor interpreting a score, is based on the notion that the text is a potential which is activated in as many subtly or broadly differing ways as there are readers, actors and audiences. Literary criticism has periodically resisted this mode of analysis. Given the need to justify its place in universities or its credibility as a 'discipline' when measured against the sciences, or simply in order to agree on certain assumptions about critical procedure, the world of English studies has made attempts over the last century to produce a 'rigorous' methodology that eliminates the variousness of response of different readers. We have had practical criticism, new criticism, common sense, Marxism, structuralism, 'the death of the author', 'expressive realism' and other –isms in an attempt somehow to settle the text down as an agreeably definite thing which is amenable to 'new readings' certainly but only within circumscribed limits. Keats's whole attitude challenges such notions, if only by implicitly allowing the validity of them all. The crucial element he introduces (following Hazlitt, who often in his Shake-spearean criticism simply quotes and 'lets the reader do the work'), is the emphasis on the creative role of the reader, leading to an individual response which need not be undisciplined or unverifiable. Every word he writes in his letters and poems is an assertion of the tight discipline of the imagination working on several levels at once, holding a rigour which is considerably more multifarious than the 'one-dimensional reading'. Interestingly, recent theorists are rediscovering the idea that the reader's unique relationship with the text must be taken as evidence in itself when speaking of the text, although modern terminology is probably a little more conscious of the need to be 'scientific' than is Keats's language:

> ... to the extent that the hearer participates in these ... discourses, he or she finds in the sentence one or more of the possible readings. In other words, the meaning of this sentence is *plural*. But this is emphatically not to say that it is subjective ...[6]

It is a fascinating, if unnerving conclusion to reach that a modest study of what one dead poet found of interest and use in the texts of another dead poet leaves us on the threshold of dealing with some of the most contemporary issues being faced by theorists of literature. Such a notion might not have surprised Keats himself, for he could find a plurality of meanings even in his own words on different readings, a phenomenon which he happily links with the name of his poetic master:

> I hope for the support of a High Power while I clime this little eminence and especially in my Years of more momentous Labor. I remember your saying that you had notions of a good Genius presiding over you – I have of late had the same thought. for things which [I] do half at Random are afterwards confirmed by my judgment in a dozen features of Propriety – Is it too daring to Fancy Shakspeare this Presider?[7]

Notes

Introduction

1 *The Letters of John Keats*, ed. Hyder E. Rollins (Cambridge, Mass., in two vols, 1958), I, 130.

2 *Letters*, II, 62.

3 The books are now in the Houghton Library, Harvard University. For textual details and information about Keats's acquisition of the volumes, see *The Keats Library (A Descriptive Catalogue)* by Frank N. Owings, published by the Keats-Shelley Memorial Association (London, 1978), p. 57. Transcriptions have been recorded in D.B. Green's unpublished PhD thesis (1953) for Boston University.

4 The copy is now in the library in Keats House, Hampstead. See *The Keats Library*, p. 55. It is catalogued 1808, and I have checked a watermark in the paper as 1806.

5 *Letters*, I, 232.

6 Keats's review of Kean's Shakespearean acting in *The Champion*, 21 December 1817 is most easily consulted in *John Keats: The Complete Poems*, ed. John Barnard (Harmondsworth, 1973), pp. 527–9. The review appeared a week before another piece which used to be attributed to Keats but is now considered more likely to have been written by Reynolds. See Barnard, p. 527.

7 See *Letters*, I, 143. The copy is now in the Houghton Library, Harvard. See *The Keats Library*, p. 27. Transcriptions of Keats's markings (sometimes inaccurate) are reproduced by Amy Lowell in *John Keats* (Boston and New York, 1925), II, 545–605. Corrections to her transcriptions are given by Norman A. Anderson in 'Corrections to Amy Lowell's Reading of Keats's Marginalia', *Keats-Shelley Journal*, xxiii (1974), 25–31. I shall not examine Z. Jackson's *Shakespeare's Genius Justified* (1819) since Keats's notations simply express irritation at the writer's crassness; nor

his copies of Shakespeare's *Poems*, since the markings are agreed not to have been made by Keats.

8 *Letters*, I, 394.

9 'Sleep and Poetry', lines 69–71.

10 J. Middleton Murry, *Keats and Shakespeare* (London, 1925).

11 Murry, p. 69.

12 'Verse letter' to Reynolds, line 75.

13 Stillinger's reading, now generally accepted.

14 See *Letters*, II, 74–6.

15 Murry, pp. 10–11. Murry regards the study of Keats 'as a sort of prolegomena to the study of Shakespeare' (p. 7). I should crucially qualify this to say that Keats guides us to *certain aspects* of Shakespeare.

16 *Keats's Shakespeare: A Descriptive Study Based on New Material* (2nd edn, London, 1929).

17 R.D. Havens, reviewing Spurgeon's book in *Modern Language Notes*, xliv (1929), 339.

18 Helen Darbishire, *Review of English Studies*, v (1929), 488. I am indebted to D.B. Green's thesis (see note 3 above) for convenient access to these reviews.

19 Robert F. Gleckner, 'Keats's "How Many Bards" and Poetic Tradition', *Keats-Shelley Journal*, xxvii (1978), p. 20.

20 For a tactful account of the nature of 'influence' upon Keats, see E.C. Pettet, *On the Poetry of Keats* (Cambridge, 1957), ch.1.

21 Proust, *On Reading*, originally Preface to Proust's translation of Ruskin's *Sesame and Lilies*, tr. J. Autret and W. Burford (London, 1971).

22 *Letters*, II,5.

I *The importance of reading Shakespeare*

1 *Letters*, I, 212.

2 *Letters*, I, 214.

3 For bibliographical information on the variants in the different versions of the sonnet, see Stillinger, *Poems of John Keats*, pp. 588–9.

4 Allott compares Gen. 27: 'And the Lord God formed man of the dust of the ground, and breathed into his nostrils the breath of life; and man became A living soul.' The phrase is so uniquely Keats's own that it would be impertinent to suggest any particular source, but it must at least be valid to connect it with the play

which is the subject of the poem.

5 To Reynolds, 19 Feb 1818. *Letters*, I, 231–3.
6 *Letters*, II, 113.
7 'I am ambitious of doing the world some good.' *Letters*, I, 387.
8 Johnson when writing on *King Lear* says, 'for it is always a writer's duty to make the world better...', *Preface to Shakespeare*.
9 *Letters*, II, 102–3.
10 *Letters*, I, 243.
11 I am grateful to Barbara Everett for impressing upon me the importance of this point.
12 *Letters*, II, 102.
13 I shall develop this important point in a forthcoming book, *Paradoxical Keats*.
14 *Letters*, II, 101.
15 J.C. Maxwell, 'Keats as a Guide to Shakespeare', *Notes and Queries*, 15 March 1952, p. 126.
16 *The Complete Works of William Hazlitt*, ed. P.P. Howe (in twenty-one volumes, London, 1930), IV, 271. (The underlining is Keats's).
17 *Letters*, I, 242–3 (above, note 10).
18 For a wide-ranging and challenging textual study of Keats's text of *King Lear*, its relationship with the Sonnet and with Shakespeare's text, see Randall McLeod, 'Unediting Shak-speare', *Sub-Stance*, 33–4 (1982), pp. 26–55.
19 *Letters*, II, 167.

II *Hazlitt and Keats's attitudes to Shakespeare*

1 Keats uses the phrase twice in *Letters*, I, 203 and 205 and on the page of Hazlitt's *Characters*, with a quotation from Launcelot Gobbo..
2 Kenneth Muir, 'Keats and Hazlitt' in *John Keats: A Reassessment* (Liverpool, 1959), p. 158.
3 See especially Roy Park, *Hazlitt and the Spirit of the Age* (Oxford, 1971) and John Kinnaird, *William Hazlitt: Critic of Power* (New York, 1978). Numerous articles have appeared as well (see Bibliography). An earlier book, M.H. Abrams, *The Mirror and the Lamp* (New York, 1953), contributed in a pioneering way to the study of romantic criticism, and I am generally indebted to it. See also W.P. Albrecht, *Hazlitt and the Creative Imagination* (Lawrence, Kansas, 1965).
4 Muir, p. 139.

5   *The Tempest*, I.ii.221–4. In Keats's text he has marked thus:

> (Ariel): The King's son have I landed by himself,
> Whom I left cooling of the air with sighs
> In an odd angle of the isle, and sitting,
> His arms in this sad knot.

6   *Letters*, I, 166.
7   *Letters*, I, 123 and 252; II, 24.
8   *Letters*, II, 24n.
9   Haydon influenced Keats in turning him away from Hunt's notions of poetic beauty, and encouraged him to study and attempt to emulate Shakespeare. See C.L. Finney, *The Evolution of Keats's Poetry* (Cambridge, Mass., 1936), pp.211–14.
10 Review in *The Champion* (Introduction, note 6), Barnard, p. 529.
11 Park, p. 35.
12 Hazlitt, XII, 246.
13 Hazlitt, XVII, 311.
14 *Ibid*.
15 *Letters*, I, 193–4.
16 Hazlitt, XII, 347 and 355.
17 Hazlitt, IV, 171.
18 Hazlitt, IV, 175.
19 G. Wilson Knight, *The Wheel of Fire* (fourth edn, London, 1949), p.l.
20 John Jones, *John Keats's Dream of Truth* (London, 1969), p. 287.
21 Hazlitt, V, 4.
22 Hazlitt, V, 1.
23 Hazlitt, IV, 77.
24 Kinnaird, p. 144.
25 Hazlitt, IV, 79.
26 Hazlitt, IV, 77.
27 Review in *The Champion*; Barnard, p. 528.
28 *Letters*, I, 192.
29 Stuart Sperry, *Keats the Poet* (Princeton, NJ, 1973), p. 9. Sperry goes on: '...Keats's approach to art is primitive and constructive: it begins with what is most fundamental to human experience and proceeds from there.'
30 Ian Jack, *Keats and the Mirror of Art* (Oxford, 1967).
31 Terence Hawkes (ed.), *Coleridge on Shakespeare* (Harmondsworth, 1969), p. 108.
32 Coleridge, *Biographia Literaria*, chap. xv, Hawkes, p. 73.
33 Hazlitt, IV, 230.

34 *Letters*, I, 189.
35 *Letters*, I, 144.
36 *Letters*, II, 167.
37 Kinnaird, p. 184.
38 Hazlitt, IV, 201.
39 Hazlitt, IV, 191.
40 *Letters*, I, 387.
41 *Letters*, I, 277.
42 *Hamlet*, I,iii.65, underlined by Keats.
43 *Measure for Measure*, III.i.119–34, underlined by Keats.
44 *Letters*, II, 80.
45 *Letters*, II, 360.
46 Jones, p. 268.
47 Park, p. 154.
48 Hazlitt, V. 3.
49 Hazlitt, IV, 238.
50 Hazlitt, IV, 210.
51 Hazlitt, IV, 186.
52 Hazlitt, IV, 221.
53 *Troilus and Cressida*, I.iii.316–17. Underlined and annotated by Keats.
54 *Letters*, II, 90.
55 *Letters*, I, 232.
56 *Letters*, I, 201.
57 Hazlitt, IV, 172.
58 See D. Nichol Smith (ed.), *Eighteenth Century Essays on Shakespeare* (Oxford, 1963), Introduction.
59 Nichol Smith, p. xxxv.
60 Nichol Smith, p. 193.
61 For a recent appraisal of this field, see Brian Vickers, 'The Emergence of Character Criticism, 1774–1800', *Shakespeare Survey* 34 (1981), 39–50.
62 See Hawkes, *Coleridge on Shakespeare*, pp. 67, 74, 78, 274.
63 Hazlitt, IV, 23 ('On Posthumous Fame').
64 Nichol Smith, p. xxxvi.
65 *Letters*, II, 344.
66 I *Henry IV*, III.iii.1–8.
67 Hazlitt, IV, 279.
68 *Letters*, I, 125.
69 *Letters*, II, 260.
70 *Letters*, II, 378.

71 *Henry V*, II.iii.9–26.
72 *Letters*, I, 157.
73 Hazlitt, IV, 172.
74 *Collected Letters of S.T. Coleridge*, E.L. Griggs (ed.), in six volumes, II, 810. Quoted in *Coleridge's Poetics* by Paul Hamilton (Oxford, 1983), p. 180.

III Keats's readings of Shakespeare's comedies

1 *Letters*, I, 140–1. The passage is underlined in Keats's text.
2 'Fame, like a wayward Girl...' and 'How fever'd is the man...'
3 London, 1969. Keats also uses the phrase in *Letters*, I, 146.
4 *Letters*, I, 128.
5 *Letters*, I, 138.
6 *Letters*, I, 148.
7 *Letters*, I, 224.
8 *Letters*, I, 324.
9 *Letters*, II, 43.
10 *Letters*, I, 142.
11 *The Keats Circle*, Hyder E. Rollins (ed.), (Cambridge, Mass., 1948) in two volumes, I, 284.
12 *Letters*, II, 101.
13 II.i.31 and IV.iii.104. Both contexts are underlined in Keats's text.
14 *Letters*, I, 242–3.
15 *Letters*, II, 187–8.
16 Hazlitt, IV, 329.
17 *Letters*, I, 258. The underlining is in his letter, and his edition.
18 *Letters*, I,, 193–4.
19 *Letters*, I, 276.
20 *Letters*, I, 190.
21 *Letters*, I, 276.
22 *Endymion*, iii, 927.
23 Christopher Ricks, *Keats and Embarrassment* (Oxford, 1976).
24 *Letters*, II, 235.
25 *Letters*, II, 299.
26 Eamon Grennan, 'Keats's *Contemptus Mundi*: A Shakespearean Influence on the "Ode to a Nightingale" ', *Modern Language Quarterly*, xxxvi (1975), 272–92. See also Ogden, Bate and Gradman in the Bibliography.
27 Hazlitt, IV, 179.

28 Hazlitt, IV, 180.
29 *Letters*, I, 157.
30 *Letters*, I, 387.
31 Hazlitt, iv, 180.
32 *The Fall of Hyperion*, II, lines 13–17.
33 Hazlitt, IV, 185.
34 Hazlitt, IV, 324.
35 Quoted by Ian Jack in *Keats and the Mirror of Art* (Oxford, 1967), p. 13.
36 Jack, pp. 211, 227, 236.
37 *The Fall of Hyperion*, II, lines 58–61.
38 'I stood tip-toe upon a little hill', line 162.
39 The Odes have been the subject of a thorough study by Irene S. Harris, 'The Influence of Shakespeare on the Odes of Keats'. PhD thesis for Boston University (1978), as yet unpublished.

IV 'Shakespearean hieroglyphics'

1 See Spurgeon, *Keats's Shakespeare*, pp. 7–20 and 55–65.
2 As an indication of the proportions of markings, there are roughly 1800 lines in *The Tempest* and roughly 2100 in *A Midsummer Night's Dream*. Spurgeon reproduces the marked lines in these plays.
3 Hazlitt, IV, 173.
4 Review in *The Champion*.
5 Edmund Blunden in a paper on 'Shakespeare's Significances', mainly on *King Lear* (Shakespeare Association Lecture, 1929) gives an interesting parallel to Keats's 'hieroglyphics' when he builds his analysis on the premise that '... all critics of Shakespeare must be cryptographers'. Since Blunden wrote extensively on Keats it is not impossible that he is remembering Keats's reference. I am grateful to Dr Desmond Graham for pointing out the essay to me.
6 Hawkes (ed.), *Coleridge on Shakespeare*, p. 183.
7 Hazlitt, IV, 233.
8 Hazlitt, IV, 259.
9 *OED* gives the meaning as 'physiognomy' which in its turn is interpreted most concisely as 'A judging of the form of a living body from the skeleton' or simply 'A representation of a face; a portrait'; or again, 'The general appearance or external features

of anything material'.

10 Hazlitt, IV, 238.
11 *Letters*, I, 133.
12 *Letters*, I, 128.
13 Havens, *M L N* xliv (1929), p. 340.
14 Spurgeon, p. 17.
15 Review in *The Champion*.
16 *Letters*, I, 214.
17 *Letters*, I, 142. The reference is to *The Tempest* IV.i.156.
18 *Letters*, I, 231–3.
19 *Letters*, I, 231. the quotation is from Wordsworth's 'The Old Cumberland Beggar'.
20 *Letters*, I, 232.
21 *Letters*, I, 233.
22 *Letters*, I, 232.
23 *Letters*, I, 129. In Keats the lion becomes a titmouse.
24 *Letters*, II, 254.
25 *Letters*, I, 129.
26 *Letters*, I, 132.
27 *Letters*, I, 136.
28 *Letters*, I, 147.
29 *Letters*, I, 158.
30 Finney, pp. 733 ff.
31 *Letters*, II, 234.
32 Hazlitt, IV, 247.
33 *Ibid.*
34 Spurgeon, p. 55.

V   Hamlet *and* Macbeth

1 Leonidas M. Jones, 'Keats's Favorite Play', *English Language Notes* xv (1977), 43–4. The evidence is a casual reference in a letter on 8 May 1820 from B.W. Proctor to John Scott. As Jones implies, it is not strong evidence.
2 *Letters*, I, 279.
3 Hawkes, p. 158 and Hazlitt, IV, 232.
4 *Letters*, II, 67.
5 *Letters*, II, 115–16.
6 *Letters*, I, 279.
7 *Letters*, I, 277–8.
8 *Letters*, I, 281.

9　*Ibid.* The phrase itself is probably from Webster, *The White Devil*, V.vi.260; cf. *The Duchess of Malfi*, IV.ii.188, V.v.118.
10　*Letters*, I, 139.
11　*Letters*, I, 179.
12　*Ibid.*
13　*Ibid.*
14　*Letters*, I, 223–4.
15　The *OED* entry is; '3. *incorrectly* for: Realm, domain. (A misunderstanding of the passage in *Hamlet*.) Obs. 1818 KEATS *Endym.* III.31 A thousand powers keep religious state, In water, fiery realm, and airy bourne.'
16　An interesting attempt to link *Hamlet* with 'Ode to a Nightingale' is made by A. Jonathon Bate in 'Shakespeare and the Nightingale', *English*, xxxi (1982), 138–41, and see also the convincing suggestion by Mark Taylor, 'Keats's "Ode to a Nightingale" ', *Explicator*, xxxvi (1978), 24–6.
17　*Letters*, II, 206.
18　*Letters*, II, 178.
19　*Letters*, II, 312.
20　*Letters*, I, 138. See also R. Ryan, *Keats: The Religious Sense* (Princeton, NJ, 1976), pp. 92–3.
21　Green, 'Keats's Shakespeare: A Second Gleaning', chapter in PhD thesis.
22　See the reminiscence by Charles Cowden Clarke, conveniently quoted by Finney, p. 19.
23　Hazlitt, IV, 186.
24　*Letters*, II, 156–7.
25　Hazlitt, IV, 187–8.
26　*Letters*, I, 201.
27　*Letters*, I, 269.
28　*Letters*, II, 82.
29　Review in *The Champion*.
30　*Letters*, II, 79. Note also that 'speculation' is a word used by Lady Macbeth at III.iv.95, underlined by Keats.
31　*Letters*, II, 81.

VI　*Tragedies of love*

1　Spurgeon, pp. 22–3.
2　*Letters*, I, 144.
3　*Letters*, I, 320.

4 *Letters*, I, 395.
5 *Ibid.*
6 Hazlitt, IV, 230.
7 Hazlitt, IV, 228.
8 I have suggested this literary connection, among others, in 'Shakespearean Music in Keats's "Ode to a Nightingale" ', *English*, xxx (1981), 217–29.
9 Hazlitt, IV, 232.
10 Above, ch. v, note 1.
11 Pasternak, after translating Shakespeare, spoke of 'the explosions of Shakespearean imagery', continuing 'His analogies represent the furthest point the subjective principle in poetry has ever reached ... The strength of Shakespeare's poetry lies in its way of being a freely done sketch, which, knowing no restraint, tosses about in powerful disarray'. *Russian Poets on Poetry*, ed. Carl Proffer (Ann Arbor, 1976). I am grateful to Dr Desmond Graham for pointing out this quotation to me.
12 *Letters*, II, 256.
13 *Letters*, II, 293–4.
14 'La Belle Dame Sans Merci' is too mysterious to comment on: we only hear opinions about her, rather than what she is in fact like herself.
15 Bruce E. Haley, '"The Infinite Will": Shakespeare's Troilus and the "Ode to a Nightingale"', *Keats-Shelley Journal*, xxii (1972), 18–23.
16 *Letters*, I, 404.
17 Douglas Bush (ed.), *John Keats: Selected Poems and Letters* (Cambridge, Mass., 1976), p. 351.
18 See W. J. Bate, *John Keats* (Cambridge, Mass., 1963), p. 215.
19 *Letters*, I, 190.
20 *Letters*, II, 281.
21 *Letters*, I, 157.
22 *Letters*, I, 325.
23 Hazlitt, IV, 253–4.
24 Hazlitt, IV, 180.
25 *Letters*, II, 80.
26 Hazlitt, IV, 248.
27 Hazlitt, IV, 249.
28 Hazlitt, IV, 250.
29 See also Finney, pp. 543ff. and Jack Stillinger, 'The Hoodwinking of Madeline: Scepticism in *The Eve of St Agnes*', *Studies in*

Philology, lviii (1961), reprinted in *The Hoodwinking of Madeline and Other Essays on Keats's Poems* (Urbana, 1971).

30 The phrase is Hazlitt's, *Works*, IV, 248, above.

31 Hazlitt, IV, 251.

32 *Ibid.* The links between Hazlitt's essay on *Romeo and Juliet* and *The Eve of St Agnes* are just as significant as those between the play itself and the poem. Hazlitt anticipates many of Keats's key images (such as the opening rose) and as I have argued he supplies a quasi-philosophical analysis of the emotions which are being dramatically and poetically portrayed. It is interesting to speculate that Keats is consciously writing an 'anti-Wordsworth' poem, since he would have read Hazlitt's suggestion that *Romeo and Juliet* emphasises the anticipatory imagination and desires rather than the backward-looking reflectiveness associated with Wordsworth's philosophy.

VII   King Lear

1 The relationship between the Quarto and Folio texts is a topical and highly specialized subject among Shakespearean textual critics, see Gary Taylor and Michael Warren (eds), *The Divisions of the Kingdom: Shakespeare's Two Versions of 'King Lear'* (Oxford, 1983) – but it is not necessary to elaborate here. For consistency and ease of reference I have here, as throughout this book, quoted in modern spelling from the conflated Alexander text. Where differences matter, I quote the Folio.

2 Spurgeon, p. 180.

3 That is, roughly V.iii.26–257, which covers the time when Lear is offstage.

4 There are occasional comments in the letters which come close to expressing such a fatalistic attitude in Keats's own words, but by and large he is more robust. See e.g. *Letters* II, 181 where 'woes' and 'grievances' are placed in a firmly humanistic context.

5 A.C. Bradley sees it as a defining quality of Keats's moral speculations that he stresses inevitable adversity and rarely speaks of human evil; see Bradley's essay on Keats's letters in *Oxford Lectures on Poetry* (2nd edn, London, 1909). In qualification, it should be said that Keats often sees evil in specifically political terms as the unjust exercise of power by those in authority – an issue which is quite central to *King Lear*.

6 *Letters*, I, 192.

7   *Letters*, II, 80–1.

8   *Letters*, I, 194.

9   *Letters*, I, 387.

10 *Letters*, I, 277. The phrase is repeated at 281.

11 Cf. also 'the Penetralium of mystery', *Letters*, I, 194.

12 *The Fall of Hyperion*, I, 303–4.

13 *Letters*, I, 277.

14 *Letters*, I, 279.

15 Hawkes (ed.), *Coleridge on Shakespeare*, p. 204.

16 I feel sure that Keats found the term 'bye-play' in Hazlitt's discussion of Kean's Richard III, 'Mr Kean's *bye-play* [H's italics] is certainly one of his greatest excellences, and it might be said, that if Shakespear had written marginal directions to the players ... he would often have directed them to do what Mr Kean does'. Hazlitt, V, 202, quoted by Stanley Wells in 'Shakespeare in Hazlitt's Theatre Criticism', *Shakespeare Survey* xxxv (1982), 43–55.

17 Hazlitt, IV, 260.

18 Hazlitt, IV, 271.

19 In Keats's Folio this is 'ear-bussing', though in some editions it is 'ear-kissing'

20 A.D. Atkinson, 'Keats and Compound Epithets', *Notes and Queries*, April (1952), 186–9 and July (1952), 301–6.

21 See *Keats: The Critical Heritage*, G.M. Matthews (ed.), (London, 1971), pp. 110–15.

22 *Letters*, I, 141.

23 Wordsworth, 'Resolution and Independence', lines 99–102.

24 *Letters*, I, 132.

25 The basis of an argument (implied, for example, by A.C. Bradley), that Keats did not really consider morals in any accepted sense would be his desire for 'disinterestedness' as a ground for action, and his preference for speaking about natural adversity rather than human evil. In fact, building upon the latter point, there is remarkably little *guilt* in Keats's letters or poems, in contrast to virtually all his contemporaries. However, on the general issue, I take it that Robert Ryan has convincingly demonstrated the searching quality of Keats's moral interests (defined broadly) in *Keats: The Religious Sense* (Princeton, NJ, 1976).

26 *Letters*, II, 101.

27 *Ibid*.

28 Review in *Keats-Shelley Journal*, xxiii (1974), pp. 152–3.

VIII   *Keats and tragedy*

1   *Letters*, I, 231.
2   *Letters*, II, 174.
3   Leonidas M. Jones, *Keats-Shelley Journal*, iii (1954), 55–65.
4   Quoted by Finney, p. 239.
5   *Letters*, II, 174.
6   Jack Stillinger speaks of 'anti-romance' and 'Keats's constant sense of the insufficiencies of romance' in *Isabella: The Hoodwinking of Madeline and Other Essays*.
7   Harry R. Beaudry, *The English Theatre and John Keats* (Salzburg, 1973).
8   *Letters*, I, 219.
9   *Letters*, II, 139.
10   *Letters*, II, 234.
11   For a convenient summary of critical attitudes see B. Chatterjee, *John Keats: His Mind and Work* (Calcutta, 1971), p. 100.
12   Murry, *Keats and Shakespeare*, p. 153.
13   Finney, pp. 662 ff.
14   Beaudry, Chapter VI.
15   Finney, p. 65.
16   Joan Grundy, 'Keats and the Elizabethans', essay in Muir, *John Keats: A Reassessment*, p. 13.
17   Beaudry, p. 184.
18   *Letters*, II, 102.
19   *Letters*, II, 101.
20   *Letters*, II, 113.
21   *Letters*, II, 167.
22   See Muir, 'The Meaning of *Hyperion*' in Muir, pp. 102–22.
23   *Letters*, I, 142.
24   *Letters*, I, 207.
25   *Letters*, II, 234.
26   *Letters*, II, 18.
27   See notes in editions by Allott and Barnard for some reference to *Lear* and see D.G. James, 'Keats and *King Lear*', *Shakespeare Survey*, xiii (1960), 58–68.
28   Murry, p. 169.
29   Helen Vendler, *The Odes of Keats* (Cambridge, Mass., 1983), p. 221.
30   Harold Bloom, *The Visionary Company* (revised and enlarged edn, Cornell, 1971), p. 432.

31 From 'Mother of Hermes! and still youthful Maia', sometimes known as 'Ode to May'.
32 *Letters*, II, 169.
33 Bradley, *Oxford Lectures on Poetry*, pp. 238–9.
34 *Letters*, I, 282–3.

Conclusion   Keats as a reader of Shakespeare

1 *Letters*, I, 188–9.
2 *Letters*, I, 190.
3 *Letters*, I, 197.
4 *Henry V*, V.Prologue.23.
5 'Ode to Psyche', line 60.
6 Catherine Belsey, *Critical Practice* (London, 1980), p. 54. There is, of course, a body of theoretical writing on 'the act of reading' which could furnish a large digression. A comparable 'theory' is presented in terms of the novel by Wolfgang Iser, *The Act of Reading* (London, 1976). For general information on 'reader-response criticism' see Robert C. Holub, *Reception Theory: A Critical Introduction* (London and New York, 1984) with its helpful bibliography.
7 *Letters*, I, 141–2.

Bibliography

M.H. Abrams, *The Mirror and the Lamp: Romantic theory and the critical tradition* (New York, 1953).

W.P. Albrecht, *Hazlitt and the Creative Imagination* (Lawrence, Kansas, 1965).

——, 'Hazlitt, passion, and King Lear', *Studies in English Literature*, xviii (1978), 610–24.

Miriam Allott (ed.), *Keats: The Complete Poems* (London, 1970).

Norman A. Anderson, 'Corrections to Amy Lowell's reading of Keats's marginalia', *Keats-Shelley Journal*, xxiii (1974), 25–31.

Matthew Arnold, 'John Keats', in *Essays in Criticism: Second Series* (London, 1888).

A.D. Atkinson, 'Keats and compound-epithets', *Notes and Queries*, April (1952), 186–9, and July (1952), 301–6.

Herschel Baker, *William Hazlitt* (Cambridge, Mass., 1962).

John Barnard (ed.), *John Keats: The Complete Poems* (Harmondsworth, 1973).

Jonathon A. Bate, 'Shakespeare and the Nightingale', *English*, xxxi (1982), 138–41.

W.J. Bate, *John Keats* (Cambridge, Mass., 1963).

——, *Negative Capability: The intuitive approach in Keats*, (Cambridge, Mass., 1939).

——, *The Burden of the Past and the English Poet* (Cambridge, Mass., 1959).

Harry R. Beaudry, *The English Theatre of John Keats* (Salzburg, 1973).

W. Beyer, *Keats and the Daemon King* (New York, 1947).

Harold Bloom, 'Keats and the embarrassments of poetic tradition', in *From Sensibility to Romanticism*, F.W. Hilles and H. Bloom (eds) (New York, 1965).

Edmund Blunden, 'Shakespeare's significances', *Shakespeare Association Lecture* (London, 1929).

A.C. Bradley, *Oxford Lectures on Poetry* (2nd edn, London, 1909).

David Bromwich, *Hazlitt: The mind of a critic* (Oxford and New York, 1983).

Douglas Bush (ed.), *John Keats: Selected poems and letters* (Cambridge, Mass., 1959).

Douglas Bush, 'Keats and Shakespeare', in *Shakespeare: Aspects of Influence*, Harvard English Studies 7, G.B. Evans (ed.) (Cambridge, Mass., 1976), pp. 71–89.

——, 'Keats' in *Mythology and the Romantic Tradition in English Poetry*

(Cambridge, Mass., 1937).

——, 'Notes on Keats's reading', *Publications of the Modern Languages Association*, 50 (1933), 785–806.

Joseph Candido, '*A Midsummer Night's Dream* and "Ode to a Nightingale": A further instance of Keats's indebtedness', *American Notes and Queries*, xvi (1978), 154–5.

Babhatosh Chatterjee, *John Keats: His mind and work* (Calcutta, 1971).

Sir Sidney Colvin, *John Keats: His life and poetry...* (New York, 1920).

Helen Darbishire, Review of Spurgeon (below), *Review of English Studies*, v (1929), 488.

Howard Felperin, 'Keats and Shakespeare: Two new sources', *English Language Notes*, ii (1964).

C.L. Finney, 'Shakespeare and Keats', unpublished PhD thesis for Harvard University, 1922.

——, *The Evolution of Keats's Poetry* (Cambridge, Mass., 1936).

M. Buxton Forman, (ed.) *The Letters of John Keats* (4th edn, 1952).

H.W. Garrod (ed.), *Keats: Poetical Works* (London, 1956).

Robert Gittings, *John Keats* (Harmondsworth, 1968).

——, *John Keats: The living year* (London, 1954).

——, *The Keats Inheritance* (London, 1964).

Robert F. Gleckner, 'Keats's "How Many Bards" and Poetic Tradition', *Keats-Shelley Journal*, xxvii (1978), 14–22.

Barry Gradman, '*King Lear* and the image of Ruth in Keats's "Nightingale Ode" ', *Keats-Shelley Journal*, xxxv (1976), 15–24.

——, '*Measure for Measure* and Keats's "Nightingale" Ode', *English Language Notes*, xii (1975), 177–82.

David Bonnell Green, 'Studies in Keats, with biographical sketches of his acquaintances Thomas Hill and Edward Du Bois', unpublished PhD dissertation, Harvard, 1953.

Eamon Grennan, 'Keats's *Contemptus Mundi*: A Shakespearean influence on the "Ode to a Nightingale" ', *Modern Language Quarterly*, xxxvi (1975), 272–92.

George Clayburn Gross, 'Keats's "Presider": The influence of Shakespeare', unpublished PhD dissertation, University of Southern California, 1963.

Bruce E. Haley, '"The Infinite Will": Shakespeare's Troilus and the "Ode to a Nightingale" ', *Keats-Shelley Journal*, xxii (1972), 18–23.

Irene Strickler Harris, 'The influence of Shakespeare on the Odes of Keats', unpublished PhD dissertation, Boston University, 1978.

R.D. Havens, review of Spurgeon (below), *Modern Language Notes*, xliv (1929), 339.

Terence Hawkes (ed.), *Coleridge on Shakespeare* (Harmondsworth 1969).

The Complete Works of William Hazlitt, P.P. Howe (ed.), 21 vols (London, 1930).

Robert C. Holub, *Reception Theory: A critical introduction* (London and New York, 1984).

Graham Hough, *The Romantic Poets* (2nd edn, London, 1957).

Ian Jack, *Keats and the Mirror of Art* (Oxford, 1967).

D.G. James, 'Keats and *King Lear*', *Shakespeare Survey*, xiii (1960), 58–68.

John Jones, *John Keats's Dream of Truth* (London, 1969).

Leonidas M. Jones, 'Keats's favorite play', *English Language Notes*, xv (1977), 43–4.

John Kinnaird, *William Hazlitt: Critic of Power* (New York, 1978).

G. Wilson Knight, *The Wheel of Fire* (4th edn, London, 1949).

——, 'The priest-like task: An essay on Keats', in *The Starlit Dome* (Oxford, 1941).

Amy Lowell, *John Keats*, 2 vols (Boston and New York, 1925).

Randall McLeod, 'UN Editing Shak-speare', *Sub-Stance*, 33–4 (1982), 26–55.

G.M. Matthews, *Keats: The critical heritage* (London, 1971).

J.C. Maxwell, 'Keats as a guide to Shakespeare', *Notes and Queries* (15 March 1952), 126.

Kenneth Muir, *John Keats: A reassessment* (Liverpool, 1959).

John Middleton Murry, *Keats and Shakespeare* (London, 1925).

James Ogden, 'Shakespeare and the "Nightingale" ', *English*, xxxi (1982), 134–7.

Frank N. Owings, *The Keats Library: A descriptive catalogue*, published by the Keats-Shelley Memorial Association (London, 1978).

Roy Park, *Hazlitt and the Spirit of the Age* (Oxford, 1971).

——, 'Lamb, Shakespeare and the stage', *Shakespeare Quarterly*, xxxiii (1982), 164–77.

David Perkins, *The Quest for Permanence: The symbolism of Wordsworth, Shelley and Keats* (Cambridge, Mass., 1959).

E.C. Pettet, *On the Poetry of Keats* (Cambridge, 1957).

R.F. Rashbrook, 'Keats and Hamlet', *Notes and Queries*, cxcv (1950), 253–4.

T.M. Raysor (ed.), *Coleridge: Shakespearean Criticism* (London, 1930).

Robert Ready, 'Hazlitt: In and out of "Gusto" ', *Studies in English Literature*, xiv (1974), 537–46.

Christopher Ricks, *Keats and Embarrassment* (Oxford, 1976).

M.R. Ridley, *Keats' Craftsmanship* (Oxford, 1933).

Hyder E. Rollins, *The Letters of John Keats*, 2 vols (Cambridge, Mass., 1958).

——, *The Keats Circle*, 2 vols (Cambridge, Mass., 1948).

R. Ryan, *Keats: The Religious Sense* (Princeton, NJ, 1976).

Harvey Scriven, 'Keats and the Shakespeare Anthology', *Keats-Shelley Memorial Bulletin*, xxii (1971), 59–61.

Ernest de Selincourt (ed.), *The Poems of John Keats* (5th edn, 1926).

W. Shakespeare, *The Complete Works*, ed. Peter Alexander (London, 1951).

Ronald A. Sharp, 'Keats' *Endymion*', *Explicator*, xxvii (1979), 24.

Harvey Scriven, 'Keats and the Shakespeare Anthology', *Keats-Shelley Memorial Bulletin*, xxii (1971), 59–61.

Bernice Slote, *Keats and the Dramatic Principle* (Nebraska, 1958).

D. Nichol Smith (ed.), *Eighteenth Century Essays on Shakespeare* (Oxford, 1963).

Willard Speigelman, 'Another Shakespearean echo in Keats', *American Notes and Queries*, xvii (1978), 3–4.

——, 'Keats's "Coming Muskrose" and Shakespeare's "Profound Verdure" ', *English Literary History*, 50 (1983), 347–62.

Stuart Sperry, *Keats the Poet* (Princeton, NJ, 1973).

Caroline Spurgeon, *Keats's Shakespeare: A descriptive study based on new material* (Oxford, 1929).

Jack Stillinger, *The Poems of John Keats* (London, 1978).

——, *The Hoodwinking of Madeline and other essays on Keats's poems* (Urbana, 1971).

Mark Taylor, 'Keats's "Ode to a Nightingale" ', *Explicator*, xxxvi (1978), 24–6.

Clarence D. Thorpe, *The Mind of John Keats* (New York, 1926).

Helen Vendler, *The Odes of John Keats* (Cambridge, Mass., 1983).

Brian Vickers, 'The emergence of character criticism, 1774–1800', *Shakespeare Survey*, xxxiv (1981), 39–50.

Earl R. Wasserman, *The Finer Tone: Keats' major poems* (Baltimore, 1953).

Stanley Wells, 'Shakespeare in Leigh Hunt's theatre criticism', *Essays and Studies*, xxxiii (1980), 119–38.

——, 'Shakespeare in Hazlitt's theatre criticism', *Shakespeare Survey*, xxxv (1982), 43–55.

R.S. White, 'Shakespearean music in Keats's "Ode to a Nightingale" ', *English*, xxx (1981), 217–29.

——, 'Keats and Shakespeare', *Notes and Queries*, n. s. xxix (1982), 214.

Porter Williams, Jr, 'Keats' "On Sitting Down to Read King Lear Again" ', *Explicator*, xxix (November 1970), 26.

Index